Interviews
with
Serge
Grünberg

David Cronenberg

Plexus, London

Published by Plexus Publishing Limited
25 Mallinson Road
London SW11 1BW
www.plexusbooks.com
First Printing

British Library Cataloguing in Publication Data

David Cronenberg
1.Cronenberg, David, 1943- - Interviews
I.Grunberg, Serge, 1948-
791.4'30233'092

ISBN-10: 0859653765

Printed by Cromwell Press
Original cover and book design by Jean-Francois Gautier
Design adaptation for this edition by Rebecca Martin
This edition published by arrangement with
Cahiers du Cinéma, Paris
Edited by Claudine Paquot

Acknowledgements

Thanks to Janine Bazin, André S. Labarthe, AMIP, Arte, INA.

Without the help of Sandra Tucker (Toronto Antenna), and Simone Suchet (Canadian Cultural Centre for Paris) this book would not exist.

Thanks to the Cinematheque Ontario, Pierce Handling, Sylvia Franck and her team at the Film Reference Library in Toronto, particularly to Robin McDonald.

Thanks to *Cinefantastique*, Tim Lucas, Gilles Gressard, also to the Recorded Picture Company, Alliance Atlantis, Laurem Productions and Lionsgate Films who have graciously allowed us to reproduce photos and documents from their films.

The author would also like to thank Mark McGovern for his help and special thanks to Anne Morin for her invaluable help and support.

This work was only made possible with the help of the Canadian Cultural Centre.

All photos used in this book provided by the Collection of David Cronenberg Papers, Cinematheque Ontario, Film Reference Library, Toronto, except:

- Collection of Cahiers du cinema : 69, 79, 104-99, 101, 135, 143.
- Collection of Gilles Gressard : 28, 33, 34, 41, 48, 49, 50, 51, 55,- 67, 72, 73, 74.
- Cinefantastique; December-January 1983/84, vol.14, n°2 : 71, 76.

Copyright of photos and documents :

- p.4&5 : portrait taken by Nigel Dickson
- From the Drain, Stereo, Crimes of the Future : Emergent Films Limited, David Cronenberg Productions, Toronto.

Poster of *Crimes of the Future*, p. 25 : photo Tom Moore

- Shivers : Lionsgate Films

Photography on set : Attila Dory
Poster of *Shivers*, p. 32 ; creature made by the hands of Joe Blasco, p. 35 : photos Tom Moore

- Rabid : Lionsgate

Photograpy on set p. 42 : Joel Sussman
p. 43&45 : Cinepix Inc.

- The Brood : The Brood Film / New World Mutual Pictures of Canada / Laurem Productions

Photography on set : Rick Porter
p.46, 47 : photos Tom Moore
p. 47 : Collection of Carol Spier and James McAteer, photo Tom Moore

- Scanners : Filmplan International / New World Mutual Pictures of Canada / Laurem Productions

Photography on set : Denis Fugère
p.56 : Collection of Carol Spier, photo Tom Moore

- Videodrome : Filmplan International / Universal City Studios Inc., 1983

Photography on set : Rick Porter
p. 64, the helmet cam made by Tom Coulter, photography by Tom Moore

- The Dead Zone : Dino de Laurentiis / Paramount Pictures, 1983

Photography on set : Rick Porter / Shin Sugino

- The Fly : 20th Century Fox Film Corporation, 1986

Photography on set : Attila Dory
p. 83 : Collection of Carol Spier and James McAteer; photo James McAteer
p. 88&89 : Storyboard and drawings by Ben Blackwell
p. 94 : models photographed by Tom Moore

- Dead Ringers : Morgan Creek Produ ctions

Photography on set : Attila Dory
p. 103 : instruments photographed by Tom Moore

- The Naked Lunch : Recorded Picture Company

Photography on set : Attila Dory
p. 108 : creation of Chris Walas, photographed by Ben Blackwell
p. 118-119 : designs of Stephan Dupuis, photographed by Ben Blackwell
p. 121 designs of James McAteer, photographed by Tom Moore

- Crash : Alliance Atlantis

Photography on set : Michael Gibson / Jonathan Wenk
p. 134 : prosthetic photographed by Tom Moore

- eXistenZ : Alliance Atlantis

Photography on set : Ava Gerlitz
p. 150 : « pod » photographed by Tom Moore.

Introduction

Of all the filmmakers who made their appearance in the 1970s, David Cronenberg ranks as not only one of the most original but also one of the most mysterious. In contrast to the vast majority of his colleagues, he cannot be defined as a 'cinephile' or a 'movie brat'. He even seems to have regarded film as just one means of expression among many others, and to have chosen it almost by default.

But this autodidact, who taught himself 'on the job', has managed to establish himself as one of the masters of contemporary cinema. This owes a lot to the fact that he was able to escape the invasive influence of Hollywood, with its recognisable aesthetic, calculated morality, love of professionalism and stifling corporatism. One could say that those who began their careers in Hollywood (even in the Roger Corman 'school') have always had to meet certain expectations: to respect certain genre conventions, to have a popular style, and to follow certain rhythms and narrative rules. On the other hand, in the Canada of the sixties and seventies, where a feature film industry barely existed, a culturally eclectic young man, with literary ambitions and a rebellious mentality, could see the opportunities offered by the various underground movements that gave rise to a socially concerned and informed audience. Like David Lynch, a very different personality who operated in the realm of the 'art film', Cronenberg – an 'underground' filmmaker – began his creative life in that seminal period. Both Lynch and Cronenberg ignored the Hollywood formula of meeting public expectation (which required a popular style, lacking in culture but receptive to the standard mythology of cinema) to create work that defined an entirely new cinema audience.

Ambient Cinema in the Era of Images

When Cronenberg began his creative adventure, television was already all-powerful in North America. We had entered the era of images, the vast domain that the Situationist writer and artist Guy Debord called the 'spectacular market'. In that respect, *Videodrome*, conceived at the beginning of the eighties, could be seen as a poetic prophecy of the massive IT corporations that now govern the world's press, publishing, television, cinema, and even, at times, its weapon systems. And isn't this – the capacity to see 'differently', and even to prophesy – the way we judge great artists? But, in thematic and stylistic terms, what really established this cinematic autodidact was his ability to attract (and sometimes repulse) spectators: his wish to avoid hackneyed images and, instead, to offer the public parables or satires that would stimulate, shock, and even aggravate. Clearly, this had nothing in common with the dominant or mainstream cinema, with its special effects and publicity machines, where scenarios based on tried and tested Hollywood formulae ('boy meets girl/boy loses girl') are adapted to meet current criteria, often by no more than a change of key elements ('boy meets boy' or 'black girl leaves white boy', for example). During one of many interviews, Cronenberg told me that he read *The Naked Lunch* by William S. Burroughs during the 1960s, and that it had marked him forever. As this was also the case for me, I felt able to say that I understood the impact the book had had on him. When I confided that one day, at the end of seventies, I had told Burroughs (about whom I was writing a book, *In Search of a Body*) that I saw only one director capable of transferring his universe to the screen, 'a young Canadian, David Cronenberg', I think we established a solid basis for a fruitful series of long exchanges. But it was only with my discovery of the Cronenberg archives at the Cinematheque in Ontario that I truly understood how much the Burroughs *Weltanschauung* was the very basis for Cronenberg's entry into the cinema. I found there, on some faded sheets of paper, his first scenarios, in which one could find the seeds of almost all the films to come. These seemed to be written very hurriedly, with the kind of freedom of tone typical of the sixties and seventies and without any self-censorship or concern about audience reaction. One can deduce that, from the beginning, the young student – so keen on sports and the classical guitar – saw in the cinema a different way of making literature. At the same time, he seemed to share the wish clearly expressed by Burroughs (when he declared, for example, 'Literature is 50 years behind painting') to move towards a 'modernisation' of literature which, as the cultural theorist Marshall McLuhan was already predicting, was going to be made by 'new media'. So David Cronenberg found himself in the ill-defined 'Interzone' that separates cinema from modern art (with its extensions into video, photography, installation and performance art, etc), even with his most apparently 'commercial' films, such as *Shivers*, *Rabid* and *Scanners*.

The 'Cinema Brain'

In Cronenberg's work, one verb recurs incessantly: 'to filter'. When he got to work on the adaptation of *The Naked Lunch* – a novel that fitted neither the fantasy genre nor the naturalistic tradition, written in a style so extremely *avant-garde* for its time (the end of the fifties) that it seemed beyond literature – Cronenberg consulted an impressive number of sources on Burroughs and his times, his reading, his obsessions, his life story, his loves and his neuroses, and filtered them all through his own aesthetic, moral and sexual values. This gave birth to a sort of 'monster', still impossible to define, within a claustrophobic setting that one might believe came from an exotic *film noir* such as were sometimes produced by Hollywood studios in the forties and fifties, and which often recalled the work of Josef von Sternberg.

Cronenberg added 'parasitical' elements such as the insect-like typewriters, invented drugs 'that did not exist' and completely twisted the hallucinatory experiences of the great junky writer in transforming him into a kind of Orpheus searching for his Euridyce in the Underworld. For the enlightened lover of Burroughs, this 'betrayal' was a stimulating one. For the young filmgoers who knew nothing of the writer, it was an experience redolent of the synthetic drugs that had just begun to flourish, totally indecipherable but strangely close, making it one of the few surrealist works of our time.

For everything in Cronenberg is in the mind: characters, settings, action, editing. He has even made a film set completely in the mind, which takes place nowhere during a period that doesn't exist: *eXistenZ*, a film so disconcerting, in every sense of the term, that it may take a long time for it to be properly grasped.

Thus, with Cronenberg, we travel back through the whole history of the cinema: from the standpoint of vision as a 'noble' sense, the brain of a man can take account not only of the world that surrounds him, but can employ all of his senses in the construction of a 'world of his own'. Since the Renaissance, every work of art has been required to present us with an individual worldview. The process is that described by the filmmaker in the course of these interviews: the filtering and distilling of a fragile and constantly changing 'reality' by all the senses and bodily organs of the director, at once receptive and revealing. The best example of this method is found in *Videodrome*. Max Renn (whose surname, as has been noted time and again, recalls the Renaissance) is an adventurer in the 'cathode world' who transforms himself, literally, into a video recorder. His emotions, fears and desires are inscribed on his body, making him Christ-like in this living proof of his martyrdom. All the hertz waves of the planet run through his body, and it is visited by virtual beings of uncertain origin.

In *eXistenZ*, Allegra Geller, high priestess of the computer game, has to travel within her own creation, through the labyrinth of her unconscious, into different 'worlds' (to use the name employed in these computer games for different levels of skill). But, from the beginning of the trip, her console is directly connected (via a bio-technological opening, the 'bioport') into her nervous system, her own body.

To her astonishment, she becomes lost in the 'worlds' she has created, to the point of not knowing if this universe exists only in a random fashion or even, in her most extreme moments of anxiety, beginning to doubt if she has any control at all. For all the films of Cronenberg are more or less metaphysical adventures, during the course of which a creator, artist or demiurge begins doubting his creation and begins to contemplate the possibility of being no more than a character in someone else's work. The hallucinating spectator discovers (perhaps for the first time) that 'there is no true or real reality'. Allegra, the creator, transforms into a fictional character who has escaped from the control of her author, and who may even perhaps never have belonged to him. She is a simple puppet in a script written by another, with the mechanical gestures and attitudes of an automaton. Just as Bill Lee, coming back from the hell of Interzone in a vehicle taken from an absurd dream, must satisfy the insistent suspicions of the Annexia border guards by putting a bullet in the temple of the woman he continues to love beyond death. These psychological landscapes are rare in the modern cinema, for they permit the existence of creatures that Cronenberg refuses to define as 'monsters'. And it is true that these creatures resemble us too much for us to be able to separate ourselves from them, even if their violent transformations offend the most intimate parts of our aesthetic and moral values.

Cronenberg is a filmmaker who works by engaging all the senses: he begins with a concept and develops it to the point where it contaminates the image and the dialogue. The cinema, an art of movement, gives the illusion of speed, and Hollywood filmmakers are past masters at setting shots and sequences to an infernal rhythm that has long been their trademark. In the face of this, a certain European tradition has established a more 'literary' cinema, marked by introspection, long takes which linger on someone or something, or lengthy dialogue scenes that frame a more subtle 'action'. What is it that modern cinema, and particularly Cronenberg's cinema, has brought to these opposing traditions?

To fully understand the answer, we need to return to that quotation from Burroughs – 'Literature is 50 years behind painting!' – and to remember that the young underground filmmaker from Toronto chose the cinema, as he has said, as a 'modern' way of writing. Tracing Cronenberg's working methods (by use of the Ontario archives), we are able to analyse, if only in a summary fashion, the filtering process that he never ceases to employ. One can take the example of an early work, *Roger Pagan, Gynaecologist – A Novel*; this describes the adventures of a young neurotic who passes himself off as a gynaecologist. Later, several revised versions went under the title *Pierce*; he is now a psychopathic serial killer who invents 'instruments to operate on mutants'. On leaving prison, he meets a young and beautiful gallery worker which whom he imagines starting his life over and recovering his mental health. These two ideas were much later fused with a newspaper item that caught Cronenberg's attention (the Marcus brothers, two New York gynaecologists who were twin brothers and incestuous homosexuals, were found dead from drug overdoses in their devastated New York apartment). This project, called *Twins* (before he discovered that the title was about to be used by his old friend Ivan Reitman), was finally released under the title *Dead Ringers*. One can follow, throughout several synopses (and sometimes full manuscripts), the slow process by which a group of ideas was refined into a mature script whose gestation period took ten or fifteen years.

But it is in his adaptations that Cronenberg shows himself to be most faithful to himself: he can take a text which may sometimes seem far from his own preoccupations and infuse it with his own aesthetic and vision of the world. In *M. Butterfly*, for example, the single association of 'butterfly' with his knowledge of the insect world led him to create a complex structure whose central metaphor finds its basis in the metamorphic stages of a creature that has long fascinated him (just as it fascinated one of his favourite writers, Vladimir Nabokov).

In this way, the political content of the play by David Henry Hwang gradually yielded to a typically Cronenbergian scenario: a seemingly simple young diplomat becomes the head of an intelligence network, only to betray it 'for the love of a woman' and finally discover that his mistress (who has 'given him a child') is actually a grotesque caricature of the ideal geisha.

But there is no weakening of the initial theme in this new reading. The fundamental incompre-

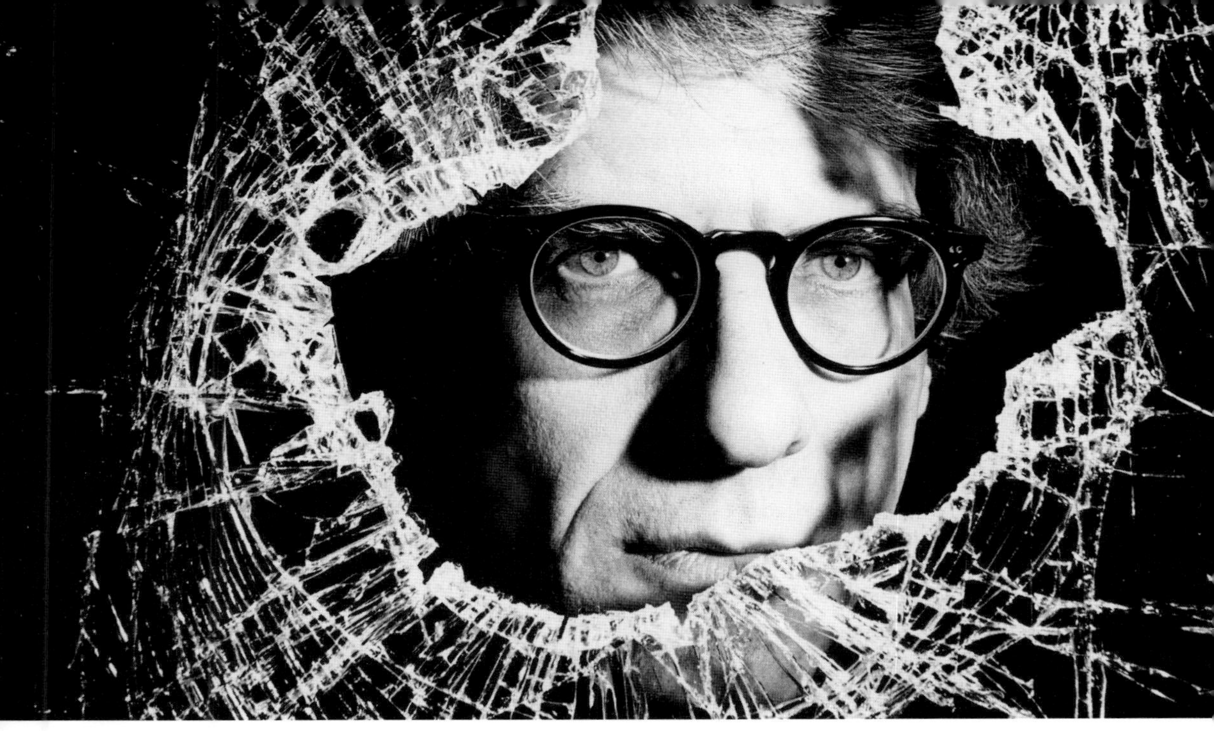

hension of the Orient by Gallimard (Jeremy Irons) is not only the result of a French civil servant's ignorance, it becomes truly existential. In his relationship with Song (John Lone), Gallimard likes to believe that he has taken on the role of the 'cruel Westerner' who has enslaved the 'servile' Asian woman, even though this belief is a complete fantasy (constructed on the Orientalist myth of the nineteenth century) which he will 'recycle' to some degree in his analysis of the Vietnam conflict. If Song Liling is an artist – a singer with the Peking Opera who plays feminine roles, who goes on to play the role of his life – Gallimard is no less of one: it is on the basis of his unconscious desires that he brings to life this unlikely Madame Butterfly, who exchanges secrets of an exotic sexuality for state secrets.

The Other, for Cronenberg, is always a shared creation. Just as the spectator, in the cinema, projects his fantasies onto the screen even as he assimilates the information the film is giving him, so the French diplomat constructs, in collaboration with his love object, a shared hallucination. The Cronenberg hero always constructs an identity for himself that inevitably leads to loss: from Seth Brundle, who literally becomes a '90-kilo fly' because of an error of computer programming (*The Fly*), to Johnny Smith, whose visions betray the despair he has experienced since his long coma (*The Dead Zone*), and Max Renn, who creates a kind of virtual 'backroom' sadomasochism in order to launch his cybersexual adventure (*Videodrome*). And, of course, Bill Lee is a creator of substitute realities, who reconstructs the world to mask his autodestructive inclinations and justify his existential emptiness, his drug addiction being only a metaphorical symptom (*Naked Lunch*). So what takes shape, in cinematic terms as well as ethical ones, is a moral vision of contemporary reality; man is henceforth condemned to make choices in a completely artificial biotopia and the problem, for him, is not how to master nature, but the technologies through which he perceives the diverse aspects of reality, all of which are, finally, of his own creation. It is to the perception and deciphering of these virtual worlds, which cannot be simply observed, that he must devote himself completely. Allowed, sometimes, to close down his 'editing suite' and to switch off his 'monitor', free to absent himself from himself, making him a prisoner who is nevertheless at liberty.

Cinema of Claustrophobia, Sphere of Intimacy

If any character is central to the cinema of David Cronenberg, it is 'the man of the crowd' (as defined by Edgar Allan Poe in the story of the same name), which is to say the very figure of modern man: he no longer belongs to a people, a tribe or a clan. Has he even come from a nuclear family? One cannot say for sure. He lives in the kind of absolute solitude that is possible in the vast cities of North America and Europe, and he does not define himself by his work. But Cronenberg is interested, above all, in the 'sphere of intimacy' – not only the apartment he lives in, but also its interior, the bedroom and the bathroom, places where he goes alone or at least only with a sexual partner. How can we forget Max Renn's den (*Videodrome*) where *frissons* of excitement from his television and video recorder await him? Or again, Seth Brundle's loft (*The Fly*), where his only companion is his computer? Or Bill Lee's bedroom (*Naked Lunch*), the scene of his strange dialogue with his typewriter? Or Gallimard's room (*M. Butterfly*), which seems entirely constructed around the hi-fi on which he places the recording of *Madame Butterfly*?

The prison that the Cronenberg hero builds for himself is that of the modern spectator, but it is also one that appears in myths as old as human culture: is he not the kind of creature born from the dreams of a demiurge? Is he the 'creator' of his own fictions? The universe into which he plunges himself, often with delectation, strips him of all individuality until he attains the nervous twitch of the cipher: in *eXistenZ*, Pikul, looking for someone who can illegally fix him a 'bioport', says to Allegra, 'Where can we find a bioport in the middle of the night? In a country gas station!' And they both arrive at the kind of grey gas station one would find, perhaps, in communist East Germany, with pumps carrying only signs that say, 'Normal' and 'Super', and with the main sign, illuminated by pallid lights, reading, 'Country Gas Station'. Isn't this the nightmare of modern man, the disappearance of the kind of distinctions represented by brand names?

Not always. When Claire Niveau (Genevieve Bujold) asks a gynaecologist why she cannot get pregnant, he replies that she has a 'trifurcate uterus'. And the gynaecologist, convinced that the universe is overrun by 'mutants', designs a set of instruments that are best suited for operating on them. The route of knowledge is never a straight line; as the Mantle brothers never cease to remind Claire, in her desperation to reproduce, 'It doesn't work that way!' For, if Cronenberg's heroes are always seeking, little by little, to be reborn and, in so doing, to travel back to the mysterious source of existence itself, in seeking to produce an ideal universe they will always be condemned to reproduce the very settings of their nightmares. There is always, behind the perfection of the ideal woman, a monster (*M. Butterfly*, *Dead Ringers*, *Rabid*, *The Brood*), or the perfect woman is 'already dead' (*Videodrome*), and even when she has been found, via an absurd and painful process, it is discovered that she has become a 'look-alike', an automaton, a character (*eXistenZ*) or that she must be killed anew (*Naked Lunch*).

This sphere of intimacy, the irreconcilable return into oneself, is both the starting point and finishing line of a crazy race. But is it futile? Torn between contradictory fantasies by indecisive sexual impulses, James Ballard (James Spader), producer of road safety films, finds ecstasy in a carwash. A woman – his wife – whom he has tried and failed to bring to orgasm, and whom he wants to climax, responds at last when spying on him via a rear-view mirror, abandoned to a stranger, and the car itself – an extraordinary sphere of intimacy – seems to participate in the pleasure, the windscreen wipers undulating under the foam jets and all the carwash mechanisms acting as accompaniment to their moaning. It is more than just a salacious metaphor, such as the one at the end of *North by Northwest* when a train enters a tunnel (resembling the carriage, with its blinds drawn, in which Flaubert's Madame Bovary receives her lovers), but is an idea incarnate: we are now *inside* the carriage, we see what Flaubert wished to suggest to his readers – and his judges – and we *feel*, through the symphonic grace of cinema, what Ballard feels. We are not alone with our mental images of desire, and even if the phrase that opens and closes *Crash* ('Maybe the next one!') constantly reminds us of the pleasures to come, even if we are condemned to repeat the same accident on the journey signposted by those who control our lives, the fictions that we and Cronenberg construct, at 24 frames a second, bring us – in spite of everything – to that unbalanced moment of completeness and dissatisfaction from which all creation springs.

Life is a Sickness

The Cronenberg hero is sick: attacked by parasites that he vomits into toilets (*Shivers*), victim of an unfortunate implant (*Rabid*), afflicted with a monstrous psychosomatic illness (*The Brood*), poisoned by a futuristic version of Thalidomide (*Scanners*), exposed to lethal rays (*Videodrome*), plunged into a coma for several years (*The Dead Zone*), dislocated by genetic manipulation (*The Fly*) or destroyed by drugs (*Dead Ringers*, *Naked Lunch* or 'The Italian Machine'), he is dysfunctional; his biological 'programme' has been accidentally disturbed, he has been diverted from the 'normal' road of existence.

Modernity was born, around 1869, with Freud – who looked for truth not in the norm, but in pathology. It was born with the cinema, where ideas are not fixed and eternal, but in constant movement; ghostly, and observable only in their impermanence and in their traces. Modernity was born, too, with the invention of the x-ray: showing us that truth is always behind appearance, inside the object that is being studied. Since then, all truly modern attempts at artistic representation have been more or less based on this perspective. From his first short film (*Transfer*), Cronenberg has given a vision of the world where Hollywood naturalism – a soulless version of the novelistic naturalism of the nineteenth century – is not ignored or forgotten, but dialectically bypassed. In refusing the vulgarly psychological primacy of popular cinema – the 'realistic' representation of our society and its times – he has rejected the slightly vain cinephilia of many other filmmakers of his generation (who, in their creation of a body of work built on film references recognisable to the public, have rejected the challenge of a post-modern cinema, stripped of a pseudo-innocent way of looking), who abdicate all invention beyond the technical (with an excess of special effects that are ever more 'perfect' and ever less poetic) and take refuge in an easy nostalgia for the 'golden age' of cinema.

During one of our first meetings, Cronenberg spoke enthusiastically of André Bazin's concept of 'impure cinema'; I am only beginning to understand what he truly wanted to say. We are now in that moment of cinema history when the substance of what was known as the 'B-movie' has become the dominant material of mainstream cinema. Any of Cronenberg's major works could be described as 'a great sick film'. But there is no morbidity in that description. Finally, it is sickness that makes the human body advance towards foreseeable perfection; it is sickness that has led to the revolutions in medical knowledge that have ensured the future of our species; it is sickness that has pushed us to invent all the various replacement limbs and organs that allow the human body to survive and, in art, it is sickness – at least since the Romantic revolution, and certainly since the Renaissance – that has freed the artist from the search for formal and ideological perfection that has always been, and will always be, in the tradition of the Platonic aesthetic.

David Cronenberg is one of those adventurers who have torn the veil from appearances, who disturb and destabilise us. Like his hero Seth Brundle (*The Fly*), who wants to revolutionise transport because he has a phobia about the means of travelling, Cronenberg goes straight through reality to see what will happen. It is often said of the great stars of cinema that they 'burst through the screen'; this is a perfect expression of this Canadian filmmaker's method. This is the kind of journey he invites us to take with him; it would be foolish to refuse.

Serge Grunberg, Paris.

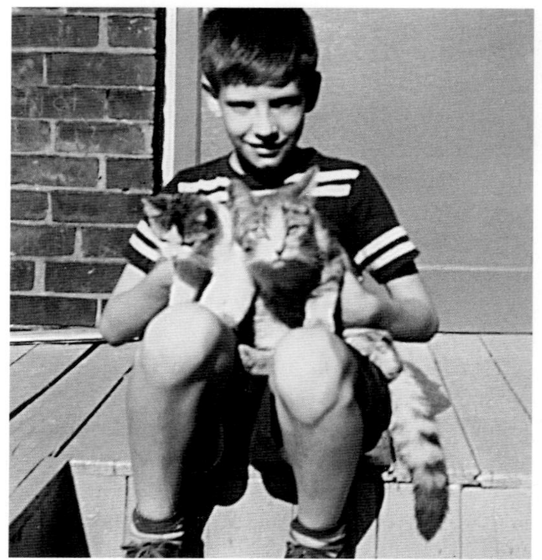

Childhood

and the formative years

Transfer, From the Drain, Stereo, Crimes of the Future

It was during his formative years that David Cronenberg accumulated the essential experience and reading that he would later use in his film work. But above all, a particular 'style' was beginning to impose itself, little by little – that of an 'amateur', in the purest sense of the term (the underground movement reserved its strongest contempt for the 'professionalism' of Hollywood) which would lead him to equal and surpass those masters he had never recognised. Cronenberg's stubborn refusal to acknowledge any 'great' filmmaker as an influence is well known, and it long struck me as a form of arrogance. But I now believe that he is totally sincere. Cronenberg is one of that breed of filmmakers for whom a film is, first and foremost, something in the mind; the visual style with which it is realised is the result of an intellectual journey and not the result of any predetermined aesthetic. This is undoubtedly the reason why, even in a perfectly baroque context, what dominates Cronenberg's cinema is its austerity, a very unusual quality within the genres he works in, and which has a strong resemblance to that of Robert Bresson.

It is very popular, these days, to denigrate the 1960s, as if they had produced nothing but an indigestible mixture of utopian sentimentality. But we need only look again at Cronenberg's marvellous television film, 'The Italian Machine' (1976), to see how the incredible feeling of liberation was still evident ten years later! Everything it deals with is thoroughly up-to-date: the machine as a contemporary artwork, man as a conceptual 'installation', the opening up of what would become cyberculture . . . But it is in rediscovering two 'underground' films, *Stereo* and *Crimes of the Future*, that one can really take the measure of what then seemed possible (what first-time filmmaker today would produce screenplays of that calibre?) and, above all, of the thematic coherence in Cronenberg's work.

With their emphasis on viral invasion, planetary epidemic, the primacy of sexuality (closer to Wilhelm Reich than to Sigmund Freud), and their Situationist-style criticism of urban planning, bound together by an absolutely black humour but free of gratuitousness, constantly transgressing the diktats of what is 'acceptable' and endlessly brushing against 'pornography', Cronenberg's early works were real 'events' – exhibiting a total lack of concern with general audience response. Perhaps it was because of his too-confident attitude in the face of 'serious' criticism that the young filmmaker would be so shocked by the puritanical rejection of his work. Puritan Toronto gave birth – as in Cronenberg's films – to a monster in inverse proportion to its Anglo-Saxon civility, born from hypocritical self-restraint and a repressive social consensus.

No doubt it is because Ontario is so calm and hard working that it clarifies, in a purely organic way, the contradictions of its huge neighbour to the south. For it is often on the steps of Empire that the sound and fury of History are heard, so deafeningly, that they cease to be events reported in newspapers and turn into metaphysical questions. Hence the way that Cronenberg's themes, while

Above: The future master of body horror caresses the animals he will one day explode in a telepod. Right: The young David Cronenberg with camera.

Emergent Films Limited

1654 Bathurst St • Suite 515 • Toronto 349
Ontario • Canada TEL: (416) 782-8365

SHOOTING DATE: January 15th & 16th, 1972

LOCATION: Apartment at 1654 Bathurst St.

SLATE: Scene 1 to Scene 10, Wild rolls 1 to 5

DIALOGUE:	Scene #	Wild Roll#	
Sacbrood	1	1	Do you mind if I eat? Uh, Do you mind if I eat?
"	2	1	The bees are our friends.(repeated)
"	3 (CU)	1	The bees are our friends, Miss Cassable. The bees are our friends, our friends.
Cassable	4 (no slate)	1	I left over a month ago. We weren't very close anyway.
"	5	2	My specialty is domestic architectural detail - in Upper Canada. I don't know what she wanted it for.
"	6	3	This is all part of - Dalgravian Birth Technique.
Sacbrood	7	4	You're Alexandra Pushpin's secretary, aren't you. (statement, not question)
Secretary	8	4	Keller Sacbrood is here. O.K.(All) Right.
"	9	4	I'm afraid I have nothing to tell you, Mr. Sacbrood.
Sacbrood	10	5	Ha, ha. Not bad! So long.

LAST SLATE FOR SEQUENCE: SATYR'S TONGUE! SC. 10, TK 1, WILD ROLL 5

TELEPATHY 2000
(THE PSYCHICS)

a film treatment
by
David Cronenberg

CRIMES OF THE FUTURE

Dialogue Transcript

(8 Pages)

A Film by David Cronenberg

Produced by: Emergent Films Ltd.
66 Hillhurst Blvd.
Toronto 305, Ontario
Canada

Synopsis: ORGY OF THE BLOOD PARASITES
(THE BUGS)
by
David Cronenberg

PIERCE (Working Title)

an original film treatment
by David Cronenberg

ROGER PAGAN, GYNECOLOGIST

a novel
by David Cronenberg

THE SENSITIVES
an original treatment
by
David Cronenberg

Opposite page: The early seventies were a prolific time for David Cronenberg as a writer. But the screenplay of Satyr's Tongue (1972) was never realised.

This page from top to bottom, left to right: the original treatment of Scanners, the synopsis of Crimes of the Future, the first draft of Shivers, an unrealised project which suggested the basis of Dead Ringers, another project which contributed elements to Dead Ringers, another version of Scanners, and the first draft of Stereo.

STEREO:

An Experiment in

Telepathy,

Sexuality,

and Cinema

not rooted in the everyday, become modern fables. The city itself plays the role of a Yankee capital, but it is only a role. Beyond it, there is no 'frontier' to conquer, only a savage and deserted vastness, practically uninhabitable. Nobody, other than Cronenberg, has better described this version of 'America through foreign eyes' – apart, perhaps, from Glenn Gould, howling alone in his recording studio, or Michael Snow, letting his camera explore the Quebec landscape of *La Région centrale*.

The guinea pigs in *Stereo* or the survivors in *Crimes of the Future* still inspire in us, 30 years later, that same profound and intimate fear, that 'disquieting strangeness'. This stems from the deformed reflexes of the *région centrale* of our psyche, as we hurry through a terra incognita to which only Cronenberg (perhaps) has the map: a utopia where the fantastic is not only present, but never ceases to impose upon us.

SG: Tell us about the beginning, and especially your activity as an independent underground filmmaker in the 1970s.

DC: Well of course it started in the 1960s with *Stereo* and *Crimes of the Future*, and then with my short films. And our inspiration really was more from the New York underground filmmakers: Kenneth Anger and Ed Eschwiller and Jonas Mekas, the Kuchar brothers. That was an extremely exciting time. And everybody keeps saying a book should be written about Toronto at that time, because they were very funny times and very entertaining times, with a lot of crazy things going on because of course it was the 1960s, but it was also film-making, and New York, and Toronto's relationship with New York. You know, Toronto always considers itself to be the Canadian equivalent of New York, even though Peter Ustinov once said that Toronto is 'New York run by the Swiss' because of its cleanliness. That was the excitement then, it wasn't Hollywood, it was documentary filmmakers: Pennebaker and the Maysles brothers. And of course it was 'do your own thing'. We were impatient.

Also there wasn't a film industry here, so there wasn't even a film industry that you could plug into and say, 'OK, if I work my way up from assistant director or third assistant director, eventually I'll be directing.' There wasn't that opportunity, and so I don't know what would have happened if it hadn't been for the 1960s and the underground film movement, I might not have become a filmmaker at all. Because I grew up assuming that I had no access to cinema, and because I was also a car and auto enthusiast, I felt it was the same [with film]: automobiles in Canada always came from some place else, even the ones that were made here were American cars made at a branch plant. And that was very different from, let's say, England, where people did make their own cars: they just decided to build a car. People didn't do that, and it was the same with movies. There was no film industry and movies came from somewhere else: Hollywood or Europe. But underground films, now that was something we could understand. We could understand grabbing a camera, we could understand buying film yourself, loading the camera yourself, cleaning the lens.

I approached it very physically because my father was a gadget freak and I had the same tendencies, so I'm very comfortable with mechanical things. And to begin to understand film-making from its physical aspects first, the film biology was important to me, the zoology of film. So I would read *American Cinematographer* magazine, which really didn't discuss the aesthetics of film, it discussed the mechanics of film – to a certain extent the aesthetics of lighting and so on, but really they were talking about mechanics. I remember for example an article that I read and re-read many times about Francis Coppola's first film, *You're a Big Boy Now.* It starred Peter Kastner, who was a young man I went to high school with. Peter Kastner and I used to play concerts: he would play the banjo

A late seventies article from a Toronto daily, combining controversy with humour, in which the young Cronenberg responds (again!) to those who find his films shocking.

The Globe and Mail

The night Attila met the anti-Christ, she was shocked and he was outraged

BY DAVID CRONENBERG

About three months ago I got thrown out of my flat by my landlady, a Protestant spinster lady of 80. She came downstairs from her own second-floor flat with a recent newspaper article in her hand. The hand was shaking, as was her voice. She was clearly upset. "I want you to listen to this," she said, and she began to read me the article in question. It briefly described my first feature film, Shivers, quoted some of the nastier bits of an old Saturday Night review of the film written by Robert Fulford, and then noted that my second movie, Rabid, starred Marilyn Chambers and would no doubt be considered a moral challenge to those same critics who had found Shivers so repugnant.

My landlady finished reading and looked up at me expectantly. I shrugged. I didn't get it. With a troubled sigh, she told me that although she had known I was in the film business, she had somehow mistaken me for a legitimate filmmaker, possibly along the lines of Norman McLaren. She had no idea, she said, that I made "that" sort of movie. I was puzzled. "What sort is 'that' sort?" I asked. "The pornographic sort," she said.

Amused, I began to explain that I made horror films, not pornographic films. She did not seem to hear me, but went on to say that she had been working quietly against pornography with a league of women for many years, that she had lived in the house we both occupied since she had been a child, and that I would have to leave no later than midnight, March 31. She could not, she said, afford to be associated with Marilyn Chambers.

No longer amused, I repeated my statement about horror films. She replied that The Globe and Mail would not print a misleading article, and that Mr. Fulford had been clearly quoted as saying that Shivers was obscene. She added that she was a friend of Bob Fulford's, and knew that Bob Fulford would not lie. She did not want to discuss the matter further, and wished me to know that it was really nothing personal.

It was, I think that "nothing personal", so rich in its historical resonances, that roused me to anger. I told my landlady that it was in fact very personal, that I was very personally insulted, and that I would personally go to the Human Rights Commission before I would leave. After all, how could someone throw you out of your only home, one in which you had just put up seven bookcases, one in

which you had just arranged a cosy room for your 5-year-old daughter and her two pet newts, solely on the basis of a half-understood newspaper article? "I had hoped we could be civilized about this," she said, getting up shakily. Civilized, I had learned in previous discussions with the woman, meant not causing trouble. "But I *am* civilized," I shouted, deliberately ignoring her definition of the term. "Look at my bookcases." "Have you nailed those to the wall?" she asked suspiciously. There was nothing left for me to do but order her out, something I could not have imagined myself doing five minutes earlier.

But even before the old woman left, resolve firm on her lips, I realized that I had just tangled with Attila the Hun, the leader of the Mongol hordes of my most paranoid dreams. I had always secretly expected him to come to my door, and now, at last, he had come. My landlady could not be expected to understand, it goes without saying. It was obvious that for her, *I* was the barbarian, the anti-Christ, the uncivilized and unrepentant destroyer of all that was holy. But she was the one, nevertheless: the pod people of Invasion of the Body Snatchers, the flesh-eating ghouls of Night of the Living Dead, the slavering maniacs of Shivers—"You can't trust your best friend, your mother, the neighbor next door. One minute perfectly normal, the next . . . RABID." The nightmare paranoia of my own films was coming home to haunt me. I was not too rattled to see the wonderful symmetry of it all.

For the first time I allowed myself to fully resent the despicable hysteria of the Fulford piece in Saturday Night, which had not merely condemned Shivers (then called The Parasite Murders) as a moral outrage, but had actually called upon the Government of Canada itself to make it impossible for wretches like me to make such films, whether passed by the censorship board of all 10 provinces or not. How dare he! This man wanted to take away both my livelihood and the expression of my dreams and nightmares—a clean sweep. I had been so cool, so fashionably calm. But I had made a mistake. I had under-reacted. For I was not, it seemed, to be exempted from the fabled insecurity of the artist, the seer, the prophet, the Jew, the alien who can live happily in someone else's house or country only until he is found out, until he is recognized. Then it's the knock on the door in the middle of the night, the one we used to joke about in high school, and the living dead take you away.

Ten minutes after my landlady left, I arranged to be shown through the house directly across the street which had been up for sale for some weeks. I had never let myself want a house of my own before. Wasn't I the nomad artist, the barbarian warrior, the Hun incarnate? The answer, though long in coming, was quite definite: no, I was not. I had a family, I was embedded in the culture of my time and place, my work was highly visible, I was vulnerable. I needed a fortress against the ravages of the Hun. A few days later I bought the house. I was amazed that my camouflage was still so good. Evidently the banks, the real estate agents, the lawyers, had not yet found out who I really was. I was to be allowed to buy a house.

Three days before I moved across the road, I heard a knock at the door. It was a city zoning inspector. There had been an anonymous complaint registered against me. "What is the complaint?" I asked. "Well," he said, somewhat sheepishly, "it says here that you have been conducting a business on the premises. This area is zoned as residential only." "What business?" I asked. He cleared his throat to make sure I understood that he was reading it all directly from his report. It was nothing personal. "The business in question is the photographing and developing of pornographic motion picture films for public sale. I am to look in the bathroom for film-developing equipment." "I think I know who made the complaint," I said. The inspector looked down at his shoes in discomfort. I smiled affably. "Come on in and have a look around." I felt confident and secure. This man would find nothing. He did not know what to look for.

Mr. Cronenberg's latest movies are Rabid and Shivers.

Shooting From the Drain, Cronenberg's second short, written, produced, directed, photographed and edited by him.

and I would play the guitar and we would sing.

SG: By the way, why didn't you become a musician?

DC: I don't know, I mean I had many members of my family who were musicians, so there was a lot of music and dance.

SG: You were quite good at guitar.

DC: Yeah, yeah. I played classical guitar from the age of eleven to 22, and before that I played piano, my mother taught me piano because she was a pianist. But my father was a writer and I really thought that I would be a writer. And when I realised that to be a musician, especially a classical musician, you were really interpreting and reinterpreting other people's creative works, that didn't appeal to me. I mean I really wanted to create my own, and I didn't think I was a composer. So I think if I had gone into music I would have wanted to be a composer, not a musician. Although I did enjoy very much the act of making music. But at the age of 22 I decided either I want to be a concert guitarist, a classical guitarist in the Segovia tradition, or I will drop it – and I just stopped right then. So every once in a while I might pick up an electric guitar. My son plays bass guitar and guitar and my youngest daughter is suddenly interested in playing electric guitar, but I was either going to do it really seriously and obsessively or I was not, and I decided I was not. I probably felt I wasn't good enough either to be a great classical guitarist. I could have been probably an OK rock 'n' roller, I did do some of that. And I can sing, I have a not bad voice really for singing, and I have a good ear for music, I mean my sense of pitch is fairly good.

But so it was writing you see, and in writing you are dealing with meaning in a way that appealed to me more than the abstraction of music. And so I really thought that I would be a writer and I was devoting myself to that, and then I got derailed by film, and primarily – you know the story of *Winter Kept Us Warm*, this film that *Cahiers du cinéma* actually gave a very nice review to as a matter of fact: *'Un très, très beau film,'* I think it said, for this movie that was made by my classmate – not a classmate, he was someone I didn't know, but was at the University of Toronto.

But I was late you know, I was in my mid-twenties really, or late twenties actually when I really thought to pick up a camera. And even then it was not serious, I didn't think it was serious, although I was obsessive about it as usual. And then it was the underground and some strange bedfellows like Ivan Reitman, for example, [who] was one of the co-founders of the Canadian Film Co-op, because he was a student who was interested in film-making also. And we modelled our co-op after the New York co-op created by Jonas Mekas. The idea, of course, in the sixties style, was to be able to produce and distribute films without making a profit: that you would make your films accessible and that you would not have to access the sort of paternalist machinery that existed at the time. You wouldn't have to deal with Hollywood or official distributors or any of that.

We learned a lot about the underground machinery because there were newsletters from the co-op and so on, and we had many people come up from New York and sometimes from LA and Chicago as well, but primarily New York, and we were very inspired by them and encouraged by them and there was a very good interchange between them, their filmmakers and us. And there was a centre, there was a theatre called Cinecity, have I ever talked to you about Cinecity? It had originally been a post office, now I think it's a Wendy's burger joint or maybe it's a Gold's gym, I can't remember. But it was a post office that was turned into a cinema, I saw *Weekend* there, they showed Godard regularly. It wasn't really designed as a cinema because there was no raking, all the seats were flat and it was quite small. But it was the centre, because it was owned by a very interesting man who is still alive and around, named Wilhelm Poolman, of Dutch ancestry. And he was a lawyer who was very passionate about film, he was – I assume he still is – a very amusing and perverse man, in a good way I think. And he put money into this small theatre and started a company called Film Canada, and he got the Canadian rights to films like Bunuel's *Simon of the Desert* and so on: things that normal distributors wouldn't remotely even know existed, never mind be interested in actually putting money into, and would show them at Cinecity. And I remember specifically the Cinethon – it was a marathon of underground cinema, and it went on for 24 hours. I mean we just showed underground films only, all day [and] all night. In the morning we would come out on the street and have croissants, and coffee was brewing out on the street, they had the coffee-makers plugged in. We'd blink in the sunshine a little bit as the sun came up, and then we went back in and we saw another eight hours or five hours of underground films. And of course underground films tended to be short, you didn't . . . Well you'd see Andy Warhol's *Vinyl*, I remember, for example, was long, Warhol would make long films, but most underground films were short: ten minutes, fifteen minutes. So you ended up seeing a hundred films in that Cinethon. And there was a real sense of camaraderie and excitement, which is an element of the sixties that I have never actually seen captured on film. Everybody's take on the sixties seems to omit the thing that made the sixties most exciting, which was that feeling when you woke up in the morning that there would be some amazing wonderful event, occurrence, discovery that was changing things in a very positive and exciting way, that opened things [up]. It's very easy to be cynical about the sixties now, but this underground film-making was all part of that.

So those are my roots as a filmmaker, even though, by the time I was doing that I had seen all kinds of films from all over the world: *Antonio das Mortes*, Brazilian films . . . Because I had a friend who introduced me to the Toronto Film Society, he's still a very good friend, and on very bleak cold winter nights, like the one we will experience tonight, he would drag me out to the film society, to some theatre that they had rented for that night, and show some obscure film like *La Strada* or *I Vitelloni*. So my introduction to the art cinema which blossomed in the late fifties and the sixties was really the film society.

Left: Poster for a screening of Stereo at Cinecity, Toronto's Mecca of experimental art-house cinema. Below: Cronenberg filming a scene from Stereo with actor Ron Mlodzik.

That was more official cinema, of course, than underground, and it was still very very distant and unapproachable in terms of actually being able to do it. So once again it was not cinema that allowed you to feel . . . that gave you access. So it was a combination of these things.

And then of course [there was] Holly-wood, because as a kid, every weekend there would be a little stream of children like lemmings going to the sea. We would be going to one of two theatres that were close to us and one was called the Pylon and the other was the College, and we would go there and see Hopalong Cassidy movies, we would see whatever was playing and cartoons. I remember my father telling me about *The Seventh Seal,* he had just seen it and he was telling me about it and I couldn't believe what he was saying. I just got that on DVD now, I'm excited to look at it. So in terms of movie influences those are the three basic [elements].

SG: I always wondered, because on one hand, for example, all the young people of the nouvelle vague in the sixties considered themselves as writers, they really felt, and it was something very French at the time, that you could write novels with the camera – it was a new thing. And on the other hand there's William Burroughs, whom you had read at the time, who was doing almost the opposite . . .
DC: Doing cinema on paper. Yeah.

SG: So was it conscious or were all these influences, let's say, in the air . . .
DC: I think so . . .

SG: . . . as a valid means of expression?
DC: I remember even quite a long time ago, and I'm looking right there [on his bookshelf] and seeing *Four Screenplays of Ingmar Bergman,* I remember knowing that Bergman felt inadequate as an artist because he was not a novelist.

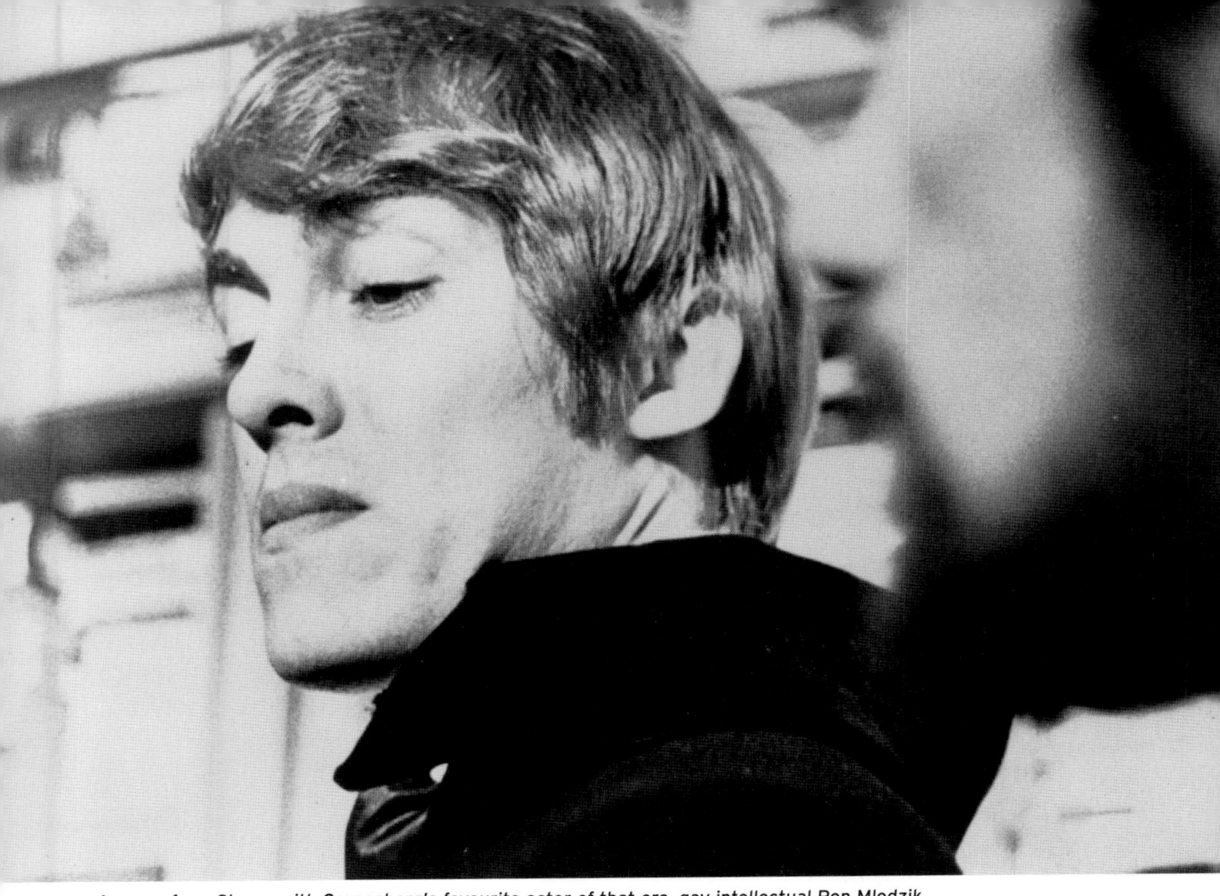

A scene from Stereo with Cronenberg's favourite actor of that era, gay intellectual Ron Mlodzik.

Even after he had made some of his early masterpieces, he felt that it was still not a real art form, that the word was really the art, where the art was. And so he has really novelised his screenplays in a kind of attempt to approach the novel. I guess I'm still struggling with that, not that it isn't obvious that the cinema is an art form, but it is an art form that cannot do the same thing as the novel. Do we have to choose? No we don't really. And in some ways, the novel goes through periods of horrible vulgarisation as does the cinema, we're in one right now, where you feel that yes, the novel exists, and yes, the cinema exists, but [that] it's almost impossible to create art in those media because of the economics of the time and the populist pressure and so on.

And I must say you have to unfortunately throw in some television there too, because we were watching television in the fifties as well. And television was an influence especially in Canada, unlike the States, because we had the CBC, which was our version of the BBC, which was government funded and therefore did not have the pressure of economics in the same way. And there were some wonderful Canadian television dramas that really affected me, very much affected me as art, as a way of art. I remember there was a production of Katherine Anne Porter's short novel called *Pale Horse, Pale Rider*, it was just stunning to me at the time. And there were some very experimental things on CBC television done by, for example, George Bloomfield, who is a director who is still around, mostly doing television and so on. He hasn't done a feature in a long time but he did do a few. And he did one called *Child Under a Leaf* with Dyan Cannon – it's amazing that I can remember this, I'm very excited that I actually can remember

The film was shot in the 'professional' 35 mm format, for which Cronenberg sacrificed colour and direct sound. He took it to Cannes on his own, carrying the reels under his arm.

these things. I thought my mind would be a blank. So that also contributed, because of course I watched a lot of TV series and comedy series, [for example] *The Honeymooners*, all the things we see now with great nostalgia and wonder how you could have looked at those horrible little black and white pictures, although they were a little better than what you see now from the kinescopes. But that also was an influence.

The question still remains, when you see a film like *Celebration* or even *The Blair Witch Project*, the *caméra stylo*: really, how close to that could you actually come? I'm very tempted now to get a digital video camera and shoot myself literally, not to make a documentary, but to create something that would be writing with the camera. You know, if you literally did not write anything on paper or on a computer, if you really did write it with the camera somehow. But at the moment the script still comes first, and the way that films are financed in general, the script comes first, so you are as you see me now, you become a literary being in a way. It's not quite literary, it's a strange, bastardised limbo, because the only words that really count on the screen are the words of dialogue. But all the descriptions and so on, there's no point in trying to find the *mot juste* because it's not to be read, you know. I was just reading Graham Greene, a little book called *The Third Man* and then *The Fallen Idol*, these were two movies that he wrote. But *The Third Man*, it was interesting, he had to write a story first before he could write a screenplay. And it's long, I mean it's a novella that he wrote

The film portrays the psychosexual experiences of guinea pigs who volunteer for an ultramodern, Sadeian environment.

with great attention, pretty serious attention to the words, which then became the basis for his screenplay. And then, with his director Carol Reed, apparently they hammered out the screenplay between them but based on this novella. But he had to write the novella first, because he had to know the background of the characters and the tone of the locations and everything, and he could only do that in a literary way. The next story, called *The Fallen Idol* – which was not his title, his title was *The Basement Room* – he said that he much preferred it because it was a story first. In other words, he didn't write thinking that it would become a screenplay, and only later did it accidentally become a screenplay. It was a literary creation and he said he preferred it to his literary version of *The Third Man.* I found that all very interesting, I'm just stumbling across that now as I am struggling with my own writing. But I have never seriously written any fiction, I have never mined the possibilities of fiction writing. I've really only written screenplays and that is basically it. And when you're writing a screenplay – for me, unlike Graham Greene, who obviously approached it a different way – it's not quite a literary endeavour. I mean, it is words but it's strange . . . Wouldn't it be odd if there emerged an art form that was the art of the screen . . . if people read screenplays? I know people read screenplays now, but they read them mostly to encourage themselves to become screenwriters. But it would be kind of very perverse and strange and not impossible, because there are all those websites that have screenplays now, people have access to screenplays, they never had access to screenplays before, except for . . . I mean, I have *Hiroshima mon amour,* and some others. I haven't bought books on movies for years. These are all ones that influenced me when I was beginning.

SG: **There's something very interesting I have been thinking about for many years now. It's really strange: there was, let's say, a Corman generation, and even if you were a little on the outside, it's interesting that at the beginning of your professional career you would be in contact.**
DC: Corman's influence was huge.

SG: **Because of Coppola, Scorsese . . .**
DC: Nicholson.

SG: **. . . Demme, Nicholson, Cameron, Dante, everybody went through Corman. Being a Canadian, maybe you . . .**
DC: Well, Cameron is a Canadian too.

SG: **Yeah, and you were perhaps lucky enough not to have to do that, but nevertheless this generation really affected the last quarter of the century because, strangely enough, what was called the 'B movie' before now became the**

dominant form . . .
DC: I know, I know, it's very strange isn't it?

SG: And you were there at the same time, maybe a little at the margin . . .
DC: Well, I was more than at the margin. Except for this trip to LA, I was just a guy who saw the movies and read about them. But it was the example that was important, and I saw a lot of Corman movies. And Corman influenced me, and not just when I was looking at low-budget films either. And you could see that some of them were like . . . what's the plant movie?

SG: *Little Shop of . . .*
DC: *Little Shop of Horrors*, you could see was quite extraordinary. And so you could see that the budget didn't necessarily mean that the movie had to be bad, or not interesting, and that was exciting. And Corman once again meant access. He was a sort of a step between underground films and official Hollywood, in between there was Corman. And in Montréal, Cinepix was the Canadian version of Roger Corman. Well in a way they were modelling themselves after him, and also some European producers as well, but as usual, we found ourselves sort of halfway between Hollywood and Europe, and so did Cinepix also. I went to quite a few places with that script and they all said, 'Oh yes we would do this, we would do this in a minute, we would finance this.' And that was very exciting to me, and that was the moment when I almost could have ended up in Hollywood. Except that when I came back to Canada, I got a phone call almost immediately from John saying that finally the CFDC (Canadian Film Development Corporation) had approved money for the film and that we could make it. So that was the defining moment, because I was beginning to realise that

the reason that Jewison and Ted Kotcheff and others had left Canada was the same reason that I was thinking I might have to leave Canada too: because I could not get a film made there, because there was no film-making machinery. But that's when it all started to change, and I have never had that feeling since. But I did feel that I had to go to Hollywood, or at least to Los Angeles, to reassure myself that I was not crazy in thinking that what I had written was a movie. Because I was getting that feeling in Canada: that it was just not – for some mysterious reason, maybe because it was very distasteful, whatever – really a movie. And I hated that feeling, and that was what I was looking for in LA reassurance.

SG: I wanted to ask you for a long time, your first movie was called *From the Drain*. Was it a manifesto, this phrase, 'from the drain'?

DC: I didn't think of it that way. In fact it wasn't my very first film. My very first film, the one before it, which I've completely forgotten the name of . . . *Transfer*. It referred to the Freudian concept of transference. In the movie there's a psychiatrist, but it's a very surreal version of psychiatry and so on. *From the Drain* was the second one. I love the idea of a manifesto. There aren't too many of them around anymore, but I never did think of it as a manifesto. In a way though, it's interesting that you say that. That's one of the things that's missing. There's enough politics per se in cinema, but right now everyone wants to be a director, a writer, an actor, win Oscars, be popular. It's a complete victory for commercial cinema. No one wants to be the Kafka of cinema. Of course it's impossible in a way, but to make films that no one has seen until after you die. And which you instruct someone to burn and never show anyone. That would be impossible and in a way that's the ideal for me. When I was thinking I would be a novelist, before discovering film-making, my desire was to be an obscure novelist. Obscure. One that you would stumble on by accident, and suddenly you would be delighted that this person had written these maybe three strange little novels that were never very popular, and you could almost never find them. They were almost always out of print, but somehow you find them. I don't think it's possible to be the cinematic equivalent of that, but in a way I wish it were.

And of course after that Cannes comes into play, because when I went to Cannes with *Shivers*, I spent a lot of time with low-budget filmmakers of all kinds: mostly sex films, horror films, not too many action films because usually they were more expensive, and felt a real sense of community and also a sense that . . . Wait a second, I was in Cannes before that, because I was in Cannes with *Stereo* and *Crimes of the Future*, that's right, and I think that's when I was talking to all of these low-budget guys. I still have some T-shirts: *Captain Lust*, it was sort of a pirate sex movie made by this crazy guy, it was very funny and very dirty and crude . . . And I have the feeling that that was before I made *Shivers*. Once again, I was just testing my sanity and my place and that was my segueway from underground film-making into official film-making, that is to say film-making where you could actually perhaps make a living doing it.

SG: **So it was quite an important moment in your career, the film was released and there were all these incredible reactions.**

DC: Yeah, good and bad. Yes . . .

SG: **Let's talk first about the bad ones.**

DC: Well the main bad one was of course the Robert Fulford one, *Saturday Night* magazine. This is very famous in Canadian folk history. The heading said, 'YOU OUGHT TO KNOW HOW BAD THIS FILM IS BECAUSE YOU PAID FOR IT,' meaning the tax-payers. And he said it was 'repulsive . . . pornographic . . . disgusting . . . hideous.' Now this was a guy who still is a major literary sort of critic figure here, and still writes for the newspapers and had been very involved in starting this magazine called *Saturday Night*. And I remember saying to the head of the Film Development Corporation, Michael Spencer, I said, 'Michael, only 100 people read *Saturday Night* magazine.' And he said, 'Yes but it's the wrong hundred people.' This was when I was trying to get my second film made, *Rabid*, they were very afraid to put money into it. They felt the public outcry would be too extreme, especially since we were planning to cast a . . . well I guess we didn't know then we were going to cast Marilyn Chambers. That would have been their worst nightmare, 'In this movie they're actually casting a porno-queen as the lead character.' There were questions raised in the House of Commons about a government funding body investing in pornography, something that a major critic called pornography. Because he wrote as Marshall Delaney, which was his pseudonym for his film criticism because he was also an editor of the magazine. But it was a really scathing denunciation of the film as 'pornography', as 'repulsive', as 'disgusting', as 'horrible' in every possible way – which in a way I would accept – but beyond that, he was saying that films like this should not get made, and in particular they should not be funded by the government. That, really, was the part that I found very offensive and which I still haven't forgiven him for, because he was [acting as] a censor basically, he was being a censor and doing his best to destroy me. This was a man whom I had shown *Stereo* to and who had actually given it quite a nice review in *Saturday Night*. He had called it 'like an elegant dream' or something like that. So I gave him a private screening, thinking that he would understand the evolution from one to the other, even though, yes, they are very different in tone, but I thought he would get it – he didn't get it.

And he still annoys me, because there's a critic

here, a so-called critic named Bart Testa, who is renowned amongst his students for saying that Cronenberg is a genius without talent. This is phrase-making, you know, critics in North America love to do that – although he's not really a critic, he's a teacher. Then I saw something in which Robert Fulford was agreeing with him, although he admits that he has not seen one of my films since *Shivers*. It's like, what? . . . assessing James Joyce on the basis of his first short story. I mean, how can the man have any credibility when he does this? So the anger in me is still there, the outrage continues; I have a sense of humour about it, obviously, but I felt very betrayed.

Now maybe he did too, maybe he felt betrayed too, I don't know, I've never spoken to him since, it's been many years. And he's around, he shops in the village. I don't see him, if I saw him I would say hello, but it was just the beginning of my understanding of the relationship between a filmmaker and a critic, and in particular a critic that you know. It's a difficult relationship, and I can tell you that you are the only – I don't exactly call you a critic, but you are the only critic who has ever been in my house, in any house of mine, because I don't trust them. It's gotten much worse, film criticism: what is it now in North America? It's a branch of marketing, it's a sort of confessional psycho-therapeutic exercise for the writer, it's so bizarre, and they are such a compromised group of people, because they all have scripts in their back pockets that they want to give you. Atom Egoyan told me of a critic here who has been relatively kind to me but very nasty to Atom, in *Now* magazine, John Harkness. And he says that John will never escape an opportunity to hit Atom over the head, I mean he could be reviewing some other movie and say, 'At this stage in his development, this director is far above Atom Egoyan's level, even in his fifth film.' And then he sends Atom a script and asks him would he produce it and direct it? Now this betrays a real misunderstanding on the part of that man of what a filmmaker's work is to him. Because they can say, 'Well why are you taking it personally?' I think that's the attitude, 'You're not taking this personally? I mean we're just doing our jobs, this is just objective.'

SG: Like the Mafia: strictly business . . .

DC: Strictly business.

SG: . . . not personal . . .

DC: 'I have to execute you and then I might need you later.' It's very personal, it couldn't be more personal, especially if you are a serious filmmaker. I mean, if you are a mechanic, then there's a little professional pride that's hurt maybe, it's like you tried to fix someone's car and you didn't do a good job, so you're upset professionally on that level, and that's what they think it is. And that means that they don't understand what you are doing at all, because of course it's personal. Rex Reed once came up to me, he was all smiling and shaking hands and stuff, I wanted to kill him because he had said some really horrible things about my movie. Being civilised, I didn't hit him, but he disgusted me, you know, and the fact that he would want to pal around with me made me sick. At least be disgusted or something. I mean, if you're offended by my movie then you're offended by me . . .

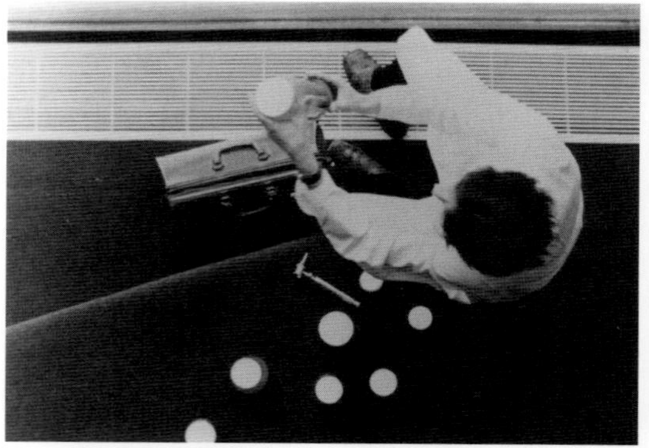

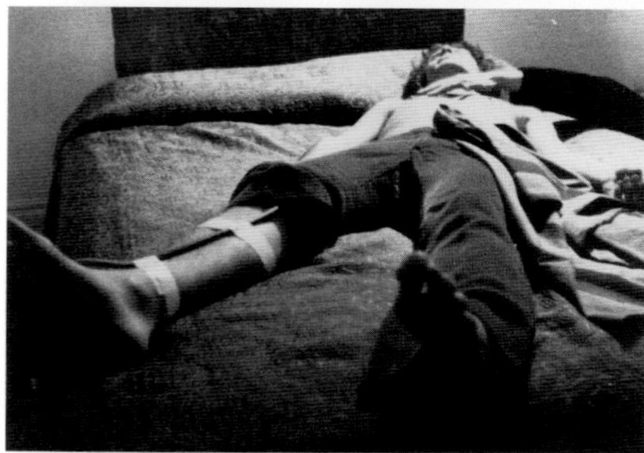

Crimes of the Future: *A science fiction film which again centres on a very Burroughsian theme: the disappearance of the female gender.*

I had some introduction to this sort thing with my other films, because they got reviewed, they got shown at film festivals and so on. And really, *Stereo* and *Crimes of the Future* were my *entrée* into the world of film festivals, because they were shown at Edinburgh. And so when I went back for *Crash*, not that *Crash* was shown at Edinburgh, but we showed some clips from it, that was I think my 25th anniversary at Edinburgh because *Stereo* and *Crimes* had gotten shown there, and they were shown at the Adelaide and Auckland festivals. I was putting them in film cans, filling out the forms, shipping the films off myself to the festivals, I did all that stuff. So I had that experience, but I had not the sort of commercial experience. I had the film festival experience before I ever had a film that played in cinemas commercially.

SG: When you are really attacked, does it make you feel that your work is of some importance, you know, if people become so aggressive it means there is something at stake at least?

DC: I still have, of course, with movies like *Crash* and even *eXistenZ*. I always have a mixture of feelings about that, because on the one hand I know that merely to be offensive does not guarantee you anything. So I know that I could offend people very easily with a movie, get a very strong reaction, but it wouldn't really mean much. All you have to do is show somebody's dog getting its throat cut on screen and you would have a lot of people very angry. But is that anger something you could be proud of? So I can't allow myself to think that just the fact that people are upset justifies the work. On one level maybe a little bit, but I've never made movies particularly just to upset people. If that had been my goal – and with some performance artists, for example, it is just to shake some people out of their somnambulence and get them to be angry or anything – then you could say yes, just the mere fact that you got them upset and focused on what you were doing was a triumph. But I have never felt that, for me I want more, I am demanding more. So I feel that if *Crash*, for example, everybody [had] loved it, I think I could accept that. I think I would say, 'Whoa! I'm surprised that everybody loves this, because it's not, you know . . .' The other thing I don't do is the converse, I don't do what Spielberg might do, let's say, I don't make a movie to be loved. I don't make *ET*, I don't make a movie whose goal is to have everybody say, 'It is the most loved film of all time,' or something like that. That to me would also be a failure. So just to get them angry, just to get them to love, neither one of them is enough, or interesting enough or complex enough. So I'm looking for a kind of complex reaction. If someone is disturbed and angry, but somehow also seduced and attracted at the same time, then that's something I would like. Then I could feel fulfilled by that. But when someone completely rejects the film, thinks it's just trash, meaningless, stupid, useless, amateurish, repulsive, whatever, it's very hard for me to say, 'Yes, that's a reaction I want,' because that's a lie. I wouldn't . . .

And so that kind of reaction, that particular Fulford reaction, was upsetting to me. And surprised me. Now I had friends who said, 'You have to understand that although Fulford writes about art and so on, nonetheless he is really a very conservative force in Canadian culture and you really shouldn't be surprised.' But he had given *Stereo* a good review and *Stereo* was not an easy film to give a good review to, if you are an ordinary film reviewer in a newspaper, which he isn't, he was a little bit more interesting than that, he is an interesting man. So I couldn't really comfort myself with that. So it was really war, I mean I really felt I was being attacked, and unfortunately it did delay the financing of *Rabid*. The CFDC really wanted to finance my next movie, but they really didn't want to have the same thing happen again. To their credit they tried all kinds of subterfuges. They did this thing which was very popular at the time called cross-collateralising, a company would make three films, the financing would go into one big pot for all three films, and then all the profits from the three films would go into one big pot. Very difficult really to do, because the participants are different on each film and so on, but they felt that if they did that they could sneak in some money. They would say, 'Well we're not really financing that one, we're financing that other one but because it's cross-collateralised, somehow some of that money is inevitably . . .', you know. And then it's up and running!

There's a famous Godard saying, 'Until you have cameras that you can keep in the glove compartment of your car, you don't really have cinema,' or something like that. Well we have those now. I think that 35mm is going away anyway, when you finally have digital video whose quality is acceptable in a cinema. *The Blair Witch* is sort of one of the first of those, because even *The Celebration* was not digital video, it was actually just Hi-8. Then you have the possibility of grabbing a camera out of your glove compartment and shooting something that you could put into your feature film. It wouldn't obviously be integrated in the normal way, and there are many other interesting questions, like if you shot some people on the street and then they saw it in your movie, these days

Poster for a festival of 'other cinema', showcasing the formative years of the young Cronenberg. Here he appears at last (via Stereo and Crimes of the Future) ranked among the great figures of experimental cinema . . . Rocha, Herzog, Mekas, Godard.

My agents tell me that there is a German company that would give me $1 million, I need give them no script, all I have to do is to deliver to them a digital video master of my feature film with my name on it, saying that it's David Cronenberg's next film. And they have the rights for Germany and that's it, I could sell it to the rest of the world. Now that is a pretty tempting proposition, because obviously $1 million is not a lot of money in terms of making a feature film the normal way, and even the independent way, that's a pretty low budget. But to create your own vision of a production where you might use your family and friends even if they are playing roles, it's stimulating. And you could decide to make it as professional or as amateur as you want. And that's a tempting proposition, even though at the moment I wouldn't take it because I don't know what to do with it. And it's nice to know that that exists. I think Gus Van Sant said he was going to do one like that maybe. And I think Doris Dorie said she was doing one like that, the German director.

So whether this will be another *Easy Rider* kind of thing or another *Halloween* kind of thing, there is a sense of *déja vu* because those were moments of great excitement, when a film like *Easy Rider* could come out and be such a huge

they would probably sue you because they weren't paid extras. So the Godardian vision is still problematical, I mean if you're shooting some birds in a tree, OK, you can probably get away with that . . . But it's an exciting time, and as I say, it does remind me a bit of the sixties, that sort of excitement about the power of the camera in your own hand. That is very sixties.

success. And even *The Blair Witch* reminds me very much of *Halloween*, even though of course they were made in very different ways. But once again: a low-budget film comes out of nowhere, it's a horror film, it makes a lot of money, it spawns a lot of imitations and . . . I don't know that it's for me.

SG: So to come back to this period of time, you – I won't even say 'directed', but you really made *Transfer* – because you were doing absolutely everything.
DC: Same with *Stereo* and *Crimes*.

SG: I began with the archives. It's very obvious you were doing everything.
DC: Even with *Stereo* and *Crimes of the Future*, which were shot on 35mm, I was haunted by the sort of professional mystique: the idea that you're not really making a movie unless you are shooting on 35mm, even though it's just a few more millimeters. And I was willing at that point, as you can see, to give up sound, to give up synchronised sound. In those days you couldn't find a 35mm camera that was light and portable, they were all blimped. That means that you would have to have a huge, awkward casing around an Arriflex. To get a Mitchell was out of the question: that was the standard Hollywood camera, it was huge, it was expensive, there was no way you could deal with that. I would have to make do with an Arriflex, get a blimp. I spent time with cameramen and in camera rental places, playing with the cameras and learning the technology. So I was actually willing to give up sound, dialogue sound, for 35mm. And in a way it sort of surprised me that I was willing to do that, but so powerful was the mystique of 35mm. Even though writing dialogue to me was a strength that I had that some of my colleagues at the time, young beginning filmmakers, didn't have: because they weren't writers, they didn't think of themselves as writers and they weren't good at it. So I was willing to give up a real weapon in my arsenal in order to have 35mm. And that was *Stereo* and *Crimes of the Future*, and of course I used voice-over and did all kinds of things. You don't see people speaking in those movies, so I wasn't trying to do a silent film thing or a dubbing thing, but that was part of the sci-fi of that.

But after two movies like that, I really . . . Well it was Louis Marcorelles – I met him and he gave me nice reviews in *Le Monde* – who said he was very surprised to see me come back. He thought that would be the end, that I made these two sort of perfect movies of their own genre, and then he didn't think that I would ever make another movie. And I know what he meant because I certainly felt that I didn't need to do a third one, you know. One of those was in black and white and one was in colour, more complex. And then I had to deal with the industry, the idea that I would make my living as a filmmaker, that meant a whole other level of commitment and involvement, it changed everything.

SG: At that time there was no real film industry, feature film industry in Canada.
DC: No, it was sporadic. Once in a while some renegade like Don Owen . . .

SG: So how come you decided not to go to Hollywood, to stay in Canada and to find the producer you eventually found?
DC: Once I decided that I wanted to be a professional filmmaker, and that I therefore was not going to be, for the moment anyway and maybe forever, a novelist or writer of any kind except maybe a screenwriter, I started to focus very much on low-budget film-making. I remember in New York I went to see *Greetings*, Scorsese, De Palma's *Hi Mom!*, their first films. I was very interested suddenly in any low-budget film, including horror films of course, because I had always been interested in horror films anyway, so I would see the most obscure horror films, the low-budget ones that came from England, wherever I could see them. And they played a lot, there were a lot of cinemas that would play dou-

ble bills and they would be the second half of the double bill. I even remember seeing *Three Murderesses* with Alan Delon, that was the first time I saw him.

SG: Have you seen *The Tingler*?

DC: I did see William Castle films, but some of them I missed, and *The Tingler* I missed. But even so, to me William Castle was a high-budget filmmaker, he was a Hollywood filmmaker as far as I was concerned, even though of course he wasn't in the normal sense. But even a movie like *Three Murderesses* interested me, because it was obviously a low-budget film and it had this gorgeous guy, I mean he was so striking even then, he must have been eighteen in *Three Murderesses,* he was really young. And I would see *Meat*, there was an English film called *Meat*. I would just see anything that might excite me in the sense that it would encourage me to make a low-budget film, to say to me that this was something you can do, people are doing it, it wasn't just that they got made, that they got shown, that they were in a real cinema . . . the fact that *Greetings*, was being shown in a real cinema on 42nd Street, even though it was a horrible theatre, still that was very exciting.

And I wrote a script which was *Shivers*, which was called many things, *The Parasite Murders* I think was the first title I had . . . Oh no, the first title was *Orgy of the Blood Parasites*. And really just because I suppose it felt more possible, I sent it to Cinepix. I had contacted them before because they were the only company in Canada who were actually making movies. And they were making low-budget movies that were sex movies, they were sort of sex comedies, very sweet, very gentle, funny and sexy and very Quebec, very Quebecois, and they made some in English too. There was Denis Héroux, whose brother Claude eventually produced *Scanners* and some other films that I did. *Valérie* was the first big Quebecois success, this was suddenly a film made in Canada in French Canadian, in Quebecois, that made a lot of money. They were high profile in Canada because nobody had ever done this before. They were distributors, like everybody else, distributing movies that came from somewhere else and they thought, 'We could do this.' That was what I was trying to do as a director, to say, 'I could do this.'

So it seemed like a natural match-up and I sent it to them. I think I had gone to them to see if they would let me direct one of their sex films. In fact I know that's what happened. It was very funny, I actually shot a test in a studio which made them feel that they didn't want me to direct. Because I was very interested in getting interesting angles and stuff, and really it was a sex scene on a swing. But they liked me and I liked them and I think it was a feeling that we really should do something together somehow. But after they saw *Stereo* and *Crimes of the Future*, they said, 'We know you have a strong sexual sensibility, we're just not sure what kind it is.' And so I wasn't going to direct one of their sex films. And I said, 'OK, I'm going to write a script,' and I wrote *Orgy of the Blood Parasites*. And when I sent it to them, John Dunning, who was the main creative guy there, really liked it and he could tell it was something special. And he was excited because his sex films never got released in the US, because they were very European, plus the States was very puritanical as it still is. So he could sell them to France and Germany, but he could never get into the US market with a sex film.

This was a horror film. Roger Corman had of course done what he was doing, so it had never occurred to them to make a modern horror film, because the films that they were distributing were all Gothic vampire films. In fact I remember one of the guys, who was a marketing guy there, said, 'I don't even consider this a horror film, I don't know what it is' – because it didn't have vampires, it didn't have castles, it didn't have moonlight, you know. So I went through a very bizarre period where they wanted to buy the script but they didn't want me to direct it. And also they were trying to get money from the

Film Development Corporation, which has become Telefilm Canada, but that was the government funding. They said, 'Without government funding we cannot afford to make this movie.' And of course the film was very extreme sexually for those days, in terms of all kinds of things, and violent. And this government agency was worried about getting involved with a film like that.

So I actually went with my friend Norman Snider to Los Angeles, it was the first time I had ever gone to LA. [We stayed with] Lorne Michaels, a friend who would do *Saturday Night Live*, and had tried to do *Saturday Night Live* here with the CBC, who were too conservative to do it. He was doing a Lily Tomlin special and he had a place in Los Angeles on the beach, he was renting a place in Malibu. And Norman and I went down there and I had my first LA experience. It was February, here it was like this [freezing!] and there it was palm trees, and I said to myself, 'Oh my God we're really in California, it really is warm.' We rented a red Mustang convertible, we got stopped by the police and frisked, I did coke for the first time in my life. It was the classic LA experience, and it must have been '73 maybe, '72-'73. That's where I met Barbara Steele. I believe that Lorne Michaels was renting Barbara Steele's beach-house. So I remember being invited to a lunch on the beach with Barbara Steele. And this was exciting to me, because of course I knew her as a horror queen, and also she had done a Fellini film, and she had been Louis Malle's lover. It was wonderful to meet Barbara Steele.

SG: You had seen the Mario Bava movie [*The Mask of Satan/Black Sunday*] with her?

DC: Yeah, yeah, so I knew her . . . and of course she is in *8½* as well. So it was exciting for me to meet her, and she was in an unusual state of mind, because she had gotten married and had a child and stopped acting, basically. Then she had a divorce and she was having to come back into acting. And she had many conflicts about all of that. But I met her, and with her was a director named Jonathan Demme, because he had just directed her in *Women in Chains*, I think it was called, or *Caged Heat*. [It was *Caged Heat*.] He had a beard, he had long hair, you know. So we're sitting on the beach and we're eating some salad or something, and Barbara is drinking a glass of wine and I'm sitting there and then I say, 'I got this script called *Parasite Murders*' – or it might still have been called *Orgy of the Blood Parasites* – 'that I'm hoping to get done, and I've come to LA because I seem not to be able to get this movie made in Canada.' And he said, 'Oh yes, I've read that script.' And I said, 'You've read my script! Here, you, Jonathan Demme who just directed Barbara Steele in Hollywood, why would you have read my script that is in Montréal?' He said, 'Oh well, they asked me to direct it.' Now it wasn't John Dunning apparently who asked him to direct it, but a man named Alfred Pariser, who was an American. He had been their lawyer and now he was producing for them, it sounded like Alfred's style. Anyway it really didn't matter, I just said, 'There's no way anybody is going to direct that script but me, I'll burn it before . . .' He really was very shocked and he said, 'Well you know, the way they talked to me about it, I thought there was something funny going on.' He was very sweet actually, and I didn't blame him about it. And of course, it put it in my mind that Barbara Steele would be great in that movie: a perfect actress, and someone who maybe I couldn't have gotten earlier in her career, but now that she was trying to make a comeback, maybe she would do this very very low-budget Canadian horror film. And I did go to Roger Corman's office, and I gave the script to Jon . . . He's the guy who I think ended up directing *Airplane*, Jon Davison may be his name, because Corman was just on his way to have a root canal done with his dentist.

First steps

into genre film

Shivers, Rabid

We may never know exactly at which point *Shivers* became a hit – not only in English-speaking Canada, where the feature film industry was in its infancy, but also in the rest of the world. There is little evidence of this moment of 'revelation', due to the fact that the film was released on the circuits reserved for the most despised forms of genre cinema: sex and horror. As a result, 'serious' critics had no chance to praise the film's Reichian undertones, its subversive quality and its thoroughly contemporary humour.

This would have to wait until the London release of *Rabid*, when the weekly listings magazine *Time Out* honoured Cronenberg by featuring his film on its cover, with a cover design inspired by the artist Robert Rauschenberg and including a comic-strip bubble in the style of the Situationist International. The English were not mistaken: just as the Situationists had hijacked the nascent art of the comic-strip for their agitprop material, so Cronenberg, a child of the rock generation, had deliberately hijacked the universes created by Val Lewton – of understated sex and horror, imagined only in the shadows – or Herschell Gordon Lewis – an explicitly gory yet paradoxically more innocent world, conceived to encourage petting among teenagers at drive-in cinemas – in order to smuggle into it some of the main themes of underground cinema: orgies, sexual liberation, the kind of contamination and viral infection dear to William Burroughs, criticism of urban planning, etc . . .

We could ask if Cronenberg might have expressed his ideas in a different form. His violently sarcastic provocations would certainly have found their place in the galleries and museums of contemporary art (in line with the work of the brilliant group of Toronto artists known as General Idea) and, in this way, remained in a cosily elitist environment. In the same way, one could imagine him as the passionate director of a co-operative of *avant-garde* video-makers. But he was the first to recognise that genre cinema could contain his ideas; it would also allow a broad public to enjoy his unique outlook on contemporary cinema, and a discourse that was so marginal and dissident that it needed the extraordinary conjunction of the permissiveness typical of the 1970s together with the launch of Canada's film subsidy.

From the very beginning, Cronenberg's films were 'events' that attacked the air-conditioned nightmare of North America, but remained unconnected to any political dogma; this undoubtedly explains the violent reaction of the politically correct establishment, which was already taking aim and in this case – found its target (see, for example, the ferocious attacks launched by an eminent spokesman for gay liberation and the Marxist left, Robin Wood). There was in *Shivers* something so

Above: *American poster for* **Shivers** *(They Came from Within in the USA), the first full-length film by Cronenberg to be distributed on the commercial circuit.* **Opposite page: Shivers:** *The ageing Professor Hobbes (surnames are never neutral with Cronenberg) performs an operation without anaesthetic on a household table, upon an adolescent girl. This scene was said to be a full-frontal attack on the general public's sensibilities.*

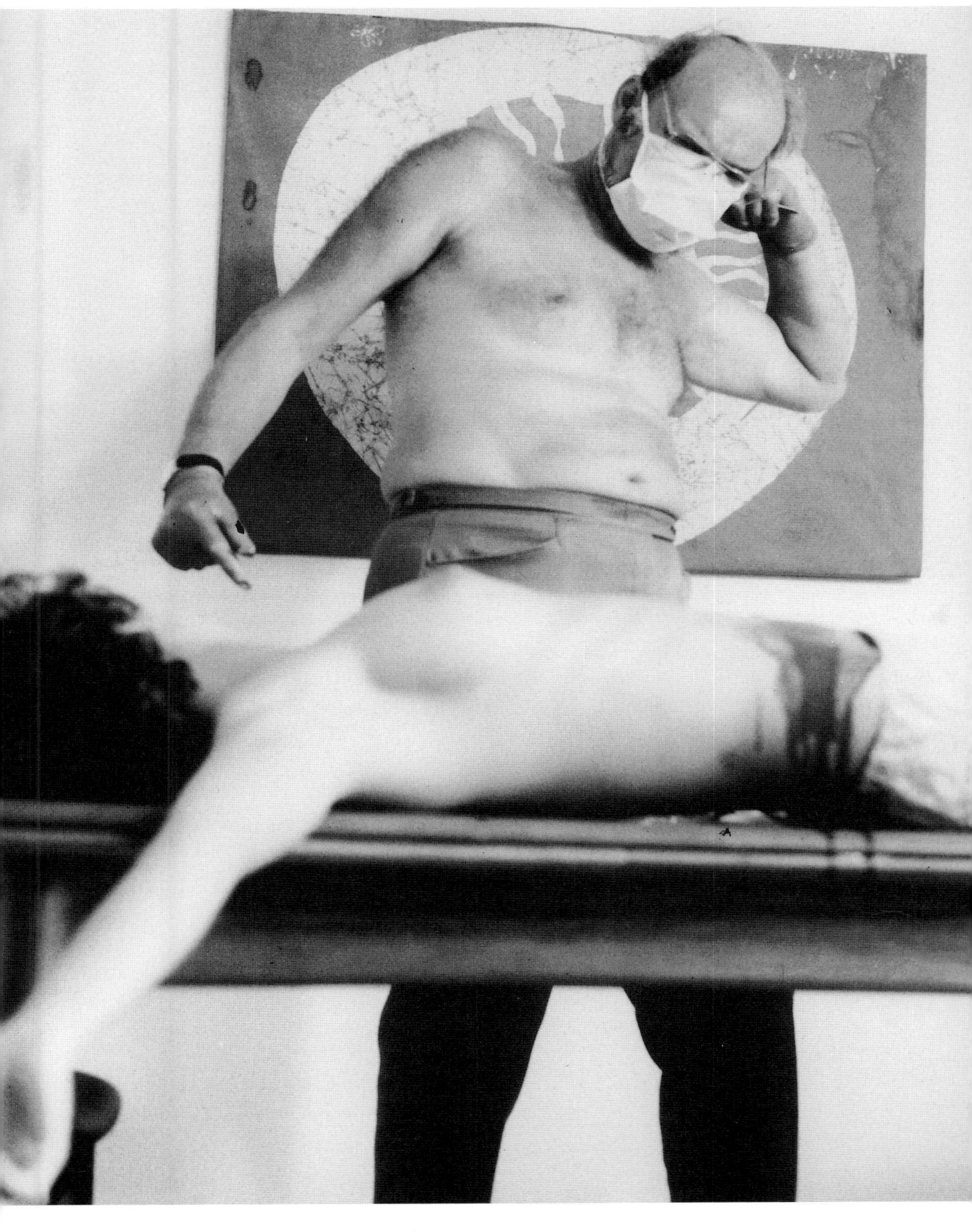

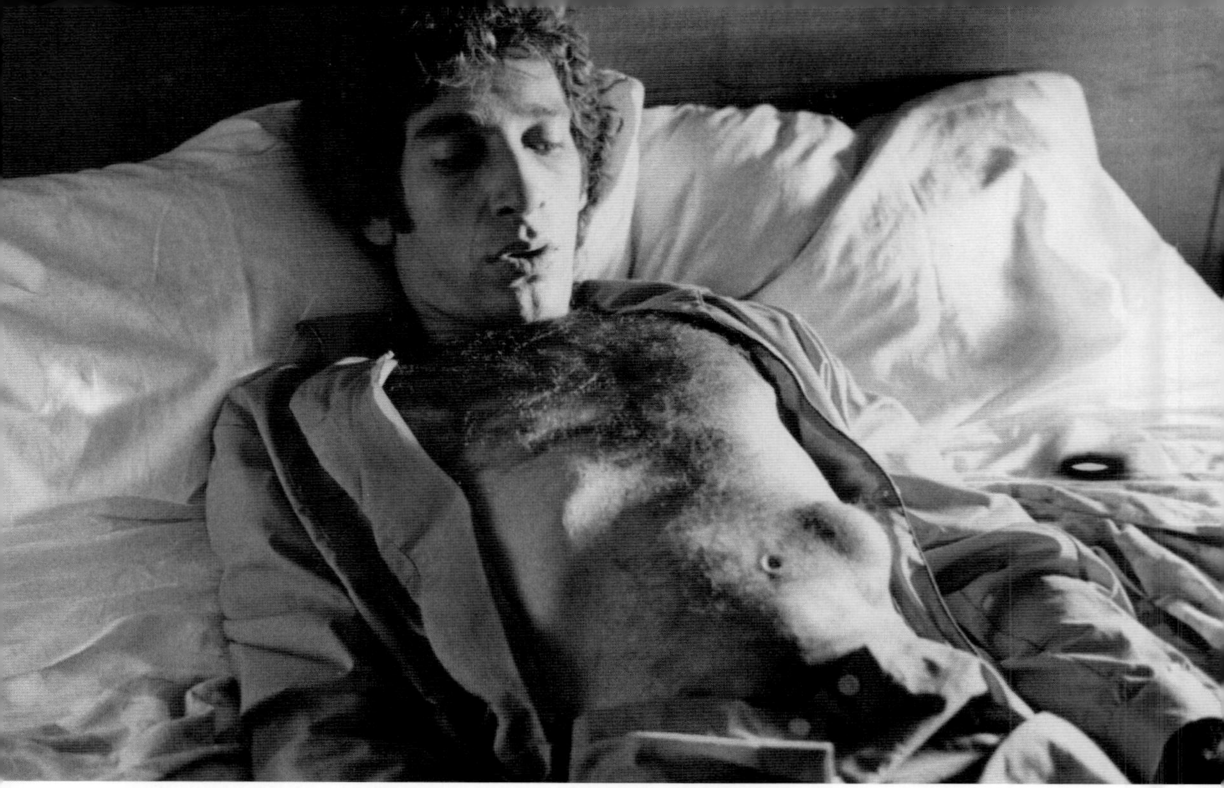

Shivers: Nicholas Tudor (Allan Migicovksy) contemplates a strange new wave travelling up and down his abdomen.

essentially radical that one cannot avoid associating it with the writings of Burroughs, with his baroque atrocities and his recklessness. These two great subversive films, *Shivers* and *Rabid*, were hugely successful with the genre audience, those fans of ultra-violent horror who despite what we might expect did not take them at face value. Paradoxically, it was because he was not interested in a 'cultivated' audience that Cronenberg, who produced dozens of crazy scenarios during those years of luminescent freedom, was never tempted to make films that could be culturally described as 'in good taste'. Certain plants bloom in shadow or, as was the case with this director, in solitude. Belonging to no group or movement, isolated in the narrow puritanism of seventies Toronto, Cronenberg began creating offbeat, unclassifiable works as if he was working in a foreign language (one thinks of Kafka, writing in the German language in Prague), free of all ethnic affiliations (along the lines of the New York-Italian cinema, for example) or the burdens of politics. One could already sense that Cronenberg would not 'go Hollywood', to tarnish his vision to make it fashionable and lightly provocative in an acceptable way. Like Sartre's hero in *Les Mains sales*, he is 'beyond redemption'. It would not take long for him to provide firm evidence of this.

SG: I can imagine at the time – was it '75 when people discovered those images in puritan Ontario ? – why it was such a scandal.

DC: Yes, it was a bit of a scandal. You know the story. I had showed it to a film critic who had liked my earlier film *Stereo*. And he was also the editor of a very influential magazine called *Saturday Night*, which still exists here. And he wrote under a pseudonym, Marshall Delaney, but I showed him the movie, because I thought this is my first movie as opposed to my first film. Professional movie. I actually got paid to make it. I thought he would understand the connection between this and my previous film and he would like this. Well he was completely shocked. And he wrote an article that

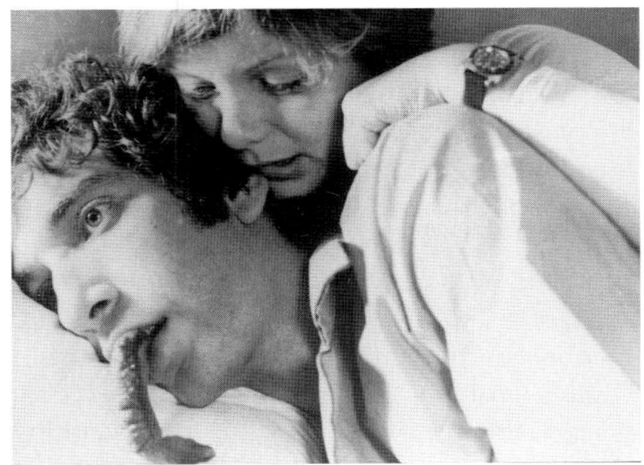

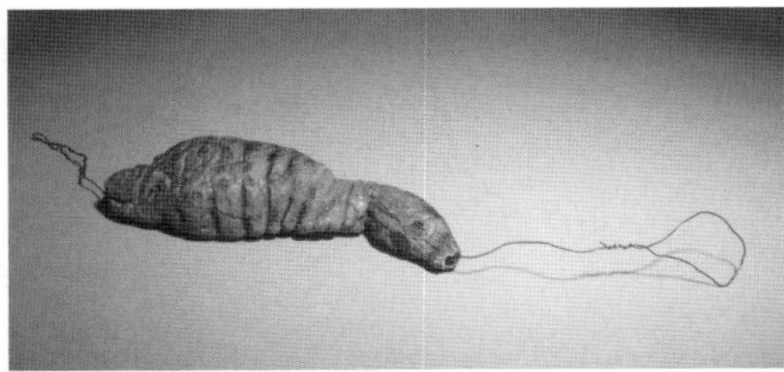

Above: A creature halfway between the slug and the penis: this special effect may have been on a small scale, but it was extremely effective. Left: Psychoanalysis translates to the cinema: the oral stage.

people still quote to this day: 'This is pornography. It's disgusting and you paid for it. You the taxpayers paid for it.' This was on the cover of this magazine and it was a huge scandal. Apparently they were talking about it in the House of Commons. Arguing about it in government as if there were nothing more important to do, because it was one of the first movies that what is now Telefilm, and was then the Canadian Film Development Corporation, had invested in. So it was the first time the taxpayer's money had gone into investing in movies. It was under a microscope. Of course it was also the first movie that made money for the government. The very first. There had been a few others that had lost money totally. It was a big scandal and my first feature film. It actually took me a couple of years more to get my next film made, because of that article.

SG: Tell me honestly, at that time you were quite young: did you consider the starting idea of *Shivers* as a sexual liberation manifesto?
DC: Yeah, because remember the seventies really were the sixties, especially in Canada. They took a little later to get here. It was very misunderstood. It was also the famous Robin Wood article, you know, a serious critic, very political, very Marxist, very gay liberation. He condemned this movie as being a reactionary movie. Of course, the mass of people who saw it who were in government, who were the real reactionaries, understood that this was not a reactionary, conservative film, but there is a sense of complete liberation by the crazy people at the end. Certainly the crew. We all lived in that building: Nun's Island. We identified with the crazy building. We actually lived in the same building we were shooting in. And the repressive atmosphere was so . . . by the time it was finished we wanted to rip off our clothes and run screaming through the halls, kicking doors down, and some of the crew did that. So we certainly understood the politics of it, even if Robin Wood seemed to be blind to it. And as I said, the reactionary forces that exist in Canada understood it as well.

SG: Which brings us back to a subject we've already discussed, but from *Shivers* to *Crash*, whether it is your intention or only the reaction of certain people, you always seem to be on the border of provoking certain people. I'm sure when you were 25 years younger, maybe your intention was more clearly to provoke. I'm quite sure when you made *Crash* that it was totally different. A lot of reactions are the same. How can you explain that?
DC: It's interesting, because I don't think of myself as deliberately intending to provoke people. I think of myself as wanting to astonish them, surprise them, delight them, by showing them some things they've never seen and making connections. You know, the metaphors and so on. And not even necessarily to shock them, but really to surprise them. And as always, there's a

part of me that's unprepared every time for the strength of the reaction, the virulence of the reaction against some of my movies. Whether it's on the grounds of feminism or more puritanism or whether they're talking about violence or whatever, grotesque, gooey, ugly. I'm really surprised, because I feel like I'm in collaboration with my audience. I'm going to show them some things.

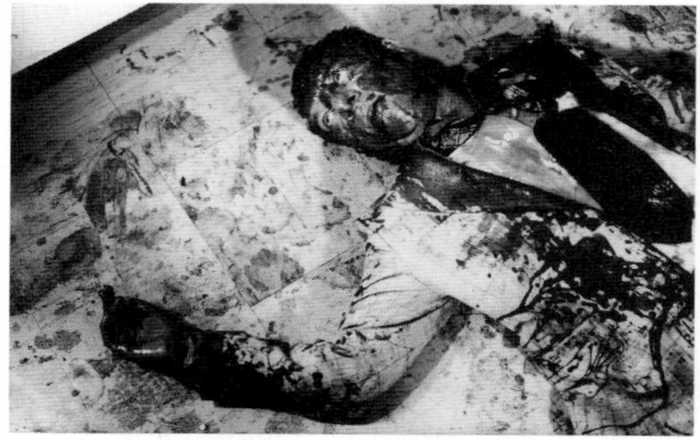

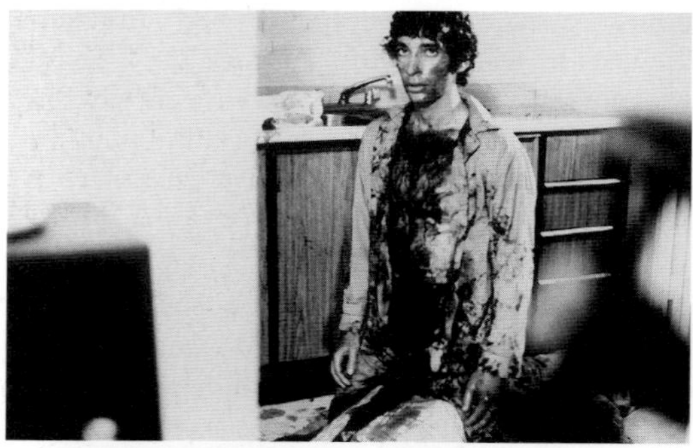

The gore is more extreme in more puritanical countries like America. Shivers enjoyed notable commercial success, but attracted a barrage of criticism from the God-fearing and the politically correct.

I'm going to do some things, but they have their role as well. I'm always surprised when it becomes an adversarial thing, when they become my opponent. It's a naiveté I have that I'd rather not lose. It's funny, when I spoke to John Dunning – who was my first sort of mentor and producer, he produced *Shivers* and *Rabid* – we talked about *Crash* and he said, 'You know, David, you haven't changed a bit.' And I guess I could have said, 'Neither has the world.' It's interesting, because in Canada *Crash* was very well accepted. It was considered strong and shocking, but it was nothing like the reaction in the UK, where the film was banned in the centre of London. People were boycotting, picketing. The film was in the papers every day, for over a year they said there was a cartoon, an article, an editorial, some polemic against it. They were vicious. Vicious. Many of them had not even seen the film. The film was based on a book by a very respected, in some quarters, British writer. Of course he has his detractors as well, as a writer. But I'm always surprised. And in the States Ted Turner was really my personal censor. He did not want the company that he bought to release the film, even though legally he had no right [to prevent it]. So it delayed the release of the film in the US for about eight months, which effectively killed the film, because any of the momentum and the publicity and excitement about it had died by that time. Similarly in the UK, the release was delayed because of the new election. They felt once the tory government was out the film could be released. So suddenly I was involved in the national politics of the United Kingdom. It's very bizarre, and I find the proportions of that very strange. It's disproportionate. Obviously, despite the Geraldos and the Jerry Springers and the TV shows and the shows about sex and vaginal reconstruction and God knows what you can see on television, those exposures of sexuality are not real somehow. And somehow these movies are touching nerves that all of this discussion, that seems so open and so free on sex and sexuality, is not really addressing. There are still taboos and I

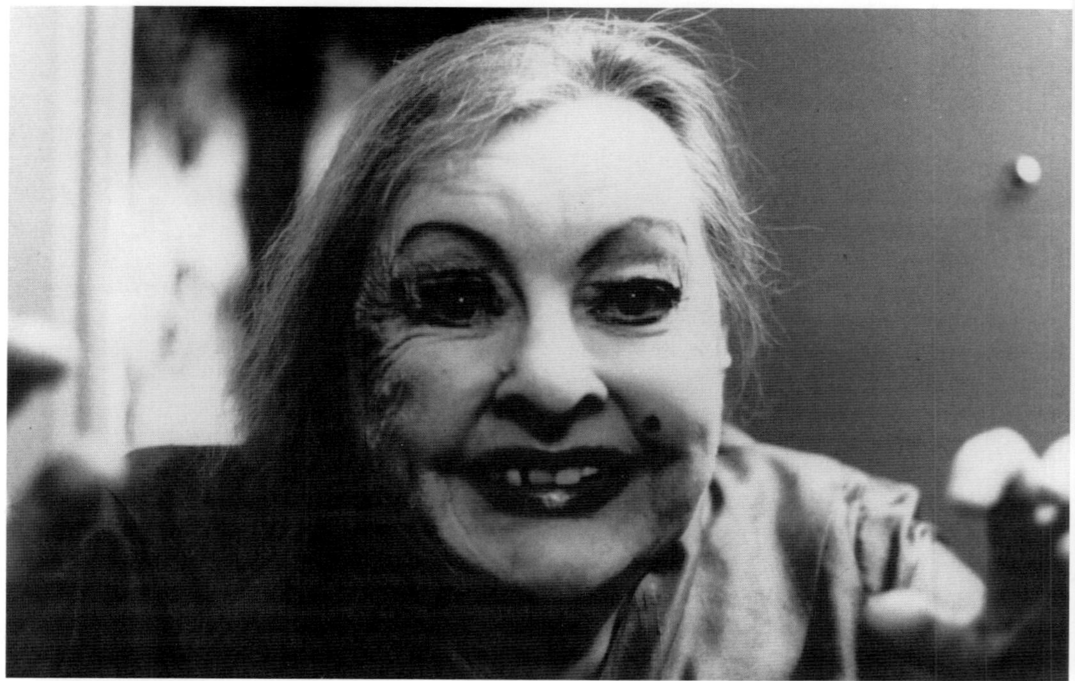

Polymorphously perverse sexuality: after the adolescents and the children, the senior citizens . . .

seem to be unerringly touching them.

SG: So would you agree with what Burroughs wrote once: 'If censorship was removed, nothing would happen and that's exactly the problem' ?

DC: Yes, I think it's true. There's this weird schizophrenia going on, because if you put what is on television now on television in the fifties, people would think there would be an atomic explosion as a result. They would think that everyone would go insane and run amok and rape and kill. I don't know what they think would happen. If you took someone from the fifties and put them in front of a television set now, they would probably go into a coma. They wouldn't believe what they were seeing, yet nothing has happened. It's not changing anything. I found that with the struggles that I've had with censorship – and Canada has still, although we keep it very low profile, real censorship. It's government censorship. And if you show a film that has been censored in its uncensored form, you can go to jail. They can take the projectionist and take his licence away. They can close the theatre. It's very strong. It's unprecedented really. The United States does not quite have this, for example. They don't have government censorship in the same way. You'd have to take the film to court and go through a lengthy court procedure. But this is, in Canada, *a priori* censorship. Somebody sitting watching your film has the power, a bureaucrat has the power to say, 'This film cannot be shown,' or 'part of the film' or 'these frames cannot be shown.' I had *The Brood* with censors in Ontario, for example. They cut the film physically themselves, every print, and kept the pieces. If those pieces had been put back in, I could have been in jail for ten-twenty years. This is very serious. There have been many attempts at certain points in the name of – you name it, whether it's feminism, or child abuse, or whatever the atrocity of the month is – to counter that with new laws that are even more restrictive and more vague, saying anything that is upsetting to anybody should be censored. You know that kind of thing. So I get into fights. That is really the only truly political act of my life, my fight against censorship.

Unfortunately I end up dealing with it in other countries, where I don't really have the right or ability to fight it. I've been in conversations with a woman in Norway who controlled all the cinemas in Oslo – and she's just a functionary. She's just a bureaucrat. She's a theatre manager and all the theatres there are owned by the city. She didn't call it banning, but she banned *Crash* just in that city. I found myself on the phone with her arguing about it for a radio talk show. It turns out that her husband had been paralysed from the neck down in a car accident, and she says that has nothing to do with her decision to not show *Crash*. So people then had to drive from Oslo to the nearest next town to see the movie. I wanted to say to her, 'You know there are probably going to be a lot of car crashes, because there are going to be a lot of people driving out of the city and you are actually going to cause car crashes.' I didn't do that. I couldn't bring myself to say that to the poor woman. So every once and a while, [with] a movie like *Crash*, I suddenly have to relive all of these battles which don't die. They'll never die. There will always be taboos and there will always be pressure to break those taboos. I suppose that's just human nature and human society.

SG: Do you sometimes feel you've made the good choice if the reactions are so violent?
DC: Not really, I believe I'm telling the truth here, because I've thought of this between *Shivers* and *Crash*. We're talking 25 years maybe. I would love everybody to love my movie. If everybody said *Crash* was fantastic, even if it was disturbing, it was great, it was wonderful, I think I'd be perfectly happy. I wouldn't feel that I had failed because I hadn't distressed anybody. I think that's true. I haven't had that happen yet. I haven't ever made a movie like, let's say, *ET*, that everybody loves. It's not my desire on the other hand to be lovable. I don't really want to make movies that are lovable because I think you've sold something out at that point. I think you've betrayed something, some toughness and some hardness and some edge that makes movie-making worthwhile to me. But at the same time, I think if *Crash* had been a huge hit, as big as *Titanic* . . . How 'bout that? Let's get really ridiculous. Let's say if *Crash* made $2 billion and everybody you talked to just about loved it, I think I'd be okay. I think I wouldn't worry about that, but maybe I would. Maybe I would.

SG: You started your commercial career with a film genre that was only budding at the time: gore. Why?
DC: It wasn't really a conscious choice. It seemed natural for me to write some sci-fi thing. I can articulate it now, but might not have been able to then, because I think that the human body is the first fact of human existence. And for me everything comes out of that: philosophy, religion. Everything comes out of the body and the fact of human mortality. It's natural that my film would focus on that. Even in my very first writings as a young kid, death, and dealing with it, was very strongly present. So it seemed natural to deal with the body and what happens to the body. So for me to invent some phantasmagoria, to create metaphors for the body and the things that happen in the body, and have part of the body outside of the body so we can look at it and deal with it, brings me into the genre of body horror. Which perhaps was not so directly recognised here, but in the context of what I did later I think becomes pretty obvious. In fact I have to say that some of the images like this ended up in things like *Alien*, which was more popular than any of the films I've ever made. But the writer of *Alien* had definitely seen these movies, Dan O'Bannon. The idea of a parasite that bursts out of your body and uses a fluid and leaps on your face, that's all in *Shivers*. So it obviously touched a nerve in the public in general, this imagery, and for me it's just natural to pursue it. I wouldn't call it an obsession, but it's just a very easy, natural thing that I get into. It's a discussion of the body. It's the discussion of

Rabid: With this film, Cronenberg reinforced his favourite theme, medical gore.

human existence as a physical event and phenomenon. Then add to that the level of metaphor I like to deal with, and you get what I do . . . It protected me, the genre. Think of *The Fly*. I've often thought of this. *The Fly* is a very difficult movie if you did it as a straight movie. Two tall, beautiful people meet. They're eccentric. He gets sick. He dies horribly and slowly while she watches helplessly, and then she helps him to commit suicide, and that's the end of the movie. Not a very commercial movie. But *The Fly* is my biggest commercial success because it's a genre picture. It's a sci-fi horror film. Therefore that plot, which is very emotional and very real, is protected. The audience feels a little bit distanced because of the invention, the science fiction stuff, the telepod, the fly, the creatures. But really it's a very strong human story. It's about aging. It's about disease. It's about death. I've been protected by the genre, unlike *Crash*, which is a genre-less picture. I mean *Crash*, it's hard to fit it into any genre. It's not a horror film. It's not a sci-fi film, even though some people like to think of *Crash* as a science fiction novel. It is in its metaphysics, but not in its physics. In its physics it's a very naturalistic novel, and so too the movie I think. So then it's unprotected and you get this hysteria, or whatever happens in some countries, because people are no longer protected by saying, 'It's just a sci-fi movie' or 'It's just a horror film.' Those genres have always been devalued in the West in general. Not so much in France, where you could have a serious literary career as a science fiction writer. I guess I mean west of Europe. [In] North America, if you were a sci-fi writer, if you were Philip K. Dick, you were a second or third-class writer, no matter how wonderful your ideas were or your actual literary style. It's interesting that Nabokov, one of my favourite writers, wrote a book, *Anna*, which is a science fiction novel but has never been recognised as such, because the weight of all of Nabokov's other works would prevent people seeing it. But it's a completely invented world, with completely invented physics and everything else. A real science fiction novel.

SG: Where were we?

DC: Oh yeah, cross-collateralising. So yes, the CFDC was attempting to finance *Rabid* in a hidden way by financing a group of films, two or three films together, so that they could say that their money wasn't actually going into my film. But at that one point the other films fell apart, and there we were left exposed and naked, and suddenly it was obvious they were financing us. And they bit the bullet and accepted that, and said, 'OK, we're financing *Rabid*.' And so they went ahead with it, worried nonetheless. But you know, given that they were government bureaucrats, I thought they were pretty bold and I had a good relationship with them. Even though, I do think that it [that one review] probably cost me a year and a half, maybe two years of delay in financing that movie. It revealed to me many things in a personal way, the power of the critic in a practical way – not that it damaged us at the box-office, because the film was

Shivers is one of the only films inspired by sexologist Wilhelm Reich to be distributed on the commercial circuit.

very successful. In fact it was the first film that the CFDC had financed which actually returned a profit. So I was actually filling up their coffers with money that could be used for other films. So that was the argument again, saying, 'This film more than paid for itself, and we'll now fund some other presumably non-pornographic films,' you see. So *Rabid* got made, and despite the presence of Marilyn Chambers, porno queen, it didn't cause anywhere near the same kind of stir [*Shivers* did], and I think it was just because society was moving on at that point.

SG: **And how did it feel to know that you had become a professional filmmaker . . .**
DC: It's interesting . . .

SG: **. . . who had reached the stage of the second feature?**
DC: Yeah, yeah, it was sort of the way it felt when I started having children, which is to say that it happened so gradually and naturally that I never had those moments that people write about where they say: 'Oh my God, I suddenly realised I was a parent,' or, 'I suddenly realised I was a professional filmmaker.' I would have to think back about those days, when I was dreaming about it. Well I can think about those days but I never . . . It didn't seem as though it was inevitable, because I could tell that there were very obvious moments when it could have all gone wrong. So I never felt that it was inevitable that it would work, and I had many moments worrying that it would never happen, and that it would just be a dream or fantasy or something. But once it did start to happen, I never looked back. I never thought about that, because it did take a long time, and it did happen gradually, and I really had my hands full with the practicalities of how to make a movie, and I was very excited and terrified by that. It seemed very natural, you know. Just like the first time I had a child that called me Daddy, it seemed totally natural. I didn't feel the slightest bit of awkwardness, which is still one of the funny things. It makes me feel that phrase that people use to death, 'I was born to do this.' There are moments when I feel, well, I was born to do this,

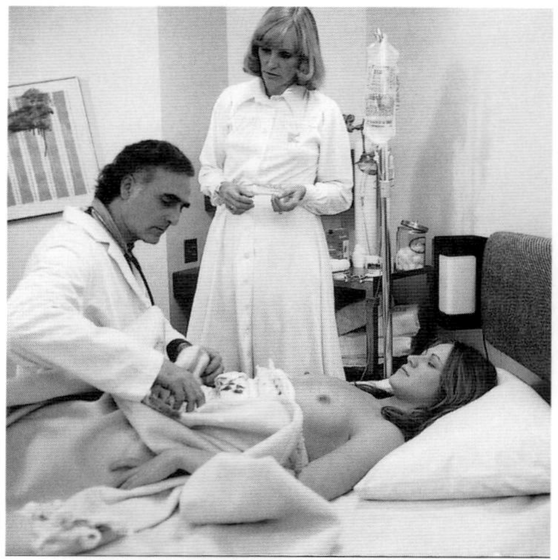

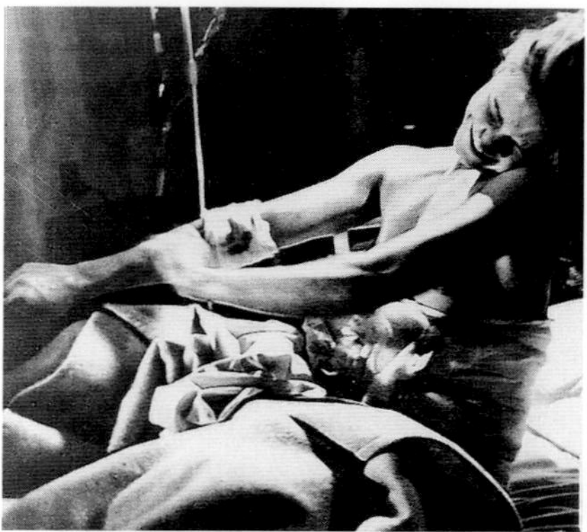

Rabid: Marilyn Chambers is transformed into a vampire by a skin graft.

and therefore that's why I don't feel the slightest bit euphoric or odd doing it, because it feels very natural to do it. I don't know, if I took a couple of years off and wrote a novel and got it published, I would probably feel more strange about that than about the movie-making.

SG: There's one thing that I always ask movie directors about, because obviously it's part of the job, especially now – perhaps there were times in Hollywood when things were different. But being a filmmaker – and especially an independent filmmaker, not in a studio system – forces you to be also the leader of a team. You cannot totally rely on a producer . . .

DC: That's right.

SG: So suddenly a young student who has been doing underground movies has to lead a team.

DC: Well I was lucky to have my mentors, who were John Dunning, André Link, and to a certain extent Ivan Reitman. Ivan had made two films, I think, by that time: *Cannibal Girls* and *Foxy Lady*. Now Ivan was into it before I was. He never made the equivalent of *Stereo* or *Crimes of the Future* because he knew that he wanted to be a big-time commercial filmmaker. That was his goal. Ivan has never sold out because he is doing exactly what he wants to do. To me that's not a sell-out. If I were to do what Ivan is doing, I would be selling out my own ideal, but he is not. So even his first film for the co-op was a gentle comedy with a goofy guy who finally ends up with the beautiful girl. He's been re-making that movie ever since, as I have probably been remaking my first movies in a sense. Ivan was hired by them to be an executive, and he was also there to help me. I very distinctly remember this one moment: sitting at a table with my production people, and I had no idea what any of them did. One of them was a production manager, one of them did props – I had no idea what 'props' was. I knew what costumes were, I didn't know what the art director did. In those days there wasn't a production designer, [if] you were the art director, that was the top. I had no idea what these people did, and I had to fake it at this meeting because they were saying, 'OK David, let's go through the script and you tell us what you want.' I didn't even know what an assistant director did, I knew what the words meant, but I didn't know what they meant in practical terms. That was my first production meeting and I was faking it totally, but I did have people who knew that I was faking it. My mentors, as I say, who were there to guide me.

Really it was a very lovely experience. It was pretty hectic, we shot in fifteen days plus two pick-up days, for wide shots and stuff. So in seventeen days I shot this quite complex movie with a lot of special effects: some ground-breaking effects, in fact, that were later stolen for

Alien, I have to say. Dan O'Bannon definitely knew my movies and he wrote the script for *Alien*. The whole idea of the parasite bursting out of the chest and jumping onto the face was all in *Shivers*. The idea of parasites living in your body was of course the basic idea of *Shivers*.

I also remember another moment that was very interesting to me, which was the first meeting I had about the script with my producers. We were sitting there and they were talking very enthusiastically about the script, and the casting, and the locations, and how we would shoot it – we were shooting in Montreal, which of course was not my city – and I had this incredible sense of loss and melancholy come over me. It was as though someone close to me had died, or as though I had left home forever, because the script which had been my own internal personal property in my head was suddenly not personal anymore. It had become a communal property and I was very surprised by my reaction. I had spent years fighting to get to that point where I had these people helping me make it a reality, and now that they were, I was resenting it and feeling incredibly depressed. It only lasted for a few minutes, but it was so potent. And that's the difference, of course, between writing a novel and writing a script. I think when you write a novel you never have to lose that other thing. Of course you [may] have critics tearing you apart and you might have editors criticising some phrases and wanting to edit, but from what I understand from the many novelists that I know, it's never the shock [that you have] when suddenly you have a huge production team taking your script to pieces, and each taking their part of it away to work on. So it's a different process. Now of course it's very familiar to me, so I don't have that shock, but I can summon up that feeling any time, it was so potent.

Whereas the faking it at the first production meeting, that was just fun. I won't say that I've never faked anything since, because every film is an experiment, at least in ideal terms. If it were just a repetition, it would be incredibly boring and it would be death, not life. So every film, you hope, will call up completely new problems, and demand new resources from you that you never knew you had, or you're not sure you have. Therefore each film is the first time you've done it, for each film there will be things that are the first time. So in that sense you're faking it despite all your experience.

Four years ago, when I went to Sundance to show *Crash*, I was also teaching and being a sort of a mentor to some young filmmakers. One of them was Tony Bui, whose film ended up in competition against mine in Berlin. That was a very interesting experience because I was suddenly forced to relive my whole education as a filmmaker. I'm not a filmmaker like some Hollywood filmmakers, not like let's say Woody Allen or Joel Schumacher. I don't make a lot of films and I don't always have twenty things on the go at one time. So I tend to downplay to myself my level of professional expertise. I don't think I'm the most technically adept director because I don't do it all the time, and I'm not making a film every year, or every two years. But when I encountered these film students who really didn't know anything, I suddenly realised how much I do know, which was one of those interesting moments. And in trying to help them through the traumas that they were going through, very basic traumas that I had long ago dealt with, [I found] some of them had never faced a wilful actor, a professional actor or actress, had never experienced that situation's potential for highly destructive psychodrama, and it was really interesting. But it was painful too, because it was like reliving birth. Just remembering having to learn all that stuff, and the moments when I learned it, that was the last time I really re-experienced what we're talking about now.

SG: Are you sometimes surprised by the result on the screen of what took so long to write as a script?

DC: Every time. I'm surprised every time. I think

some people certainly expect you to have an ideal movie in your head and then you match it. You come as close as you can. And then you can run the two side by side, one in your head and one on the screen, and you can say, 'How close did you come?'

For me that doesn't happen at all. I don't have this ideal film in my head. Even if I've created every word. Whether it's based on something or not. It doesn't really matter. It's a very organic, almost sculptural process for me, making the film. It's putting each little piece of clay here, then smoothing it, feeling it, gradually. That's why I don't do storyboards. I know that that's a very common technique, especially when you're doing special effects. And I have done one or two little ones for special effects sequences. I can't imagine doing that. I need the real actors. I need the real costumes. I need the real space. Space is very important. And the people around me who are going to make it. So I can't really sit in a room alone, the way you could if you were writing a novel, or the way you can when you're writing a script. I have to have all that physical stuff to make the film with, and so I'm always surprised with what turns out. So of course, when we're editing there are more surprises. When we're doing the soundtrack, the effects track, the music. It's very rarely anticipated by me, and in a way I don't want to. I think I would get very bored if I knew exactly what I wanted, and then tried to match it with some physical reality. All those little rectangles of film. That would be very boring. So the process has to be scary and dangerous and unexpected. When I despair about cinema and my art, the despair usually takes that form, either that everything has been done, or there are amazing things to be done and I can't do them. That's the fear. That's the despair. Or that I could do amazing things, but the structure of cinema today, the way it is – what with the domination of Hollywood and the budgets being what they are – will make it impossible to achieve something that I feel I could achieve, but because of the state of cinema today I never will. All of these things, when I'm in a despairing mode about cinema, that's usually the form it takes.

SG: I would like to elaborate a little on this subject of contamination, because what is absolutely obvious in your cinema is that we almost never see images that come from other movies, other contemporary movies, which is very rare.
DC: I would love it if that were true.

SG: My explanation would be that you are a writer and director so you do not conceive your movies in terms of images. You build them. I have the feeling that lots of other directors, even decent ones, do storyboards or at the start of the process build the movie as a combination of sequences.
DC: Well, that could be true. For me the movie starts from the inside out. It really does start with concepts, and sometimes with characters, but even the characters are conceptual. It isn't really very visual to begin with, although there is sometimes an image in my head that's a central image . . .

SG: Maybe that's the main problem of cinema as an art form, not to use the images that are everywhere.
DC: That is another part of my despairing-of-cinema-moment, that there is too much imagery. That we're overwhelmed with imagery, and that imagery has lost any possible meaning or impact or force it could have. And to try to give it artificial meaning, artificial force, which is what many people try to do, just makes it worse. I can feel it when I'm behind the camera. I can feel the history behind every shot. And you say, 'How do I make this unique?' or, 'Does it have to be unique?' In a way you have to clear your mind of that, and in a way it becomes a matter of faith. It is almost a religious thing. You have to have faith that you will find the shots that will have a meaning in context, and that you don't have to be so tricky. You see a lot of directors now from rock videos and commercials, and

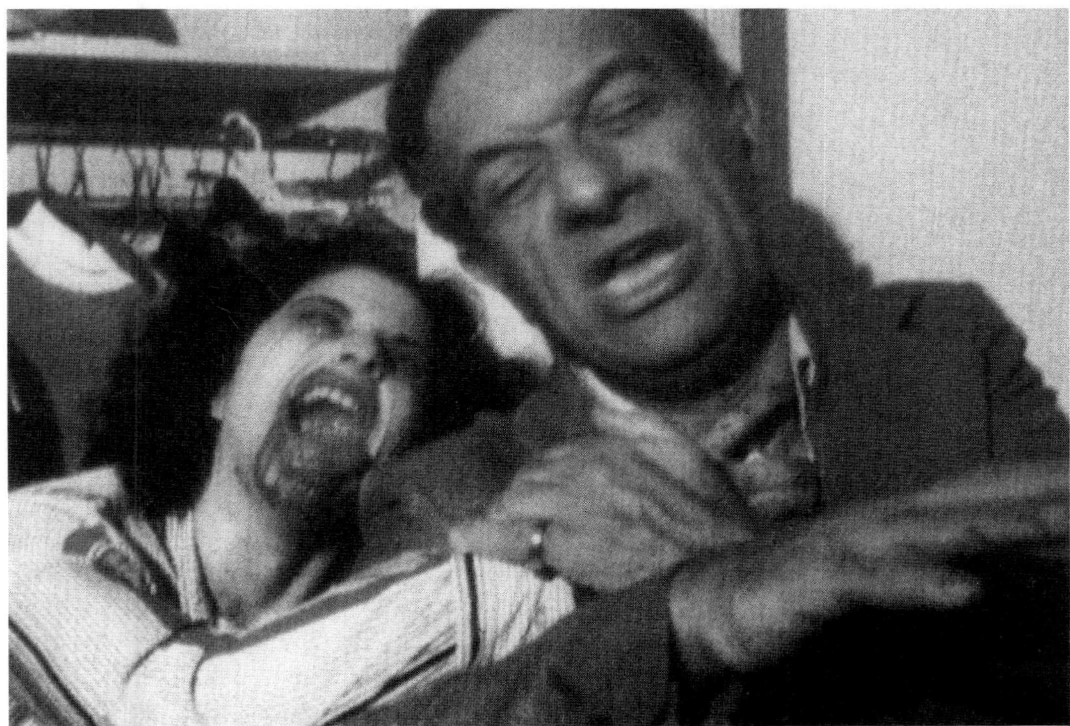

Rabid: *The theme of universal contamination. Later, certain critics ill advisedly reproached Cronenberg for 'predicting' Aids.*

they're very clever. And they do wonderful tricky stuff. It very rarely works within the context. You could say, 'My God, that was a great shot. How did they do that?' And I've been going the other way. I just read a book by Samuel Beckett called *The Last Modernist*. And I have the feeling that I'm a modernist as well, because I'm trying to simplify. I want my movies to be very still and pure and get to some kind of essence of each shot, rather than trying to constantly be exciting in the chemical sense, adrenaline. And yet I want my films not to be boring, of course, and to be engaging and to be challenging, but how to do that and keep that triple mind going at the same time? As I say, [you have] to be aware of every shot: you're using a 25mm lens; you're going to think of every shot you've ever seen with a 25mm lens. Low, moving in, backlit, smoke, whatever. You think of all the shots you've seen. It can overwhelm you and it can paralyse you. Now I think of that as a possible writing problem as well. It's not so much when you write a screenplay, because in a screenplay, of course, the quality of the writing, except for the dialogue, is meaningless except as a seduction for someone who will make the film, produce the film, or an actor who will come into the film. But in terms of the actual quality of the writing, it's not very relevant. Whereas [in] writing a novel, I can see where being obsessed with the word 'the' or 'and', how many times has it been used before, if you want every word to count you could drive yourself insane, which sometimes I do.

Have you seen this girl?

Five year old Candice Carveth, daughter of Frank Carveth of Toronto, has been missing since early this morning. Last seen near the Krell Street School, she was wearing a red two-piece snow suit. Police ask that anyone having information pertaining to the whereabouts of the missing girl to contact the nearest police station.

Towards professionalism

Fast Company, The Brood, Scanners

There were limits to the kind of support that Ontario gave to film production: it was not designed to encourage 'auteurist' works, but rather the development of a kind of national cinema in which Cronenberg had no obvious place. He therefore had to begin dealing with Hollywood, while remaining 'exiled' in his native Canada. The films of that period oscillated between the straightforward commissioned work (*Fast Company*), the astounding settlement of personal accounts found in *The Brood*, and the film that would propel Cronenberg toward a wider audience and the attention of the major studios, *Scanners*.

Cronenberg would continue to work from the basis of material accumulated during his youth; this was a means of staying faithful to himself, of avoiding becoming attuned to Hollywood's passing fads. His apparently adolescent preoccupations never let him fall into the pathos that the dominant commercial cinema requires of the genre he was working in – contemporary tragedy.

The Cronenberg hero is an artist, 'oversensitive', a creator who never manages to believe in the reality of a world beyond his own perceptions. And the filmmaker himself, ceaselessly questioning the medium in which he works, adopts a purposefully documentary tone for filming the fantasies, hallucinations and dreams that constitute the universe he depicts. Thus, in *The Brood*, which is based on some very contemporary subjects (the 'new psychiatry' and psychosomatic illness), he steers us toward an hallucinatory vision of a nuclear family founded on absolute hatred, the desire to kill one another. The incredible imagery of *Scanners* is based on a similar idea: the fight to the death between two telepathic brothers – an echo of which can be found in *Dead Ringers* – is less personal than existential. And if the public and critics, in part, declared themselves disgusted by Cronenberg's imagery, it is less because of its visceral realism than its striking proximity to what we call our unconscious. For Cronenberg does not content himself merely with working on our phobias, like so many lesser genre masters – he gives them flesh.

It is in its revelation of the disturbing proximity between our ideas and the mental images they sometimes generate that Cronenberg's art insinuates itself into the spectator's psyche, without always allowing us the possibility of filtering these images. And it is for this reason that he had no licence to disdain the gore genre in which he was working at the time: the filmmaker was preparing himself for the works to come which, despite their much less extravagant style, would lead the same spectators to experience the same sense of shock, the same disgust. If Cronenberg has affirmed himself more and more as one of the only contemporary artists in cinema, it is because he practices a kind of inverse sublimation: he does not transform our crude realities into something ethereal and impalpable; on the contrary, he gives our unthinkable thoughts, on the genuine violence

The Brood: *An autobiographical film, inspired by the separation of David Cronenberg from his first wife, and the resulting battle for the custody of little Cassandra Cronenberg. Right: Distorting tabloid sensationalism. The first collaboration with* Carol Spier, *who became Cronenberg's regular art director.*

EATON'S
Makes news on page 9

WEATHER
Wet, cold. High 7

15
FIN
20¢ OUT
METRO TRADI

OL. 8 NO. 26 • October paid circulation 202,997 TORONTO, ONTARIO, WEDNESDAY DECEMBER 6, 1978 • 104 P

BIZARRE SECONI KELLY MURDER

—REPORT, PICTURES SEE PAGE 3

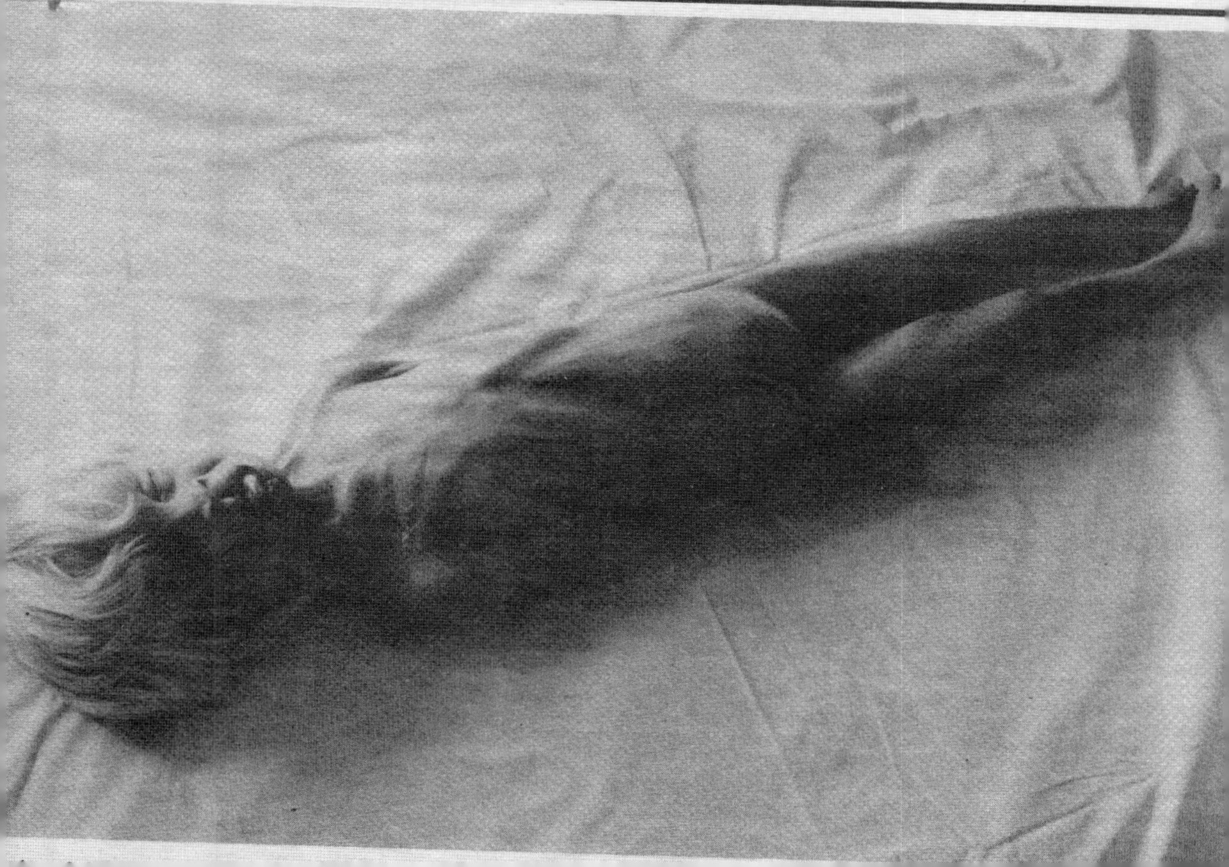

Poster for Fast Company, *an anomaly in the career of David Cronenberg, but made about a subject which remains one of his passions: motor racing.*

that we try to filter through morality and ideology, the unbearable substance of a nightmare. It is an approach that we find in the paintings of Francis Bacon and, of course, in the work of William S. Burroughs, but which, in the world of 'entertainment', is especially provocative. It is in this dimension, too, that David Cronenberg establishes himself as one of the only moralists of his generation. It is a position that creates isolation, if not total misunderstanding.

SG: **David, I know it's not an easy question, but I'd like you to answer very sincerely. When you see one of your old movies, can you learn something from it, watching an old movie one more time? What do you feel generally and does it teach you something?**

DC: No, I usually react with horror. If I'm switching around the TV and I suddenly see one of my films I immediately switch it off and switch it somewhere else. It's painful and I can't really say why it's painful. I find it very difficult to watch my old movies. So I don't do it. It's not the old cliché of I see things that are wrong, that I think I should do better. In fact, just watching some of this I'm thinking: 'Hey, that was actually pretty good!' I like what I saw. But I don't know why it is. At a certain point you're so obsessed with a film, you're so close to it that it consumes every moment. And then there comes a point where you have to let go of it, and I think you let go so deeply that suddenly it's out there. It's on its own. It's severed. It's no longer part of you, but it has a strange relationship. You can't watch it like somebody else's movie, but you can't really watch it like your own movie. I don't really think there's anything you can learn. It can only be sad things that are not very productive, like you weren't as good as you thought you were, or perhaps you're not as good now as you were. I mean all bad things. So I don't think it's very productive. I find it very difficult to watch them. When I have to do a voiceover for a laser disc or a DVD now it's very painful. At least those are more recent films. Sometimes you have to go back to do a very old film. I find that very hard, very difficult. In a way too, it's impossible to watch as a real movie. It's a documentary of what happened that day. Each shot, I remember where I was, what was happening on the set that day. It's not really cinema in the pure sense, so I try to avoid it.

SG: **So for instance you wouldn't be tempted to re-edit parts of your old movies?**

DC: No, no, it's somewhere in the past. It's gone. For good or bad, it's what happened then. It's a record of that, the mistakes as well as the good things. It's not that it's a sacred thing. I mean, if I were forced to remix because of some sound problem and somebody wanted to restore a film . . . I heard that Kubrick was redoing *Paths of Glory*, quite some time ago. I think it was for a French version because it had been banned in

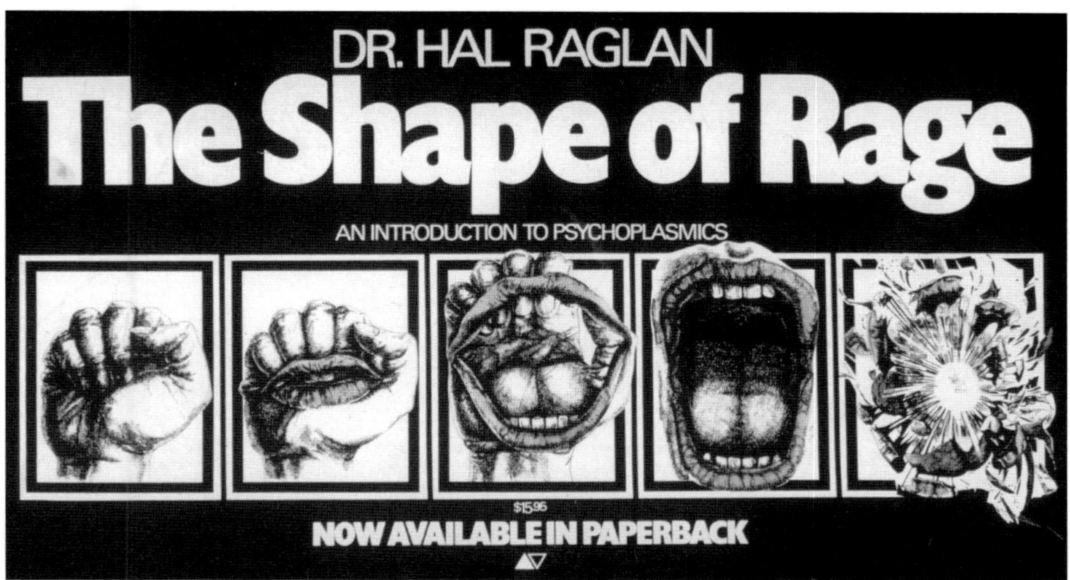

Above: The poster advertising the book written by Dr. Raglan (Oliver Reed). The film is a sincere testimony, a lament and a parody, all derived from the 'new psychiatry'. Right: The Brood – Art Hindle and Oliver Reed, a big star at the time, in his role as a psychiatric guru.

France, I think. And the sound mixers told me that he didn't like the mix and he wanted to redo the whole thing, which he apparently did. Completely differently. And I'm sure I would do the same thing. You have to, rather than do a historical restoration, you would remake it. But I would pray that I would never be in that position to have to do that. I wouldn't want to go back there.

SG: And then I think there was an interesting turn in your career, when you made a movie which was close to what you had done before but at the same time a very personal movie, *The Brood*. So was it your first attempt to create a more personal cinema ?

DC: Well I can remember very directly how it happened. I actually had made this movie *Fast Company* first, which was in a way my least personal movie, even though it had to do with cars and dragsters which I loved, but it was a project which was brought to me, and I hadn't written the original script, although I was very involved in rewriting it. It was a difficult but fun shoot out west. I had never been out west in Canada before, and I went to drag strips and met these guys who did race these cars. And I often rewrote parts of the script a second time the day before the shoot. That was something I also did on *Scanners,* although this script had a little more there. I was incorporating what I was learning from the drag racers into the scripts, so it was kind of a documentary in some ways. I'd hear them say funny things like, 'You can suck my pipes,' that was dragster talk for 'exhaust pipes'. So I would have a character say that or talk about that, because the script didn't really have any of those kind of details. It was written by a Jewish boy who didn't know very much about that scene. One of my complaints was that he made the lead, who was definitely not Jewish, and who was supposed to be a tough rough-and-

The Brood: *Samantha Eggar finally lifts the veil on the unspeakable horror of procreation.*

tumble drag racer, played by William Smith, like a Jewish character from a Saul Bellow novel. And I was saying, 'I don't think this is going to work, either he's that or he's this, but I don't see William Smith saying these lines and making them work.' So rethinking these characters was part of the rewriting. It was very interesting and it was the first time that I shot anything on a film set. The trailer that the drag racers travelled in was a film set, and that was my first experience of shooting on a set of any kind. [Before then] we had only ever shot on locations, maybe we re-dressed them a little but they were not real sets. Actually I worried about that, because I wasn't sure if I would like it.

Fast Company was also a very important movie for me, because I met Carol Spier and I met Mark Irwin, these were people that I was going to work with for a long time afterwards. Even the sound recordist became a regular crew member on the movies that I made later.

I remember Carol Spier asking me, 'Do you want the refrigerator door to open from the left or the right?' That felt odd, like a luxury and burden all at once. In *Shivers* we had to fit the characters to apartments that already existed because we couldn't afford to create new ones. We put up notices in elevators asking people to rent us their apartments for the shoot. And then we would have meetings to discuss all these apartments where we we'd say, 'Well this character could conceivably live in that apartment with that decor, that one couldn't live there . . .' It was a game of matching the location with the character. So there were many important things for me as a developing director that happened on *Fast Company*. I did a lot of outdoor shooting, which I had only really done in *Rabid* before.

I took *Fast Company* because I was being a professional filmmaker and I had a child to support and a wife. I really did it for the money, although I loved the subject matter and I also got into the idea of making a real B-movie, which normally wouldn't be an attraction to

The belly is still fertile . . . with The Brood, *Cronenberg established his style, based on the systematic inversion of base values. Here, maternity = horror!*

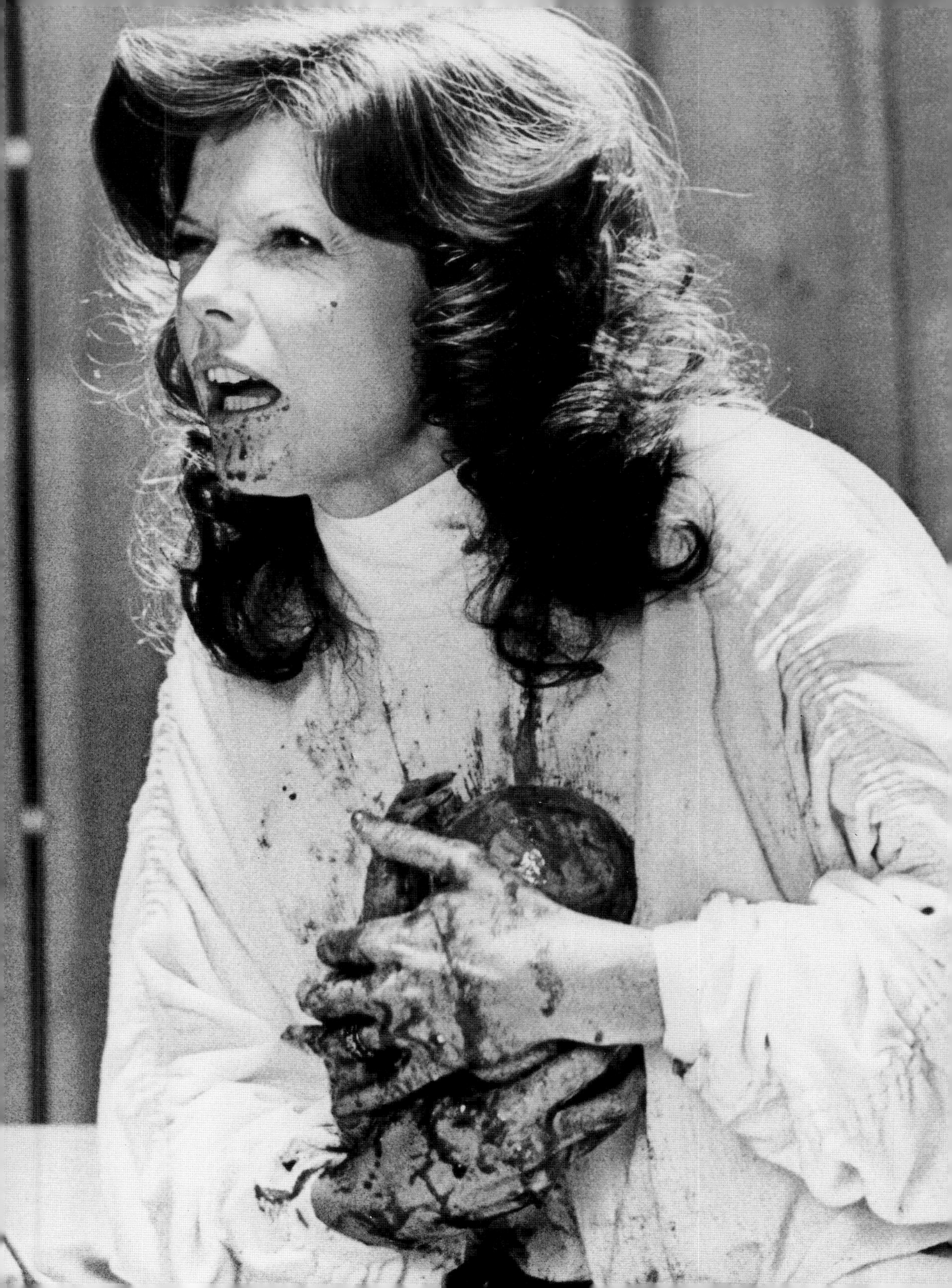

The Brood: The presence of the child (Cindy Hinds) and her monstrous 'brothers' makes the film worthy of the brothers Grimm, in every sense.

me. But I had John Saxon and I had Claudia Jennings and I had William Smith, so I got excited about that.

Immediately we finished that, *The Brood* got financed. [In fact it was even earlier.] Suddenly, without even finishing *Fast Company*, I was shooting this other movie. The writing of *The Brood* was one of those moments, I've never had an experience like it since. I absolutely did not intend to write something autobiographical, but I was in the throes of a divorce and a very painful part of my life. I had just moved into a house with my second wife Carolyn, and I was writing a script for what was to become Filmplan, this was for Victor Solnicki and Pierre David, who's now in Hollywood. He's been there for many years, but he wasn't then. He's a French Canadian from Montréal. And I had told them I was going to write something else, it wasn't exactly *Scanners*, but this idea just pushed that right out of the way. It was written with great intensity and emotion and it demanded to be written first – it needed to be written then. I don't know what provoked it, but the fact that I had remarried obviously triggered off the need to express this in a movie, and it was a very unique experience for me. Now what's interesting is that normally one thinks of that as the tradition for a first time novelist: that he writes a youthful, autobiographical novel firstly, because he doesn't have much of a life to write about, so it has to be close to his own, and secondly because a lot of what pushes many people to become writers is the need for that catharsis, to distance themselves, to examine it, to get it out on paper, perhaps for vengeance, to attack and so on. I never approached writing in that way. Even in the little writing that I did, it was always a more fantastic, inventive, creative thing: quite different from, you know, Saul Bellow's first novel or whoever. So this was in a way the closest I have ever come to that autobiographical first novel. And it had that compulsion behind it which was pretty unique, I've never experienced that since.

SG: Although the basis of the film is psychosomatology. It's very serious. I've never seen another movie which resembled *The Brood* in that way. Of course you go further than, say, a

The 'creator' devoured by his creatures; unjustly underrated, The Brood is without doubt the most crepuscular film of David Cronenberg.

documentary would, but it is almost a documentary not in any pejorative sense but in the manner in which it sets out to study 'new psychiatry', which was very strong at the time.

DC: Well that was all a kind of an extreme exaggeration of what I was seeing happening with my ex-wife, and with my daughter. So in my usual style, I didn't go out and do research, which I could have done. However, in a sense I had already done that by living through the situation with my ex-wife, and worrying about groups which might have been cults that she was involved with – it actually turned out that she wasn't [involved with them]. Still, even when she was living with a Zen group or Buddhist group who were established and not a cult, I worried about my daughter because the group was not set up to deal with young children, and my daughter was not having a good experience in the ashram or wherever they were. This was also very typical sixties stuff, even though it was the seventies. It also called up a real ferocity in me: a possessiveness and a desire to protect my child. It was my first child, so I had no idea how I would react to these things and actually I was pretty ferocious. And you know the story about it, I kidnapped her and did all that stuff to prevent her from being taken to California. [laughs] I hadn't moved to California and my ex-wife and daughter were going to move there. I didn't think my ex-wife was in any shape to take care of the kid, because she had her own struggle and she had her hands full taking care of herself. And that's what happened: I got custody of my daughter and my ex-wife went to California. And all of these things provoked this desire to examine this in the film. There was a real sense of vengeance in it, I can very distinctly remember the scene where one of these creatures is beating the grandfather to death. Shooting it was a really cathartic moment for me. It was also very private, no one else knew

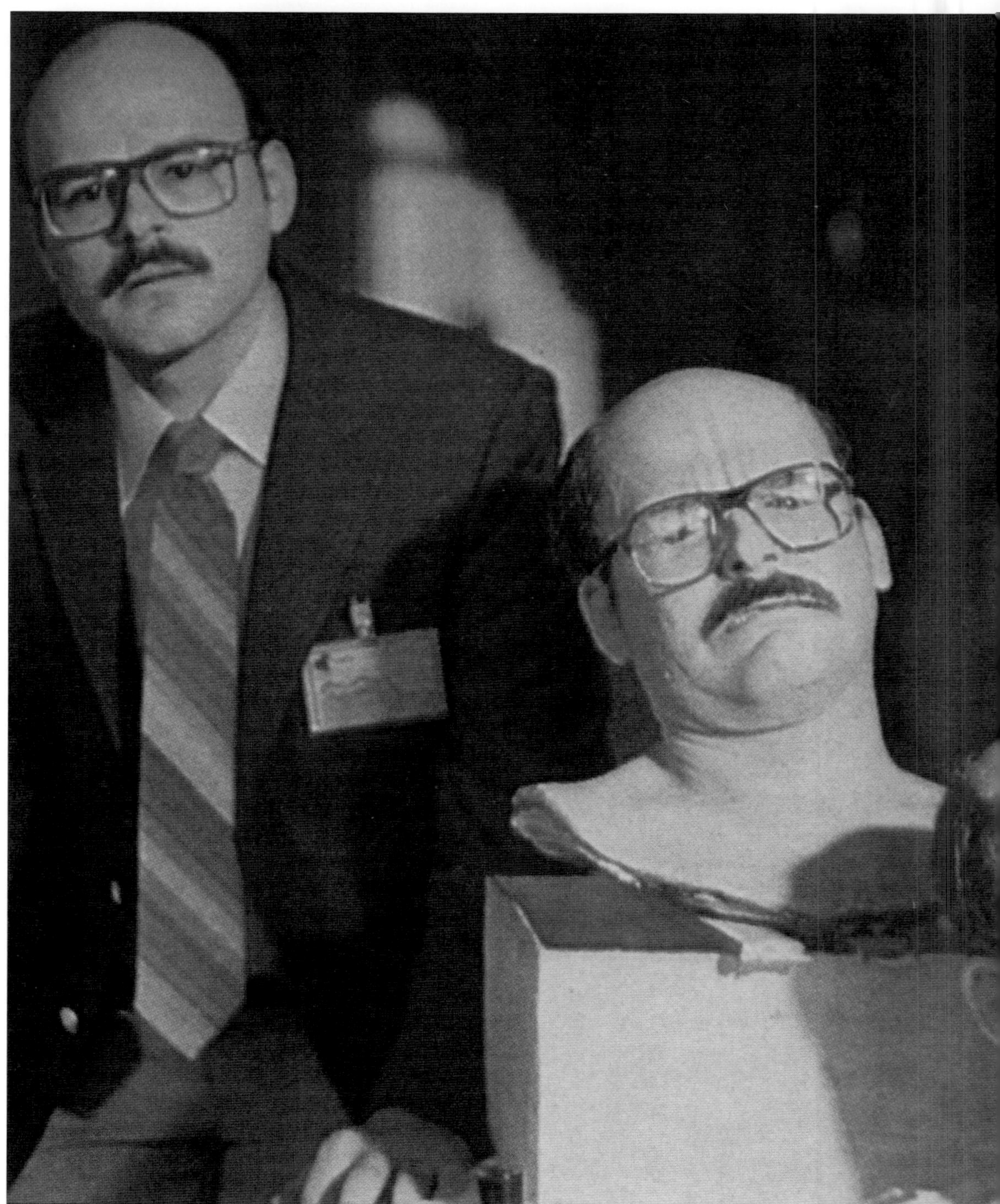

The famous exploding head of Scanners, which Burroughs appreciated so much. Cronenberg admitted utilising the most simple, archaic special effects in the cinema, directly borrowed from Georges Melies.

about it really, but I had in my own mind implicated the grandfather character with [that of] my ex-wife's father. An implication which was later proved to be fairly accurate, by his inaction and by a lot of other things. Anyway, it was incredibly cathartic for me, in the scene the creature was using a glass ball to beat him [the grandfather]. And when my editor said, 'Well maybe we only need two of those [blows],' I said, 'No, I think four or five would be better.' It's pretty unwatchable and the sounds are very . . . But it was very emotional, it was vengeance, it was definitely catharsis in a very personal way for me. That explains my famous statement, that this was 'my version of *Kramer vs. Kramer*', which was a movie about a divorce with a child involved, a Hollywood version of that situation with Meryl Streep and Dustin Hoffman, that was very popular then. I thought it [*Kramer vs. Kramer*] was the most false, sentimental, bullshit movie ever – and people were loving it, you know. That also made me realise, in a very forceful way, that you could make a movie that had people weeping and crying and very emotional but which was a complete lie – and that it would sell, and I didn't ever want to do that. You get movies like *The Sixth Sense* and so on, which are great button-pushers, they push the buttons and the tears spring out, like Pavlov's dog, except instead of saliva you get tears. Obviously to me that's not art. I guess it's entertainment or machinery, I don't know what it is, but it's not art. So that was *The Brood*.

SG: One can feel in *The Brood* that it's a very serious movie. It may be the only movie where you – I'm sure that it was unconscious on your part – used imagery that comes from fairy tales and mythology. Obviously the female creature at the end really comes from mythology. The evil little creatures really come from Grimm's tales . . .
DC: Like the seven dwarfs.

SG: That's not really typical [of your work].
DC: No, no . . .

SG: It's also perhaps the only movie you made where humour is almost absent.
DC: There's just about no humour.

SG: But the film is very powerful and I think it's getting more and more [powerful]. I see that with a new generation of students, they really react strangely to it. Perhaps it's a cathartic movie for everybody.
DC: You know, I don't really know. If you are not doing the very obvious button-pushing, then you are not sure that what you are feeling is universal, or that everyone would feel that way in those circumstances. It doesn't really matter though. You are trying to communicate to people something very personal that perhaps they would never feel themselves, but at least they can understand it or relate to it.

It is the artist's fate to expose certain things of himself without really knowing whether it will strike a responsive chord or even a sympathetic chord. So it's possible that you expose yourself only to have people say, 'That's quite repulsive,' but of course it's the risk you must take. So it would be very interesting if *The Brood* has somehow struck that universal chord even though, as I say, it was ferociously personal. I did know at that time. I mean my constant comment was, 'I'm living in a soap opera . . . I'm living in a really bad day-time soap opera and I hate it. I would really like it to be a more interesting series that I'm living in, because it's just like everybody else who gets divorced and there's a child involved and the pain is . . .' You've heard these stories and suddenly you're in it, and you never thought it would happen to you, and all that stuff. Very banal, except that when it's happening to you it's not banal.

SG: No of course.
DC: It's like death, I suppose. I guess in a way, from that point of view, it's [*The Brood* is] not surprising. What is surprising is the fact that I

chose to frame it [my emotional trauma] in a sort of fantastic, rather than what we would call a naturalistic, mode. That people could still relate to it in that way [as an expression of an everyday trauma] pleases me, of course.

SG: **Oddly enough, not very long ago I was reading something like a dictionary of world cinema, and there was an entry for David Cronenberg. I know the guy who wrote it, he's an old critic and not a very interesting one. Anyway he said, 'Nevertheless,' because he thinks you're a good director, 'I will never forgive David Cronenberg for having desecrated Samantha Eggar the way he did in *The Brood*.'**

DC: Well you know, I never thought we would get her. Samantha is an interesting story, because she had been a rising star and then suddenly disappeared. When I approached her she had not really been a star for quite a while. The story that I heard was that she had gotten involved with a very powerful man in Hollywood, was his mistress, and when she left him he said, 'I will destroy your career,' and he proceeded to do that. That's the story I heard, whether it's true or not I don't know. I was very surprised when she agreed to do it because I was kind of despairing about casting that role, because it's a very difficult, strange role. She never moves, she's physically in the same spot for the whole movie, and of course it has its grotesque aspects. She said to me that she related very strongly to it. Now I had no idea what she meant by that. And I saw her many years later – not that long ago, it might even have been at Cannes in the last couple of years – and she said, 'Oh there's that man who had me doing that strange role.' I said, 'Samantha, don't you remember what you said to me at the time?' She said, 'No.' I said, 'You said you did it because you really related to it.' She said, 'I said that!' Maybe she doesn't remember, but I never wanted to ask her why she related to that particular role: whether as a mother or a child, or whether it was the child abuse aspect of the film, or what.

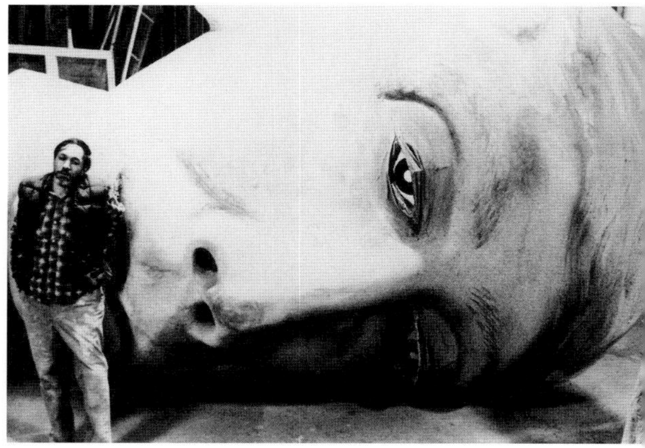

The cinema of the mind: on the set of Scanners, with Cronenberg's old collaborator Robert Silverman, playing the role of the artist lost in the labyrinth of his own nervous system. In Scanners, the deviant thought is literally a deadly weapon. Cronenberg presents his theme of the creator facing both a society and creations that are beyond his control.

I didn't really want to know and I particularly didn't want to break the spell, I didn't want her to give it a second thought, and maybe turn me down because I desperately wanted her to do the movie. And by whatever strange magic it is, she is, in terms of her looks, very similar to my ex-wife, who is also of Irish descent and had very white skin with red hair and with freckles. You know, that very Irish kind of look. It was strange to suddenly have an actress who really does look

Scanners: *Pastiche publicity poster by Carol Spier, informed by the vision of Cronenberg; Ephemerol, a pharmaceutical medicine inspired by Thalidomide, also evokes 'ephemeral art', which was very much in vogue at the time.*

[like my ex-wife], whereas Art Hindle doesn't really look very much like me, I have to say.

Anyway, that was *The Brood*. I wrote it in a house that I had just bought, where I ended up living for twenty years, the one before this one. I've only had two houses. I was writing on the third floor and I had started to tear the house apart. So I was writing in a room where – it was an old house too –the lath and plaster was there like a skeleton. Freezing! I was actually writing in sheepskin gloves that I had cut the fingers off. I was so cold writing it, and was very driven to go up to that room and write every day; write that script that was just forcing its way to be written. So even physically, the writing was a kind of unique experience.

SG: **There's a very very famous text by Sigmund Freud which is called – I don't know how it was translated into English – 'A Child is Beat.' Someone is beating a child, it refers to a nightmare . . . I think *The Brood* is the best dramatisation of that. I mean the girl, the little girl, is not even a character in *The Brood*, but she's central and you can see the movie as her nightmare, which would be unbearable.**

DC: You notice that I almost never have child characters. Just at the beginning of *Dead Ringers*, you see the twins as children, and in *Shivers* I had some children in jeopardy, but once I had a child myself it became unbearable, and now I find it really difficult. So I'm very reluctant to create child characters. But in *The Brood*, because it was cathartic, I had to do it, but I have never done it since.

SG: **Now we'll skip to Scanners. This morning and yesterday, I was looking through the files at the library in the [Paris] Cinemathèque, and there were things about *Scanners* which showed that the first draft was not even a script, you were putting down your ideas.**

DC: Really, they have that? I don't even know what they've got, it's terrifying.

SG: **No, it's very interesting.**

DC: Is it?

SG: **There are a lot of ideas you didn't use, and which you may have used afterwards. And some other ideas which are very, very close to Burroughs and *Naked Lunch*. But there are other documents showing that it was a big hit at the box-office.**

DC: Yes. Number One, my first Number One hit.

SG: **So *Scanners* is a very interesting film. I know sometimes you say it was your most commercial movie, but at the same time it's very, very close to your personal imagery and imagination.**

DC: Well I agree, I didn't ever feel that I was selling out or anything like that. It's just that it was a kind of a high-concept movie, which I suppose my first three or four movies were [too]. In other words, a movie that you can describe in one sentence, and the commercial appeal of it would be: 'A war between groups of telepaths'... 'telepathists' . . . 'A telepathic war.'

SG: There are some lines, where you try to define characters, etc., which seem to be *Blade Runner*. Totally.
DC: Really?

SG: Someone who hires professional killers to kill telepaths.
DC: Yeah, yeah. Well once again it was time to make another movie. I think Pierre phoned me as usual – this was what happened in those days. He'd say, 'Look, it's getting to be the fall, and all the doctors' and lawyers' and dentists' money is coming in, because they suddenly realise they need a tax write-off' – this was in the old tax write-off days – 'we need to start shooting in two or three weeks. Have you got something ?' So I said, 'Well, I'll come to Montréal and I'll give you a couple of possible things.' And I went to the airport and the flight was cancelled, because a Russian satellite had come through the atmosphere and was breaking up. Everybody was freaking out because they thought it could land in Canada and hit a plane, so they cancelled all the flights. So I jumped on my Moto Guzzi motorcycle and I rode to Montréal. I did that regularly, when I was shooting *Shivers* I commuted on the weekends on my Ducati 750cc every week, back and forth whether it was raining or whatever – because I was a diehard Italian motorcycle freak then. And so I said, 'Screw this! I'm going to go anyway.' So I remember meeting Pierre at an outdoor café, and I pitched him three ideas and I said, 'You pick which one.' So he picked *Scanners*, which wasn't called *Scanners*, I hadn't named them yet. I didn't know what I was going to call it at the time – maybe *The Telepathists*.

SG: I think I saw it called *The Sensitives* on one of the drafts.
DC: Yes, that's right. I called it *The Sensitives*. It was a working title which I knew wasn't good because it was too wimpy. And I remember when I came up with the idea of calling them 'Scanners', I was very excited because I thought that was very strong.

SG: You were right.
DC: Yeah, yeah. The idea of a telepathic war [appealed to] Pierre [who] was a high-concept guy, we later called him 'Pierre Hollywood'. But he got things done, he was enthusiastic and the money was there. So literally it was, 'We're going to shoot in two or three weeks.'

SG: And you had already made the connection between the telepaths and the drug, 'Ephemerol'?
DC: I can't remember, I probably hadn't because I don't think I'd gone that far.

By the way, I just thought of something really funny that I hadn't thought of for a long time. When I went to LA and was talking to Corman, I also had an idea for an exploitation film which was about an insane gynaecologist [*Roger Pagan, Gynaecologist*]. That was of course going to eventually develop into *Dead Ringers*. It stayed dormant until I read about the Marcus twins, but I had that idea when I went to LA. I remember talking to some producer, because I saw quite a few low-budget producers: some of them were sleazy, some of them were funny, it was a real [education]. And he said to me, 'You're sitting on a concept, aren't you? You're sitting on a concept, what is it?' And I said, 'I'm not going to tell you.' And the concept was that: an insane gynaecologist. Now I hadn't thought of that for years, but for some reason [it came back to me just now, probably because of] the idea of pitching ideas. Of course my basic concept was totally exploitation: there's a gynaecologist who is insane, but his patients don't realise that he's insane. I had no idea of where I would go from there, but as a high-concept exploitation movie, it's got power. Funny, huh?

Scanners: *The early films of David Cronenberg (*Stereo*, *Scanners*, *Videodrome*) often speculate on the power of the big industrial corporations.*

During my year in the south of France, in Tourettes-sur-Loup, I did sculptures. I went there because I was invited by two Canadian sculptors, Robert Roussil and Jim Ritchie, who is now in Reims or outside of Reims. They encouraged me to make sculptures in aluminium and discarded Styrofoam, and one of my ideas was surgical instruments for operating on mutants, not mutant women but mutants. I just saw *Sleepy Hollow,* did you see *Sleepy Hollow*?

SG: **Yeah.**
DC: Those instruments, I mean . . .

SG: **Absolutely**
DC: It's pretty obvious . . .

SG: **Did you know he's [Tim Burton is] a great fan of yours?**
DC: I know, I know, so I don't resent it, but it was a shock because even the way he [Johnny Depp] plays with them, when he goes like this, it's just like Geneviève Bujold.

So back to *Scanners* . . . So he chose that one and I think, as I say, I had probably not worked out the details properly at that time. It was really just the idea of people who were somehow telepathists. I knew that I would have them be artificially created telepathists, though. I did some research, I must have done it afterwards, into psychic phenomena and stuff and I totally don't believe in it. I have some books upstairs, Russian books on psychic phenomena.

SG: **Yeah, they [the Russians] were very excited about that.**
DC: And they did tons of experiments and they were all failures, absolute failures. And just by perverseness as well, I wanted it [the telepaths] to be artificially created, but I didn't like the idea of it being a military experiment where they blah, blah, blah . . . And then the Thalidomide [a prescription drug of the sixties, given to pregnant women, which created deformed babies] connec-

tion occurred to me: the idea that it was accidental and it had repercussions like that. And I might even have [been influenced] by a film called *Blue Sunshine*, did you ever see that movie? It was a low-budget horror film about a bad batch of acid that ten or twenty years later causes people to go violently insane. That was the gimmick in that movie: suddenly people who were normal a moment before were freaking out and killing people. It might have been made by Zalman King actually. You know Zalman, who did *Wild Orchid*, he's just totally into sex now. He seems to do nothing but sex films. [King acted in *Blue Sunshine*, the director was Jeff Lieberman.] Anyway, I don't know if that contributed to the idea of a drug which had repercussions later, but primarily I was thinking of Thalidomide.

And of course, once again as with *Fast Company* but not *The Brood*, I was writing the script while we were shooting. Because it was a very complex story with a lot of effects, it was the most difficult shoot I have ever had, for about twenty different reasons: my relationship with Patrick McGoohan, my relationship with Jennifer O'Neill, the writing. [On top of that] it was freezing in Montréal, I've never been so cold. It wasn't snow but it was damp and cold, and we were shooting, as we usually did in Canada, without a real studio. I think we were on Expo Island, so we were surrounded by water, it was damp. And we were making sets inside some abandoned buildings that had been built for Expo '67 and they weren't insulated. It was physically and emotionally the most difficult movie. Emotionally difficult, though not in the same way as *The Brood*, which was not difficult on the shoot. On the famous first day of our shoot [the *Scanners* shoot], two women died. It had been a ludicrous day anyway, the schedule said we should be shooting so we went out even though we had nothing to shoot. We had nothing prepared. So it was a disastrous beginning to a very difficult shoot. Often I was writing stuff at 6 a.m. and 7 a.m. and trying to make it happen during the day, and shooting out of sequence, as

The two enemy brothers of Scanners: the first is named Vale ('the veil'), while the second is Revok ('cover' in reverse).

you normally do, but with this very complex thriller plot built in, and the necessity to make special effects happen which you can't do on the spot, it takes a lot of time. We did end up doing re-shoots some weeks, or even a month later, in Toronto. So you can actually see: the scene in the subway, that's the Toronto subway not the Montréal subway, even though the other stuff was in Montréal. And there were scenes that had to be shot to make sense of what was going on. Once we put it together we saw where the gaps were, so it was a miracle that it ended up making sense. It was one of my great editing triumphs, I have to say. Working in the editing room, sometimes I can remember distinctly taking the last word in a sentence that Stephen Lack

The battle to the death between two brothers: Michael Ironside concentrates all his telepathic energy into causing his brother to explode.

said, and using it to be the first word in a new sentence that I would write. In other words, I would have him say that word and then cut away to someone else and continue with new dialogue that I wrote and recorded later, just to sort of make sense out of the plot and everything else. So it was a catastrophe . . . I mean, we knew that we were getting some good stuff, there were some good scenes, but it was amazing that the film did as well as it did and that it still lives, you know.

SG: And how did you react to its success at the box office? It must have felt strange in a way.

DC: It was very abstract, because it wasn't like *The Fly*, which was the next movie that I did [which was a big box office hit], because I was not connected with Hollywood really, I wasn't in Hollywood. I mean the best thing that you can do in Hollywood is walking around and going to Morton's and going to various restaurants the week that your movie is Number One. I remember with *The Fly*, people, studio executives I had never heard of, or some that had disdained me before, would come up and shake my hand and congratulate me because I was in LA the week that *The Fly* was Number One. So you're on top of the world for ten minutes, you know, but to me, it seemed superficial and casual because I was not a kid. It's one thing if you're the *Blair Witch* guys. I read that somebody, maybe it was the head of the distribution company that distributed *The Blair Witch*, said to them, 'You know guys, enjoy this because it will never happen again.' And that was good advice, because those sort of things are a miracle if they happen, it's by accident. I've had so many disappointments, especially in the US. Even with my last film, *eXistenZ* . . . when you're going with Miramax and Dimension and the Weinsteins, you figure that you're going to get a decent distribution at least, and [then you have to put up with] broken promises and reneges. So that you make the movie is a miracle, and then that it should actually be well-distributed is a miracle, and then that it should do well is the third miracle. So you need several miracles for those moments to happen. It seems to happen every week for somebody's movie, but in terms of my experience, *The Dead Zone* could have been a Number One film but it was not well-distributed for various reasons. So not knowing any of this, when we were Number One on the *Variety* charts, we just had a party at Victor Solnicki's house, which was not far from here – but he doesn't live there now – and everybody got a little card showing the top of the *Variety* chart.

SG: Yeah, I've seen it

DC: I didn't know if I still had those. But it was only that, it was a party, it was theoretical. I was in the habit of tracking the films, you know, like *The Brood* and stuff. I would clip out that page of *Variety*, and it was just [the expression of] my desire to connect with the industry, to feel like I was part of the industry. So I did that even though I had an uneasy relationship with the whole word 'industry' and 'industrial', but obviously I had a yearning to connect with it, because it meant in North America that you were a real filmmaker. I did do that, I have to confess. But it [the success of the film] didn't do much more. It didn't make me crazy, it didn't make me egomaniacal, it didn't make me secure, it didn't make me overly happy, just a little bit, you know. It didn't change my life, it wasn't as though I suddenly got $1,000,000 through the door when I had been living on $5000 a year. That didn't happen, not like some rock stars who have a hit and suddenly they are getting these amazing cheques and stuff. It didn't really have a huge impact on me.

SG: **What is perhaps remarkable is that, unlike a lot of filmmakers and especially Canadian filmmakers, you were not tempted to go to LA where a Number One hit at the box office can make you part of the family, people would have adopted you, but you were not tempted.**
DC: I think then it never occurred to me. I thought it might mean that I might have an easier time getting the next film financed: that people would know who I was a little bit, walking through the door. But you have to remember that it was a horror film, and there was still at that time – OK, it was a sci-fi horror film – [a prejudice against the genre]. A movie like *The Brood*, for example, would never be distributed by a major, the only time you would ever get that would be a film like *The Omen*, where it was based on a bestseller and you had Gregory Peck. There was a real disdain for the genre amongst major studios, which of course doesn't exist now. But at that time there was a real class system, so I was still a second-class citizen or even a third-class [one], despite the fact that, by accident, because there was no major opposition that weekend and so on and so on and so on, this little horror film or sci-fi film from Canada became the Number One film in North America. It wasn't a big deal that way, I was still a second-class citizen and I knew it. And there wasn't the euphoria and the craziness that surrounds box office, at least there wasn't in Canada. For example now, Atom Egoyan gets a nomination for the Oscars, oh my God, he's elevated to the level of God here. On the one hand, people will have a proper disdain for the Oscars, and yet on the other they are dazzled by it. Atom has never come remotely close to having a Number One film in North America. But I think if I had a Number One now . . . Even when *The Fly* was Number One, it was not [a big deal] in Canada anyway. And I think it was because of the vehicle, because it was a horror film. So I was still a second-class citizen, but the difference was, of course, that *The Fly* was distributed by Fox, a major, and hell, *Scanners* had a lot to do with that, and some other low-budget horror films which made a lot of money. That money made the majors realise that they couldn't afford to be snobby and elitist about the genre. But I can tell you that when *Scanners* and *The Brood* came out, they were definitely considered to be second-class and there was no question of a major picking them up. They absolutely refused to touch low-budget horror films.

Stephen Lack experiences a Christian 'passion'. Cronenberg likes to include references to sacred art in his films.

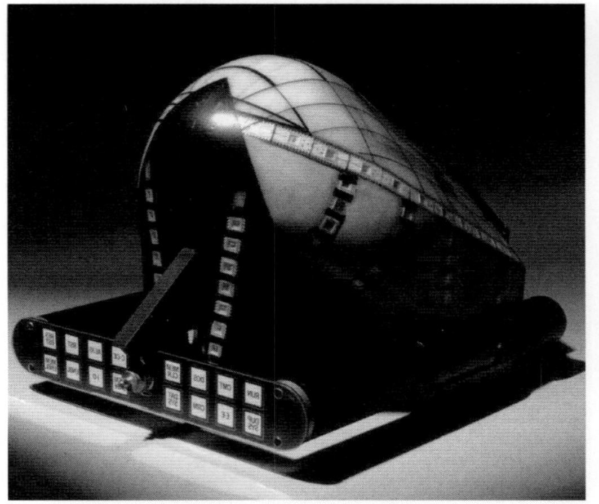

Birth of an auteur

Videodrome, The Dead Zone

One may think of *Videodrome* as a unique one-off – like *The Night of the Hunter* or *The Honeymoon Killers* – in that it wants to say *everything*, within its concentrated 90 minutes, not only about all the main themes of its era but also those of the era to come. Those who saw it on its first release were neither very many nor very influential, but they would never look at a television set or a video recorder in the same way again. The film was based on the interiorisation of 'new images', and, at the same time, put a definitive seal on the loss of the innocent gaze. Midway between Guy Debord's *The Society of the Spectacle* and the aphorisms of William Burroughs (O'Blivion borrows a line from *The Job*, made in relation to the tape recorder – 'an externalised section of the human nervous system' – and applies it to television), the film announced the arrival of *homo technologicus*, that being who fuses the organic with the mechanical, in an apocalyptic atmosphere.

Videodrome avoids the trap of 'denouncing voyeurism' into which it might have fallen, by probing, with the pertinence of a philosophic tale, the essential virtuality of all sexual and/or romantic relations. No work of art had ever shown, with such strength and elegance, that which has become the private sphere of post-industrial civilisation. Cronenberg said once that he had tried to imagine what happens when a man returns home alone and puts a pornographic tape into his video player. It is a situation that is typical of our times, just like the hypothetical 'snuff movie' from which he conceived a contaminating hallucination that does not spare the viewer. This fantasy logic would make the viewer doubt everything, even including the implicit contract he had formed with the filmmaker.

Videodrome was the first film where Cronenberg refused to play the game of 'suspension of disbelief', but, instead of simply setting a rational trap, at the same time he implicated our affectivity. For despite its tone, *Videodrome* – like *Crash* – is a film about sensual passion, about the abandonment of self. Max Renn, like Seth Brundle, the hero of *The Fly*, always wants to 'go further', reaching beyond the flesh by passing through the flesh. What was undoubtedly scandalous about the film was its refusal to return to that *statu quo ante* that is the very essence of Hollywood spectacle. Intensity in Cronenberg is contained less in acts than in thoughts (to the point where we should take the most striking scenes in *Scanners* at face value), the all-powerful thoughts that are radiated by the body. From this comes the ineluctable movement that leads to total bodily and psychological possession.

In *Videodrome*, the style achieves its maturity: the Cronenberg hero follows a path of initiation, a succession of metamorphoses that, literally, wear him out; the chromatic palette of *Videodrome* starts with the red of the clay wall, passes through the red of Nicki's hair and lips, and finishes with the reddened oxydisation of the rusty vessel with which Max 'pierces' the television screen. And, in a magnificent metaphor in which thought is incarnated, the television no longer appears only as 'the eye that watches us', but in the form of a mouth which attracts us with its siren song and, finally, as an explosion of entrails that sets us free. This unique confrontation of the violence of desire, the diffuse harshness of a spectacle that addresses itself to each spectator and punches

Videodrome: *The 'Image Accumulator Helmet', or 'Helmet-Cam', created by Tom Coulter, anticipated, in the 1980s, the virtual reality tools that would be developed ten years later.*

them in the guts, makes *Videodrome* one of the most necessary films of contemporary cinema.

SG: So we were talking of your débuts, as we say in French, with *Scanners* and *Fast Company*. I have the feeling that then you were getting to the core of what would become your style and your oeuvre, *Videodrome* obviously. So how did it start? Because I have seen a lot of notes, a lot of short stories and synopses, but *Videodrome* seems to come from somewhere else.

DC: It came out of two things, I suppose. The first was remembering, as a kid, watching TV late at night, and of course it was black and white television, and when all the regular stations would go off the air you could get these distant, strange stations that were probably all American. The airwaves would be quiet, so you could pick up – and we had a rotating antennae, you know, so we could rotate the antennae on our house and get this stuff. But they were always very bad images, and they would fade in and out, and where they came from and what they were was very mysterious. That was many years before I was making movies, I was probably fourteen or fifteen or sixteen. Anyway, these strange late-night channels, plus bits of Marshall McLuhan, plus I have no idea what, combined to create the initial premise that someone receives images on his television set that are fascinating to him, and seem to have an element of danger which makes them more fascinating. I don't even think I knew, at the time that I started writing, that I would be examining the influence of television or that I would create a character based on Marshall McLuhan [O'Blivion], none of that was really in my mind to begin with. And I can't really remember how I proposed this to the guys at Film Plan. It was the same thing, you know, the tax money was coming in, they wanted to do another movie, Pierre David and Victor Solnicki. I remember renting a room right across the hall from where Ron Sanders was editing, it was downtown near the waterfront. It was in an old building that had been rented, but it had sand-blasted brick in the Toronto style and beams. And there was nothing in the room but a table, a chair and an IBM Selectric, that was it. It was quite a big room, and I was just in the middle of it and I would go there every day and write. And that's where I wrote *Videodrome*, I can remember that, but I don't remember any more of the details other than just the normal way that things accumulate around a central concept.

SG: If I had to sum up *Videodrome*, I would say that there are three major themes: something which would eventually become – I'm sure at the time it was a bit too novel to speak of it in these terms – cybersex or virtual sex, and of course the power of the media and in particular television, and this very Burroughsian idea of control, in this case a big company which exercises general control. Do you have any recollection of how these three themes began to meld in your mind ? Were you conscious of that at the time?

DC: No, no. Obviously there was a local TV station called City TV, which still exists. Station director Moses Znaimer – he wanted to sue me because I named a character Moses, you know, all that silly stuff. But it's true that I did model Civic TV after City TV, just because the cinema was always sexual for me. I can remember the first time I saw a nipple, a breast, a pubic hair. Of course, that was part of the fascination of European film-making for someone in North America, because North American film-making was very prudish and very repressed, European cinema was not. So we were fascinated even by *Ecstasy* with Hedy Lamarr – of course that was an old film. I still have books called *Sex and the Cinema* and all that kind of stuff. But I transposed that to television, even though at the time there was very little sex on television. It was even more prudish and of course it was mostly American. But City TV did show what they called *The Baby Blue Movies*, which was softcore but you could see simulated sex and you could see naked people. It was very popular and it wasn't really very controversial. So that, plus the whole idea of that kind of sex, and the idea of sexual torture, and the idea of performance, and the idea of sado-masochism and all of that kind of stuff. What would be forbidden? What would you see on your television set that would be attractive and seductive and yet dangerous and forbidden? But why this came together, how this came together, that's the magic of what happens when you sit down and start writing. Things that I am interested in separately come together to form a new thing. So I could see where all the separate things came from, but why they should have combined at that moment, I don't know.

You know, I went to the university of Toronto when Marshall McLuhan was there. I didn't ever actually go and take any classes with him, but his influence as teacher was very strong in the late sixties and early seventies. And then of course he got famous, which if you are an academic you are not supposed to do. First of all, everybody else is jealous, and then everybody questions your credibility. But suddenly Marshall McLuhan was the guru of communications, and was on all the TV shows and in all the magazines. And 'the medium is the message' was his famous line. So all these things were in the air, but no-one had really done anything about them. The people who were most interested in it were advertising people. They were the first to take him seriously because they felt that he was really onto something, and they wanted to use it, of course, for their own venal advertising purposes.

But other than being aware of where all the elements came from, and why I was interested in them, I can't really say why they happened to coalesce into that movie. And it was very difficult as well, because once again I was writing it while we were shooting. I had set a lot of complex things in motion, but I didn't have a script which had been very carefully considered, and mulled over, and so on. So I was writing it as we were shooting, and, of course, when you do that, you as a filmmaker are very vulnerable. It leaves you open to the madness of many people, and the obsessions and the fears of many people, including your actors. Suddenly you might be writing a scene for them, and because it's something they haven't seen before it's something they don't really want to do.

I sometimes presented possible scenes to some of the actors, and they didn't want to do that stuff. So I couldn't make it happen. It wasn't as though you have a script and everybody agrees upfront that they will be involved in whatever is in the script. And I'm not really talking about nudity necessarily, but just narrative stuff and what happens to their characters and so forth. So it was difficult that way, not as difficult as *Scanners*, but still difficult. I remember distinctly having to apologise to my crew, because we moved to one location and then I decided I wasn't ready to shoot there, so we moved back to another location and then I wasn't ready to shoot there either. And they were getting very frustrated and beginning to wonder if I knew what I was doing. So I actually had to make a little speech to the crew to explain what was going on and why we were in the position that we were in. They were mostly people that I had worked with before, but still there are moments when there are questions that have to be answered.

And then, of course, there were a lot of effects, and these things are difficult if they are not planned ahead of time. And then there were some sexually edgy scenes of sado-masochism and so on, which really my actors were pretty comfortable with, because they had already been made aware of them. And then there was Debbie Harry, who I think had really only done one movie before and was not really an experienced film actress at the time. Although she really wanted to be good and wanted to learn, and we did get along well. There were some strange moments with some members of the crew because she was a famous rock star, and certain people, I don't really want to get specific, although I could . . . but there was a hairdresser who got very strange with her. I think he was the first crew member I ever fired, I had to do it.

Videodrome: Max Renn (James Woods) and Nicki (Debbie Harry) during the preliminaries to their S&M scene. Feminist groups accused Cronenberg of giving a 'politically incorrect' image of female sexuality.

He was just messing with my star, I don't know what his story was exactly, but anyway. That was difficult to deal with. The American style is you fire somebody every week in order to keep everybody on their toes, but that's not my style. I'm very faithful to my crew so it was a difficult thing for me to have to do. So I was learning a lot of interesting things as I went along, and trying to make this very difficult, strange movie that had a lot of quite complex effects.

SG: Can you be a bit more specific about the re-shooting and the editing? I mean did you re-shoot some of it?
DC: No, I don't think I re-shot anything in the same way as *Scanners*. I mean, *Scanners* was the only movie where there was a hiatus of let's say a month, and then I went back and shot more. That was an unusual thing for me. I know Woody Allen sometimes now schedules his re-shoots. I don't think that I did that with *Videodrome*. I had to make it all work in the schedule that we had, so I wouldn't really call them re-shoots. Somebody could probably remind me of something I'm forgetting, but I don't think we ever went back. We never reassembled everybody after the crew had been disbanded, that's always a very difficult thing to do.

SG: But you had to suppress some things when you edited the movie?
DC: No, no. Well yes.

SG: The ending, no?
DC: Not the ending, not the ending. This really happened more when the film was being released. It had to do with Bob Remy, who was then head of Universal. As I say, for some reason

the movie was being released by this very conservative company. I wasn't really involved in the negotiations, but it had to do with the relationship between Pierre David and Thom Mount, who was the executive there. He was a very well-known executive at the time and has been an independent producer for quite a while. I think he did Polanski's last movie, or the one before that. I think he does more Europe now. And Verna Fields, the famous editor, the woman who edited *Jaws* and so on, was now the post-production supervisor. And I had these very supportive people. It was interesting, it was a weird movie but they were very supportive. It was certainly not a Verna Fields kind of movie, she was an older lady, an old Hollywood lady, but she was very sweet to me. And we were trying to solve some problems in the film, just because it was difficult: trying to make it accessible and make people understand it.

I remember, it was my first preview, my first real official studio preview, I had never done that before. We went to Boston and Ron, my editor, was there, and we had a screening and it was the most disastrous screening you can imagine. There was a transit strike in Boston at the time, the weather was very bad, which makes it difficult to get people to come, and then Ron and I, in our madness, had made a version of the film which was about 72 minutes long. We thought we had cut it really tight, but it was totally incomprehensible. I mean, as difficult as the film is to some people now, [that version] was so incomprehensible that you didn't even know that Max Renn worked at Civic TV, I'd cut out all the footage that explained that. I don't know what possessed us to do it. That's my natural tendency anyway: to cut very tight. I've just been looking at *Magnolia*, it's three hours and eight minutes. I've never even made a two-hour film. I like to make them dense and tight, but I'm not interested in making a three-hour movie. And maybe I go overboard on that. As opposed to some directors, who can't bear to cut out any shot that they've done, I can't wait to get rid of shots. So we had this totally incomprehensible thing.

In the meantime, women were coming with their babies, who were crying. It was an R [rating], which means that parents can bring kids, so that was also an introduction to that problem. I had noticed it with *Shivers*, and it's still a problem with the R rating, kids can come if their parents will bring them. So you always have to make a movie as though children were watching over your shoulder, which is why the NC17 rating is desperately needed. But of course, at the moment it's invalid and doesn't work – you know that whole story. Anyway, I was running into that problem, and I didn't like the idea that there were kids watching this movie: especially this one woman whose baby, who wasn't really watching the film because it was a baby, was crying. She probably was a single mother who just wanted to get out of the rain. The [audience questionnaire] cards [were terrible], it was a disaster. Everybody hated it, nobody could understand it.

SG: I read some of the cards.
DC: Really, they still have those ?

SG: Yes, but now that you're telling me about it, it's very obvious why people wrote that they couldn't understand anything.
DC: Yeah. Well it's not the version that anybody has ever seen since then. And I have to say that I was treated very well by Universal, I wish all of my screenings that didn't work out were handled as well, they were very mature about it. We were mainly dealing with Thom Mount and Verna Fields and we just sat and discussed what was wrong, how Ron and I had overreacted and what we could do [to improve it]. Of course, Universal didn't have a lot of money in the film, so it wasn't as though it was *Heaven's Gate* or something. And Ron and I went back and we built it back up to being a real movie again. And I don't think we had a second preview, I can't remember having one. Obviously it wasn't a big release, and probably after this disastrous screening they just weren't interested in doing much with it, but it

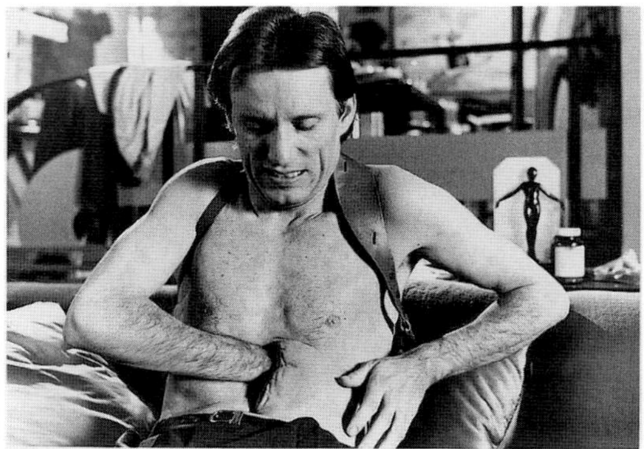

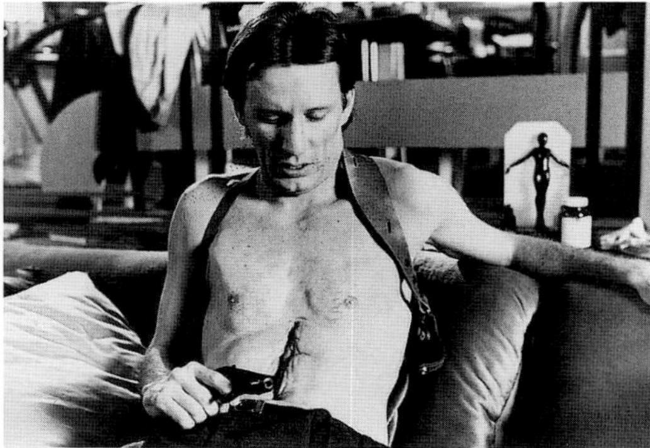

Max Renn, the human VCR, extracts a phallic arm from his vaginal orifice. The desires created by technology are driving him insane.

didn't matter. I knew it was going to be a difficult film, I just wanted to make sure that it existed and that it got released. Then when we were releasing the film and the MPAA asked for cuts in order for it to get an R [rating], that was my first serious interaction with them . . .

So the MPAA was asking for cuts: they were worried about the torture scenes and all the obvious stuff, and Debbie Harry, with the cutting and the burning, they had a lot to worry about. So I was struggling with that, and in the middle Bob Remy suddenly said, 'Oh, and by the way, while you're cutting those other things, I'd like you to cut a couple of other things too.' And I was so upset, I still haven't really forgiven him – not that I've seen him much, and he's head of the Academy, or was. At a moment when I was totally vulnerable and bleeding and fighting, he weighed in on the side of the censors and asked for extra cuts. What he wanted me to cut was the scene in *Samurai Dreams* where she lifts up a little Japanese figure which turns out to be a dildo, it's a phallus. He didn't want to see that, he wanted me to cut before she lifted it up. I said to Thom Mount, 'The MPAA didn't even ask me to cut that. Why is he asking me to cut that?' He said, 'Ah, I guess he has a problem with cocks, I don't know.' And I go, 'Thanks, that helps.'

And I had to cut it and I was really upset. I was very happy to see that when they released the videotape, it was back to its original version. Thank God, because I was worried then that the cut version might in fact ultimately become *the* version. That was why I was so upset with *Crash*, because as soon as a cut version exists, it exists and people can see it by accident . . .

Anyway, I think I talked about this in Chris Rodley's book in great detail, about what happened with *The Brood* and so on. Other than that, it's normal editing stuff, you know: just trying to make the scenes work and to get the best performances and so on. I don't know what else to say.

SG: Perhaps just one more thing. Obviously the sci-fi aspect of *Videodrome* is quite significant, especially because most of the things you were dealing with in the movie became so important afterwards. How do you react, now that it is clear that the movie really did have a deep sci-fi quality? I know that long ago I used the expression 'prophetic quality', and I was not alone in doing so. How do you personally feel about that? Do you sometimes think that you did in fact foresee something?

DC: It's funny, because all that stuff seemed obvious to me, it just seemed obvious. I didn't think I was being a prophet, I thought I was just describing what I thought was obvious: that it was happening. I thought I was describing what was existing then. And I think it did [exist then],

Deborah Harry (cult singer of the group Blondie) in the role of Nicki Brand (as in the branding of flesh), a virtual goddess of the sadomasochist cult.

but it was just the beginnings of what became much more universal and much more recognised. Maybe that's the way it is with prophecy. I was never an Arthur C. Clarke, it was never my interest to be able to say there will be satellite communication and so on. My inventions were all metaphors that pleased me and conceits, intellectual conceits and toys, that felt juicy to me: provocative, full of some kind of meaning, but not really an attempt to be a prophet in any way. [As far as I was concerned, an invention] would suffice if it had meaning within the film. If it had no meaning outside of the film that would not really matter to me, as long as it worked within the film. So I wasn't really thinking of prophecy at all and, as I say, it felt obvious to me. Like when I was doing *Shivers* and using the parasites and stuff, it seemed obvious to me.

SG: **Wouldn't it be your desire to, say, open a third dimension in cinema? I'm thinking of the hand penetrating the stomach of James Woods in *Videodrome*. I know image is not the ultimate thing for you, but this is an image that will survive for many decades, or maybe centuries.**
DC: Imagery is important to me, ultimately because of the metaphor. In a way, imagery is not even imagery. It has a metaphorical weight for me. So it is very important to find the images. In a way, if I don't have the invention that is possible in science fiction, then I feel that my weaponry has been taken away. If I have to shoot in very mundane circumstances, I feel where are the images that will illuminate things, that will become metaphors? And for *Dead Ringers*, which except for one dream sequence and the instruments and my version of what surgery is, is fairly naturalistic, it has to be using the more traditional means of cinema to create these metaphors of twinness of identity. Then you're doing it with lighting, with camera angle, with choice of lens, with how you shoot things. But I keep coming back to wanting to invent things that don't exist, to become my metaphors. That leads me back into the genre . . . when I made *The Dead Zone* some people said, 'He's going towards the mainstream.' Even though there's a supernatural element in *The Dead Zone*, it came from Stephen King. Then I made *The Fly* afterward, which was completely a sci-fi horror film. So I feel that I have to forget about the genre, really, because that's not what drew me to it. It's not an obsession with making a sci-fi film or being a horror film director, which a lot of young directors have at times. It was just very second nature to me to do that, and still is.

SG: **David, I wanted to show you this reproduction of a famous Caravaggio picture. It seems very pertinent to what we've discussed before: the relation between truth and the body, the flesh. As they say in the rhetoric, of 'palpable flesh'.**
DC: This is a terrific painting.

SG: **Of course it makes us think of *Videodrome*, but do you think that in art, and cinema is definitely an art, there is a relationship between truth and the flesh, the body?**
DC: Definitely. I think ultimately you have to go to the body for verification of anything. You go to the body for verification of life. You go to the body for verification of death. That covers every-

David Cronenberg in front of his 'organic TV'.

thing. This is a painting of *Doubting Thomas* being convinced of Christ's physical resurrection by being able to actually put his finger into the wounds, Christ's wounds. It makes perfect sense. It makes body sense, because really everything else is abstract. Everything but the body is an abstraction for us. So [the sense of touch] keeps returning to the body for ultimate verification. Whether you're talking about a murder or a presidential sex scandal, it's always the body that everybody goes to. They would like to strip everybody naked and see them do what they did and replay that, but it's all body. They want to see what the bodies did, what they were doing, what was done to them. It's also the post-mortem, the dissection, the autopsy. It's the autopsy [in] which you try to find the truth. Of course, an autopsy means that you have a dead body. It's not a living body, so there are only certain things you can verify with a dead body. And all of medicine is concerned with truth as it applies to the body. So much of what we think, in our understanding of human relations, is totally a satellite around the body. So it makes sense to me, and it's true I hadn't really thought of it this way, but you have to go to the body for truth. I suppose, in a sense, that's what I'm doing in my movies, constantly.

SG: So if we ponder on that very strong image that is at the centre of *Videodrome*, that penetration of the hand inside the body, would you

say that, consciously or not at the time, you meant to say cinema becomes flesh?
DC: That would be the ultimate trans-substantiation. The Eucharist. The blood and body of humans made cinema. Of course, in cinema it's still a representation of flesh. It's not the real flesh. I'd say it's an image of the flesh, a reflection of the flesh, and so it's still an abstraction, obviously. But it's like a lover wanting to find out if his lover has been unfaithful to him, and he goes to her body or his body, she goes to his body for verification of the betrayal or the loyalty. Even with cinema it's an abstraction. It's at a remove, but we're able to make that translation ourselves. It's a force of will to be able to believe that wine is blood and that cinema is the human body.

SG: **There is something also very ironic in this Caravaggio painting, when it's compared to *Videodrome*, because this was a religious painting obviously commissioned by the Church and nobody at that time, the seventeenth century, felt disgust when confronted with the body of Jesus, or whatever form this body was representing. But your movies are supposedly giving way to disgust, physical unease. Why is it so?**
DC: I think it's a reflex reaction, and of course there's a built-in terror of seeing the innards of a body outside, because that means there's death, there's violence, it's not the normal, healthy way that bodies should appear. That's the natural reaction to it. But beyond that, it's quite beautiful to think that we understand. There's a great desire that Christ should be real, should be a flesh human being. I remember when I read the book *V* by Thomas Pynchon, and as I was getting into it there was a point where I felt myself saying, 'I hope that V is a real woman, that she's an actual living human and not just an abstraction, not just a metaphor.' It's the same impulse, because if Christ is just a metaphor, an abstraction, then suddenly our relation to him is also an abstraction and does not have the force, the strongest force we have of a human touching another human. That is the strongest relationship we have: physical presence of one another, humans.

SG: **So in a way, we should accept the fact that either your sex imagery or your organic imagery gives birth to those strong physical reactions in a certain part of the public? It means that they're not totally abstract.**
DC: I would never stoop so low as to just get a reaction. I'm not desperate for a reaction from the public no matter what. I mean, you can always kill a pig on screen, as many filmmakers have done to get a reaction. To kill an animal. To depict a human being killed or torn apart is a way of getting a reaction. But if it's a reaction that means nothing, it's in a vacuum, it's just a reaction, then to me it's not interesting. It's the meaning of that that's important to me. It's the context of, and the metaphorical value of the film event, that I'm striving for. Trying to distil its meaning to something very forceful, but that is not an abstraction, that is quite palpable and real. That's the struggle. It feels like an abstract thing when I speak of it, but when you're actually making a film it doesn't feel abstract at all. It feels like an actual struggle to get this thing on camera.

SG: **Now I'm discovering stuff . . .**
DC: I'm trembling in fear here.

SG: **No, no, no, there's nothing to be afraid of . . . but how did you get acquainted with De Laurentiis? Not only concerning *The Dead Zone*, but also I discovered how much you were involved in *Total Recall*. I'm sure it's not a great memory for you, obviously you lost . . .**
DC: A year, a year, at least a year.

SG: **So maybe let's start with *The Dead Zone*.**
DC: I don't think I had met Dino. What had happened [is that] I was sent the book. I was asked if I would be interested in doing *The Dead Zone*, and I read it and then I said, 'No, I'm not interested.' And then, Debra Hill was producing it for Dino – she had done a lot of John Carpenter stuff, so I had heard about her. I think I might

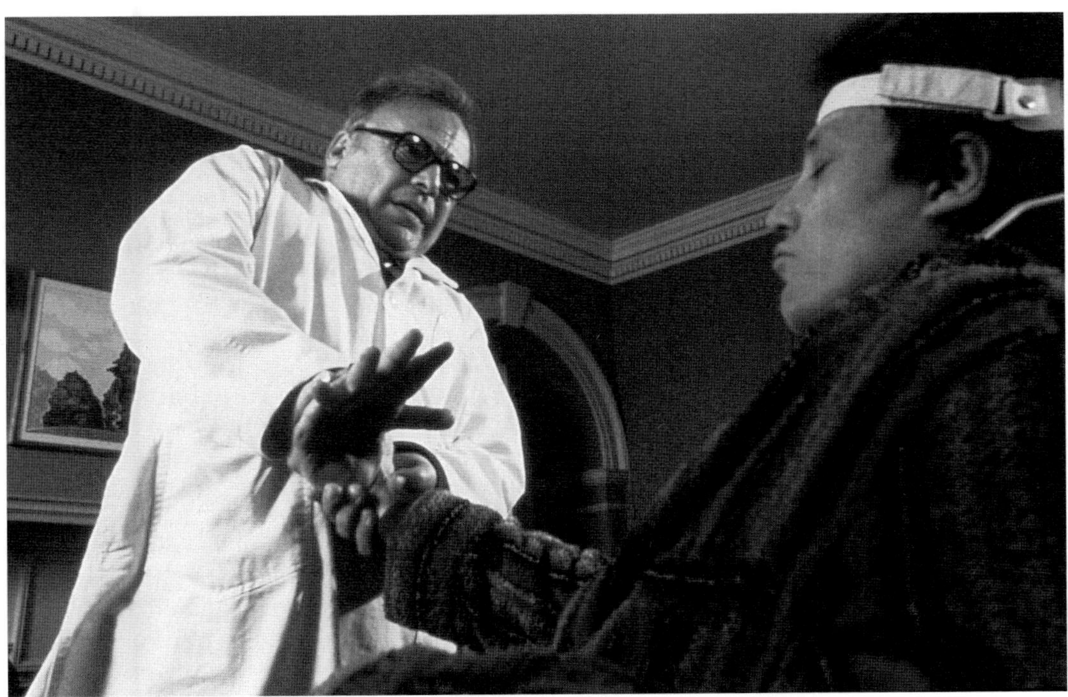

Herbert Lom and Christopher Walken: 'The hand that sees.'

have met her actually as well and I said, 'I don't want to do it,' for various reasons. And then I met her at a party in LA, which is not something I do very often, and I can't remember the occasion, and she said, 'I'm now doing this with Dino De Laurentiis.' I think that's how it went: the first time it came from her but not from . . . No, I think that maybe it's the reverse, I can't remember. I think maybe it came from Dino the first time and she wasn't involved, and then the second time she said, 'I'm now producing *The Dead Zone* for Dino and I'd really like you to do it.' I'm not even sure if she knew at that point or if she had already been asked. And I said I would be interested, which is one of those things that happens, you know. I mean, in a different way it happened with *Crash* as well. Somehow – and it might have been a year later that this happened, that I met her, I can't remember at all, but it was a good chunk of time – it had sort of settled in me. And somehow it went from something that I wasn't interested in at all to something that I was interested in. And so that's really when I started to get involved with Dino. She must have introduced me to him, and we met. I spent a lot of time with Dino, I really love Dino, a lot of people do, you know. He has a very controversial reputation, but as a human being that you sit down with and talk, he's actually great. And I did like him a lot.

Anyway, I can remember when David Lynch was in the middle of his *Dune* agony, he said, 'Dino is a nice man, but he is no help.' But I found Dino to be – despite the fact that his English wasn't perfect, and everybody does an imitation of Dino, including me, it's almost irresistible, in his office with the big desk that everybody talks about, which was not quite Mussolini-size, but nonetheless very big and he's a small man – just an interesting guy. He really could

The Dead Zone: Nicholas Campbell (in his second Cronenbergian role) as a serial killer in his final moments; an evocation of The Death of Marat by J. L. David?

read a script, but translated into Italian. And I realised that you had to get a good translator, because especially with the humour . . . Sometimes he'd say, 'There's no humour here.' And I'd say, 'But Dino, this is a joke, this is a joke . . .' 'Oh,' he'd say, 'that's a joke, I didn't know.' You don't know what the translators translate. Still, he was pretty savvy when it came to reading a script and talking about the structure. That surprised me, because I was used to the new generation of studio executives who were mostly from marketing or agents, and they were not necessarily good with any of that stuff. It was the beginning of that sort of breed of studio executive. Dino, of course, was a throwback to the old mogul school. And I could see why people got nostalgic even for Harry Cohn, when they thought about the way things were going. He may have been a horrible man in many ways, but still . . .

So I got five scripts that had already been written, including one by Stephen King which was the worst one by far. I didn't like any of them, but I picked one of the writers, Jeffrey Boam, because I thought that was the best script of the five, and then we did another script. And this was interesting for me, because this was my first adaptation of a book and it was the first screenplay I hadn't written myself. Even for *Fast Company*, I had hands-on [input], me typing stuff. On this one I didn't do any typing and Jeffrey did the writing. Nonetheless, I retained control over what was included in the script and what wasn't. There were things that worked in the book but would not have worked on screen. There were some things in the book that I thought didn't even work in the book, and I certainly did not want to deal with them on screen – I could be very specific about those . . . So I was working intimately with a writer for the first time since *Fast Company*, when I had done a little of that. This was seriously working with the writer in the Hollywood style: this was as close to a Hollywood movie as I was going to come.

And I wrote the script, and I had many discussions with Dino, and met Dino's daughter, Raffaella, and his new wife – well actually, I'm not sure if he had remarried then. But anyway, with Dino you get involved with the family too, and in a nice way. When he was opening his new restaurant, I came to the opening and he tried out some food samples on me and he made me cappuccinos. I have very fond memories of that aspect of it. Then we had Americans here producing in Toronto, Debra Hill in particular and a couple of other people. That's when I first realised that Americans get funny when they're in Canada. They get quite funny and paranoid because they suddenly realise that they are different from Canadians. Recently, my assistant director was working on a John Travolta movie in Montréal, and he told me that the Canadians were treated like shit. Once again it's like, 'You're not Hollywood, we're supercool and you guys are the sticks.' It's sort of a class thing.

But at the same time, it was also my first movie which did not have Canadian content. It was a totally American production, although I used a lot of Canadian crew, but I had no restrictions in terms of actors, for example. That's why there are so many American actors in *The Dead Zone*, because it had no Canadian financing at all. It was Dino for Paramount, and Paramount was footing all the bills, and therefore it was an American production basically. So it wasn't eligible for any Canadian Genie Awards and so on.

Psychic combustion: Christopher Walken enters his own vision. The Cronenbergian art of illusion is simple in its conception, but with maximum effect.

And I had a lot of actors like Anthony Zerbe and Martin Sheen, who I probably wouldn't have been able to get otherwise, because they were the fourth, fifth and sixth American actors. It was kind of exciting for me, because it's a huge gene pool: America is so much larger than Canada that I had ten times more actors to choose from than I usually did. Usually I had to restrict myself to primarily Canadian actors, so it was very interesting in that respect.

Martin Sheen said to me, 'You don't know how good you have it here in Canada, you're so lucky to be able to shoot like that,' and at the same time my producer was yelling and screaming about how incompetent all Canadians were, and stuff like that. Sheen also told me, 'Don't even bother shooting in LA, you'll hate it,' because he could see that the crew was very tight, everyone was involved in the movie. There were no teamsters and no union muscle tactics. Everybody was very interested in the movie: I give my gaffer the script to read. Everyone reads the script, it's not like in America where they don't know what they're doing. They don't care, they just show up. And it was a thrill to work with guys like Chris Walken and Martin Sheen and Anthony Zerbe too. So it was my American production, and the story was set in America and involved some American politics. All of these things were the reasons why I wasn't interested in doing it initially, and then they became the reasons why I was interested in doing it. And it still has a very Canadian feel, as you can imagine. It was set in New England, which I can relate to, because southern Ontario feels very much in some ways like New England, and it was all shot in Canada. It was a very potent experience.

I can remember the second day on the set, I

Elect
DZ-5134-10

got a phone call on the set from Dino saying that I was shooting too much film. And I said, 'Well Dino, you know, during the first few days, when you're beginning to know your actors and so on, you tend to shoot a lot because you're feeling your way through.' And he said, 'Oh, Ingmar Bergman said the same thing to me,' because he had produced *The Serpent* or something with Bergman [they worked together on *The Serpent's Egg*]. I think he did maybe just that one film. So I thought well, that's good, the difference was that I never stopped shooting that much film. And Dino got mad at me, and I remember at one point Debra said, 'Dino is going to fire you,' and I said, 'Thank God.' And she said, 'No! Don't say that!' They couldn't threaten me, they couldn't change me by threatening to fire me. I said, 'Thank God, take me off this picture.' It was a difficult picture in many ways, although in terms of the actors [it was] fantastic. Chris [Christopher Walken] was wonderful. It was a great experience with the actors in that movie. In fact it went pretty smoothly, all things considered, I have to say.

SG: **And strangely enough it really is a Cronenberg film, it doesn't feel like a Stephen King-inspired script.**
DC: Yeah.

SG: **I know that King said that it was one of his favourite adaptations of his novels, but you can feel it's different, I don't exactly know why. I've read the novel and I noticed all that you ignored . . .**
DC: Yes, I filtered out a lot of things. Still, the basic concept of the film I would never have done, and really I was in two minds about it. Because the whole idea of prophecy and that sort of supernatural thing that King does all the time, I avoid it because I don't believe in it – although you don't have to believe in it, obviously, because it has metaphorical value. Once I started to think about that, first of all it amused me to think that the whole film could be interpreted as the fantasy of a crazy person, and secondly, it is a very good analogy of an artist who creates and has visions of some kind, and is an exile from normal society because of that. So it had honourable roots for me, and I got into it. And even some of the American politics – of course, in Canada we're obsessed with American politics even more than the Americans are – was [of] legitimate [interest to me].

And it is a film which I am very proud of, and very fond of, and the irony is that I think it had the potential to be the most popular of all my films by far. It is the only film I have ever had a good test screening for. Actually, now that I think of it, they had a test preview somewhere, I think it may have been in New Jersey. Anyway, it scored the highest scores that Paramount have ever had [on] a film score, the highest on every level. But they blew it, and at that time Paramount was considered the strongest distributor, but I unfortunately got into a nightmare with the marketing people, and they were in the middle of a huge scandal. A guy named David Rose, the head of marketing there, was arrested and taken out in handcuffs because he had been scamming them. He had been siphoning out money that was supposed to go into making trailers and so on: he would pocket the money and make a really shabby, terrible trailer – all kinds of stuff was going on. So they were in complete disarray in terms of their marketing, and I unfortunately happened to be right in the middle of it. And I had one or two very unpleasant experiences with, for example, a young lady in the marketing department there . . .

Anyway. They didn't market the film well. I ended up renting my own theatre in Toronto and installing Dolby stereo equipment. That was the only time I ever rented a theatre, it was a very interesting experience for me too. It was

The Dead Zone: *Despite giving the appearance of a political film, it marks the first incursion of Cronenberg into the supernatural, or fantastique – but a subverted form of the genre that usually sits at odds with his atheism.*

Chris Walken the visionary sniper. All of the film centres on an ambiguity: is Johnny Smith really a psychopath whose point of view we are forced to share?

being distributed by Cineplex and they weren't going to put it in a stereo cinema. It was my first stereo picture. Now, of course, everything is stereo, but at the time most films were mono and only the flagship theatres would have Dolby stereo. So I said, 'All right, I'm going to run it myself in my own theatre and I'm going to install stereo and I'm going to advertise the fact that it will be the only place where the picture is shown with Dolby stereo,' and I did. And they immediately put it in a Dolby stereo theatre. So I ended up with what was an old neighbourhood theatre – they were all disappearing, but this one still exists on Mount Pleasant Avenue. I rented it from this guy who usually showed softcore porn – well, not just that, he showed all kinds of stuff. And I put out the money to do this because I was so upset about the sound.

We had mixed the sound in LA, and that was another Hollywood experience for me, because I was mixing in a very big, posh Hollywood mixing stage with some very well-known mixers. I had never done that before, all of my films had been mixed in Toronto. That was a major thing, the sound was great and it was my first stereo mix. It was the first time we could afford to mix stereo. So I was damned if they were going to show it in Toronto in mono.

That was also an interesting experiment [the theatre rental]. I took my daughter Cassandra, and we would go every night. We sat and watched to see how many people came in, and how they were when they came out and how much popcorn they would buy. This guy [the landlord] retained the rights to the popcorn. Of course, I didn't realise then that that was where you made your money, with the popcorn – but money wasn't my purpose in doing it anyway. I realised that that movie could have been hugely popular, because it's the only movie I've made that grandmothers love, grannies love it. What can you say? I mean, as I said before, it's a miracle when it all works all the way to the theatre. So that was *The Dead Zone*.

SG: **So now . . .**

DC: And the beginning of my relationship with Dino, which went on . . .

SG: **You don't have to go into minute details, but how come – given that your closeness to Philip K. Dick was so obvious – you couldn't direct *Total Recall*?**

DC: You know, I hadn't read Philip Dick, at that time I was not a Philip Dick fan. I knew about him, but I had stopped reading sci-fi when I was a kid, probably sometime in the 1950s – that was when I started reading guys like Burroughs and Nabokov. So I missed the beginning of Philip K. Dick's reign as one of the supremos of sci-fi. It was the script of *Total Recall*, which Dino gave to me, which got me interested – the first third of it was great, though after that it fell apart.

SG: **Who wrote the script?**

DC: It was Dan O'Bannon, I think, and Ron Shusset, or it might have just been Dan O'Bannon. And I had a funny non-relationship with Dan O'Bannon, because I've never met him, but I know tons of people who know him and have worked with him. John Landis told me that he [O'Bannon] knew very well what he called 'the Canadian films', by which he meant *Shivers* and *Rabid*, when he wrote *Alien*. And so I know that he stole all that parasite stuff from *Shivers*. And Ron Shusset says, 'He never saw those

Greg Stillson (Martin Sheen), the fascistic demagogue politician, takes a child hostage on the podium and uses him as a shield.

movies and knows nothing about it and I believe him.' Dan O'Bannon later denied that he had ever seen those movies, but John Landis swears that he talked about them all the time and knew them very well. So I remember, at the film festival in Hof in Germany, I had a little retrospective there and we showed *Shivers*. This was many years ago, maybe *Shivers* and *Rabid* were all I had to show, with *Stereo* and *Crimes of the Future*. Anyway, afterwards, when I was talking to the audience, this man stood up and said, 'How dare you show this movie when it is so obvious you have stolen from *Alien*?' And I said, 'Well, this movie was made three years before *Alien*.' He said, 'What?' I said, 'Yes.' Then he said, 'Now we know who the thief is.' So that was my vindication, somebody knew then. I had a chance to say that. So it was odd for me to read a script from Dan O'Bannon. Not that I minded, I mean everybody obviously steals from everybody else, but he apparently was a very aggressive sort of hostile character. I don't know. I never met him.

But the script had this very wonderful beginning which was pure Philip Dick, and then they didn't know what to do with it. So I was intrigued, because it felt very close, it felt good. And as I say, I had no preconceived ideas of Philip Dick, I hadn't read anything of his then. I read him much later. Now I have a Philip Dick collection of original [editions].

So I spent a year, and it was interesting because it was the first script that I wrote on a computer. It was a Xerox 860 dedicated word-processor, a very big machine with big eight-inch disks, but with a beautiful screen that was page size, it would hold a whole page, and it even had a touch pad. That was a long time ago, before anyone had seen those things. Xerox was very ahead, as computer freaks know, and then they blew it. They had all kinds of possibilities: they could have been Apple, they could have been everything, and they didn't know what they had. But they did make this wonderful system.

Anyway, *Total Recall* was the first script that I wrote on a computer, and it's a good thing I had a computer because I did about twelve drafts in about twelve months. I was constantly fighting with Ron Shusset, and meeting with him. I liked him, but basically he was wanting to do *Raiders of the Lost Ark Go to Mars*, and I had a much darker, complex, more sophisticated idea in mind. In fact, at one point he said to me, 'You know what you've done with this draft?' I said, 'What?' He said, 'You've done the Philip K. Dick version.' And he was saying it angrily, like I had done something terrible. And I said, 'Isn't that what we wanted to do?' The story that it's based on, in typical Dick fashion, doesn't really carry through or finish off: it sets in motion some wonderful things, but never resolves them in a way that a movie in particular has to do. It really is a very short story.

So I was doing all these drafts, and basically the problem was that Dino was siding with Ron Shusset. And at a certain point I went to Dino and I said, 'Dino, I think we have to stop because we're obviously talking about two different movies, and we might as well acknowledge it now. I don't want to make your movie. It seems that you don't want to make my movie. We should stop.' He was rational, but he was telling me he was going to sue me. I was surprised he even cared, but it was like he had a deal with me . . . So I basically said that I would make another movie with him. I mean, I obviously wanted to work with him, but that project was clearly not the right one. And my vindication there was that, some years later, Dino came back to me and said, 'OK, we'll do it your way, let's do the movie.' And I said, 'It's dead for me now, I can't get back into that now. I just can't go back to working with Ron and fighting the same old battles and doing all that stuff.'

So he did offer me a chance finally . . . I think as part of my making peace with him, I was bringing him *Dead Ringers*. That was the third project that I had Dino involved with. And Raffaella was going to produce it, but there was another similar moment. This was different. I walked into Raffaella's office and I could see her hair was up and she was looking very executive suddenly, and I knew something was wrong. And she basically said, 'We can't finance *Dead Ringers*.' And it was because they had just had a movie called *The Million Dollar Mystery* or something. They had had about five total flops in a row which had cost a lot of money. Basically DEG, De Laurentiis Entertainment Group, was going bankrupt. So I was caught in that and I remember saying to her, 'I hope this isn't another *Platoon*,' because everybody knew that Dino had had *Platoon* and that he quibbled so much about, I think, just the money, the budget, that he had let go of it. And then of course it made a fortune and won all those Oscars. It probably would have saved his DEG. So I had to give her that little dig. I said, 'Well, *Dead Ringers*, I don't know. It might be one of those movies that you decide not to do . . .' But really they were in financial trouble.

Dino had some input in *Dead Ringers*, some good input. I had the idea and the concept and I knew the original twins, but he told me about some dentists that he knew in Italy who were very handsome identical twins, and how they swapped sexual partners. One of them was shy and one of them was aggressive, and the aggressive one would do the seduction, and then the shy one would move in. Now that isn't quite in the Marcus twins story, but it is obviously in the movie. So Dino did have some creative input into *Dead Ringers*, despite the fact that he wasn't really involved ultimately in making it.

SG: I know that maybe it isn't very important, but what was your reaction when you eventually saw *Total Recall*?

DC: I remember meeting William Hurt in Dino's office, because I wanted him to play the lead. And we discussed it, and that was my meeting with William Hurt. He liked the script, he didn't trust Dino, but we had gotten that far. I met

Richard Dreyfuss about it as well. So when you imagine that they cast Arnold Schwarzenegger, you can see the difference. I really thought it was a bad movie, although there were one or two moments that were true Philip Dick moments in it – they were good. But they weren't good, because it was Schwarzenegger still: first of all as an actor for that kind of role, and secondly as that character. The whole point of that character was that he was a unique, shy, mild character. And you know you can't hide that [physical] part of Schwarzenegger, it's just impossible. They tried to compensate by making him a construction worker, but they gave him this beautiful Sharon Stone wife. That was, I think, the first time I really saw Sharon Stone. Also I thought it was very tacky, very visually tacky and messy. *Robocop* was good and very tight, but I thought that [in *Total Recall*] Verhoeven didn't do a good job with all the effects and the mutants and all of that stuff. You know, there were several moments that were good, they were all in the trailer. But I didn't think it was good, and I also thought it betrayed the promise of the basic premise, which had some implications in terms of memory and identity and all kinds of things. They went for the action stuff purely and that was it: it was an action gimmick. So I didn't really like the movie and I didn't think much of it.

SG: I guess it must be sad to spend a year on a project and then . . .
DC: It's heartbreaking, it's heartbreaking.

SG: . . . seeing the project . . .
DC: Well by the time . . .

SG: Honestly, *Total Recall* is not a good movie.
DC: No, I know. But by the time I saw it, I didn't care. I was pretty neutral, I mean if it had been good in a different way it would have been fine. And of course it did well, it made money. By the time it came out it was years later, so I was over it. I had made other movies, it was OK. It happens all the time.

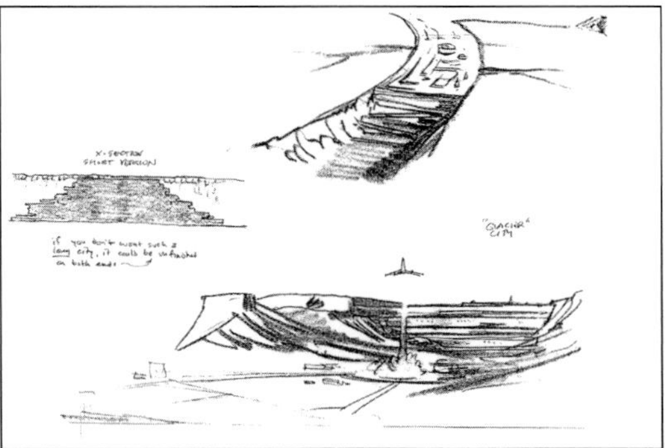

Total Recall (unmade): Sketches of the sets for Total Recall by production designer Pier Luigi Basile, the project on which David Cronenberg spent two lost years – after being tempted by Dino De Laurentiis to impose a personal vision that was closer to the universe of Philip K. Dick. To his eternal regret, we never got to see Cronenberg's version of red days spent on the planet Mars.

FLY PRODUCTIONS LIMITED

TORONTO INTERNATIONAL STUDIOS, 11030 HIGHWAY 27, BOX 430
KLEINBURG, ONTARIO L0J 1C0 TELEPHONE (416) 893 2222/(416) 893 1911

The beginning of recognition

The Fly

Made between *The Dead Zone* (1983) and *Dead Ringers* (1988), *The Fly* (1986) occupies a special place in the life and work of David Cronenberg. First of all, because it is halfway between an original screenplay and an adaptation, the two positions between which the director has veered throughout his life, and also because the film, entirely financed by Hollywood, was and remains his greatest commercial success. It shows how the most improbable challenge can, in the hands of an authentic artist, result in a masterpiece. It may have originally been conceived as a remake of a classic horror film (even though Cronenberg had always turned down this kind of typical Hollywood exercise), but he succeeded so well in twisting a conventional science fiction scenario (featuring teleportation) with its corresponding imagery (a creature half-man and half-insect, in the image of those archaic mythical divinities whose quasi-animal life preceded the organisation of the universe by *logos*, i.e. rationality) into an anxious closed world where two lovers are confronted by decay and death. We find ourselves faced with a modern tragedy (an 'opera', in the proper sense of the term) where a computer plays the role of implacable destiny and human passions obey the rules of bio-chemical formulae.

David Cronenberg's rewriting of this contemporary fable where, once more, the body is the theatre of existential drama, confirms yet again his importance in contemporary art. For the monstrous mutation of Seth Brundle (Jeff Goldblum), even though it occurs organically, is presented as a technical aberration, a mistake by an artificial intelligence unaware of the 'mystery of the flesh'; it strikes us on two levels: that of the computer screen which, like the idiot in Shakespeare, tells a tale 'full of sound and fury ... signifying nothing', and that of a body that becomes, literally, mad, and produces a disorder that seems to have come directly from nightmare, an unscientific teratological hypothesis which is, nevertheless, close to our childhood fears. Is it by chance that Brundle's metamorphosis follows the description of human destiny that the Sphinx gave to Oedipus? (The triumphant Apollonian body of Brundle, a demigod emerging from an egg as in one of Ovid's tales; the pathetic spectacle of a scientist eaten away internally by an insect, who leans on a cane, and eventually reaches the infantile stage of the new-born crawling on all fours.)

We have come a long way from the fundamental good-and-evil dualism of the fantasy genre! The polluted air that we breathe here has much in common with that in the room of the hero of Kafka's *Metamorphosis*. And when Veronica (Geena Davis) – who has introduced the somewhat virginal researcher to the pleasures of the flesh – cries out to abort the 'thing' that her lover has implanted in her belly, the viewer finds himself violently projected into the morally ambivalent universe of the unconscious, cruel and sometimes terrifying. For it is certainly a birth, with all the pain of human childbirth, that we witness: the vision of the masked filmmaker giving birth to a trembling larva (in a sequence that, in its dreamlike way, encapsulates the drama of the film as a whole – I have never known any audience member to laugh during this scene) further

Above: David Cronenberg creates ad hoc production companies for each of his films. This is the card for his co-production of The Fly, made with Mel Brooks and Stuart Cornfeld.
Opposite: This Ducati motorcycle engine is the motor that drives 'the dream machine' in 'The Italian Machine', Cronenberg's 1976 TV short, and also served as the model for the telepod in The Fly.

DUCATI

Part of the Ducati motorcycle cylinder that provided Carol Spier's initial blueprint for the telepod.

defines the films of Cronenberg as 'forceps cinema' – where the director, the perverse master of a new form of midwifery, realises our darkest fantasies, rendering them almost tangibly 'real'. Here it is a question of death; more precisely, of a slow agony, with no *deus ex machina* arriving to provide miraculous release. It is the Cronenberg theme *par excellence*.

It is hard to say exactly why critical recognition should at last begin for Cronenberg with *The Fly*, but the film's widespread public success (and an Oscar for technical excellence) showed that audiences were finally beginning to understand the work of a director whose demanding harshness might otherwise have condemned him to the art-house circuit. Cronenberg was now able to go on to even more audacious projects, with sufficient means to realise his visions, but without renouncing the fluid austerity of his style.

SG: And then came *The Fly* . . . Just one point: you've worked with De Laurentiis and with Brooks, as Lynch did. So it shows in a way that those producers were a bit different in that they were interested in, let's say, interesting directors. That's unusual in Hollywood . . .

DC: No, no, Brooks is . . . They're very different guys, of course, but they're both short – little. What happened with Brooks was, when I finally told Dino I can't do *Total Recall*, I was in LA. I phoned my wife Carolyn and I said, 'I don't think I am going to come back until I get a movie because we're broke.' I had spent a year writing for not a lot of money, because it was a rewrite and so on. She came down with the kids and I told my agent, 'I'm now a filmmaker looking for a movie.' I don't know if it happened at the same time, but ultimately it was *The Fly* which was the project that was around. They were interested in me, and I had met Stuart Cornfeld who was producing it for Mel. I remember reading it and the first sixteen pages were awful. Of course I knew the original film, I saw it when it came out when I was a kid.

SG: They just wanted to do a remake?

DC: Yeah, that's all. The first sixteen pages were terrible. I thought the dialogue was terrible, the characters were terrible, everything was terrible. But then it got interesting when it began to deal with the concept of genetic fusion, and some of the details of what became like a disease rather than a big head, a fly head like in the original, and so on. And I saw a lot of potential in that, and it really felt like me, that was interesting. But the characters were terrible, the structure was terrible, everything else was bad, the dialogue was bad, everything. But the rethinking of it, the basic rethinking of it was pretty good. So I said to them, 'Well, the first thing I would do is throw out the first sixteen pages establishing the guy.' He was married, as in the original, and it was all boring stuff. I said, 'Get rid of it. Who cares about that?' And I told Stuart what I would do with it and they said, 'OK.'

It was complicated, because I was also talking to Ivan Reitman at that time – Ivan, who I knew of course from Cinepix days and before, underground days in Toronto, had come down to LA and made some successful films. He was producing some other films and he was wanting to do *The Hitchhiker's Guide to the Galaxy.* So Ivan and I were working on that, just on the idea of what we would do. Then Mel offered me twice the money that I got on *The Dead Zone* to direct *The Fly*, which was quite an extraordinary thing to do.

By that time I was thinking that I should do *The Fly* anyway, so that sealed it for me because money was an issue at the time. Ivan was mad at me. He said, 'You're just doing it for the money' – this is Ivan, you know, the irony. I said, 'No I'm not.' He said, 'Yes you are.' Then, when he saw the movie, I said, 'Well, Ivan?' He said, 'No, you're right, it wasn't just the money,' because he could see what I was doing. But at the time he was mad at me – you know, a little bit.

So that was what launched me into doing *The Fly*, that and the fact that they were willing to do it my way. Now they had had a director whose name I have forgotten, but who has done stuff since. He was going to do the movie and then his child was killed. I think a tractor rolled over on her, or something like that, so it was really pretty horrible. Obviously he couldn't work, so that's when I stepped in to do this. But I said, 'I want to do it my way, I want to shoot in Toronto,' and so on. They agreed on everything. Basically Mel really wanted Pierce Brosnan to be the lead and I didn't.

SG: He was not that famous at the time.

DC: He was not, he was just doing *Remington Steele*, but I think Mel thought it should be a handsome guy and he was a handsome guy. For some reason, he really thought he was good, and obviously he has had a good career since then. And he's done some sci-fi too, he did *The Lawnmower Man*. Anyway, he wasn't my idea of the main character.

So I rewrote the script and had a couple of script sessions with Stuart and Mel. I met Mel and I got along very well with him. We had some discussions, some arguments, whatever, but basically the script-writing phase went well. And then we started shooting in Toronto and it was really . . . There were many complex things that happened and there were some shaky moments and some difficult moments . . .

SG: Who decided to cast Goldblum?

DC: Me. It needed to be agreed upon but I approached a couple of people.

SG: Where did you meet him?

DC: Oh, I had seen Jeff at the Toronto Film Festival. He had been here with *The Big Chill*, and I remember that somebody was attacking him because they said that that was just a remake of *The Sarcophagus*, a John Sayles film [he's thinking of *Return of the Secaucus 7*]. And I was defending the film because I liked it. So Jeff thanked me for doing that. So we had met each other. But I did approach one or two other

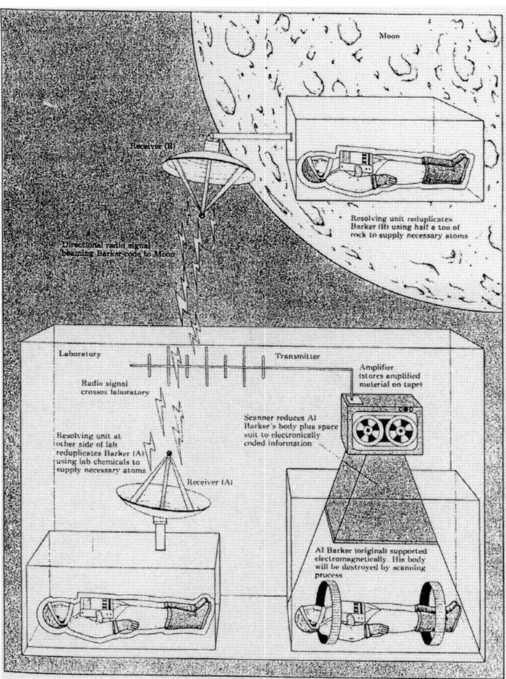

Reproduction of an article on teleportation which served as Cronenberg's inspiration. The article reaches a different conclusion on the virtual impossibility of teleporting matter.

actors, and I think Dreyfuss might have been one of them because of the *Total Recall* thing. He said he didn't want to act with 30 pounds of rubber on his face. And there were a couple of actors who were very intimidated by the idea of having to act with rubber on their faces. Jeff had no problem with that. He knew he could act through the rubber. He loves science fiction and we got along very well. So that was Jeff.

I remember casting Geena Davis was a more interesting thing, because many actors were suggested to me for Geena's role, but I couldn't find anybody who I thought worked with Jeff. I mean, once you've got Jeff you have to take into account the fact that he's a very specific guy, and he's very tall. And I knew that Geena was his girlfriend, but he never mentioned her. She was very unknown. She had had one nice moment in *Tootsie*, and some limited success with a comedy TV series which I had seen, but I knew she was funny and I knew she was pretty. We still hadn't made a final choice. I was having to audition a TV actress that Stuart insisted I audition, Shelley . . . I forget her name, who was sort of big at the time. And it was a disaster, I didn't want to do it and he made me . . . Oh, actually that was after Geena. So at one point Jeff said, 'Well, what about Geena Davis?' And I said, 'OK, I'll audition her.' So she came to Toronto, to that office that you know well on Avenue Road, and she auditioned and she was just great. She was funny, she was beautiful, she was smart and she was a lovely actress. So I said, 'Great.' I think finally that she was the first actress that I actually auditioned.

Then I ran into the whole . . . Stuart had a whole idea of what it is to be a producer in his head. It was a very American and to me a very perverse idea. His idea was, *Whatever the director wants, you don't give him right away because he must be wrong.* So he made me audition this other woman and it was a horrible audition, because she was trying so hard, but she just didn't have it. And he was there too, and he could see that it was wrong. I felt so uncomfortable. And I knew Geena was the one and there was no question [of anybody else]. So that, to a certain extent, was Stuart's and my relationship. I was very sure about many things, because as a director you have to be sure. You make your decision and you go with it, but he felt he had to second guess me on everything – and this was one of them.

Finally, of course, we ended up with Geena, who was great, and then a year or two later she won an Oscar for *The Accidental Tourist.* Once we had those two we had most of the movie, because it's basically just three people in a room, and the rest was making the special effects work and the script and so on.

SG: And they were not afraid of the idea of just having three people ?

DC: Well, you see, this was the amazing thing: no-one ever mentioned it! They loved the script. Mel said to me, 'Don't hold back. When it comes to gore, extreme whatever, don't hold back.' And I said, 'Don't worry, I won't.' Because that's what that movie was, unlike *The Dead Zone*, which was very discreet – there wasn't much blood, but the whole tone of *The Dead Zone* was different – *The Fly* was a horror film, so no one even noticed what a depressing plot it was. No one noticed how it was like a little opera in a room, or a play. And in fact when people saw it, they didn't notice those things either. I have said this many times, but of course I can say it again, I was protected by the genre in making this movie. It is really about death: it's about love and death and aging. A lot of people afterwards thought it was really about AIDS, and in retrospect they thought that *Shivers* and *Rabid* were also about AIDS, but basically it was a movie which, if you had made it straight, would have been so depressing that no one would have ever gone to see it: an eccentric, interesting couple meet, fall in love, he gets a horrible disease, she watches him dying, finally helps him to die, kills him, and that's the end of the story. That's really what the story is, and you can throw in an abortion or two in the middle of it, and you have a fairly depressing story. But in fact people don't respond to it as though it was depressing, that's what happens when it [a movie] works.

And of course it did, and it remains to this day my biggest box office success. It was the Number One film, I think, for three weeks in a row in North America. And it also did that amazing thing of also getting very good reviews, which was surprising because it's a horror film.

SG: It must have in some way accessed our deepest fears. I remember the first time I saw *The Fly* was at the Avoriaz [Film] Festival, and I was sitting near a male producer. I remember, when I left the theatre, I had the mark of his fingers printed on my skin. He was my age and he was totally frightened. I'm sure that the ultimate horror is something that is very deep inside us, even if we are not conscious of it. It's true that it is a wonderful film.

DC: Well, the funny thing is, people tell me it's a wonderful love story, and I think it's not a wonderful love story. To me it's not a wonderful love story because, once again, I feel that the love story is just set up: it goes through the motions of a love story, but it's not really examining the love story. People love the idea that she stays with him even though he becomes ugly and diseased. There's truth in that, there are those moments, but if I were going to do a love story it would be quite a different thing. But it's a death story, it's a very serious death story about physical death, death as a physical event.

SG: And even death as a virus, with the abortion theme, etc.

DC: Yeah, yeah. Well it's the virus we're born with. So even the idea that he bites his fingernail and he's looking at himself in the mirror and the fingernail comes off, I mean, how many times have you heard stories about someone who just discovers a lump or a bump or a blemish or a blotch or something, and it's the beginning of the end? Bob Marley has a mole on his toe and eventually it becomes brain cancer . . . So it does touch all of those things, as well as, of course, *The Fly* becoming a dangerous creature and that whole element too. And I had seen John Getz, who was the third actor in the triangle in *Blood Simple*, the Coen brothers film, and I liked him and so . . .

SG: He's very good.

DC: Yeah, he is good.

SG: By the way, there is something we have not discussed yet: the musical score . . . I think with *The Fly* – I'm not saying that you didn't have musical scores before, the score of *Videodrome* is very good – but in *The Fly* the score seemed to become very important.

DC: Well, we had some money for one thing, and also I saw it as an opera. The film was very operatic so I wanted a big operatic score. The thing about *The Fly* was it was mixed in England, and that was my first experience of that. We felt at the time that there wasn't a place in Toronto that was good enough, and since Canadian content once again was not an issue, because there was no Canadian money in the project, we could have gone to LA or we could have gone to London. London was cheaper and so we went there. Going to London was a whole interesting experience and, as is often the case, the most ferocious struggles were fought in the mixing theatre – struggles with both Mel and Stuart, I was fighting them both at that time. Sound is more subjective than anything visual, and when it comes to music, music is very subjective. People have associations with music that other people don't have, if you have a bad association with music then you don't like it . . . Well, Mel said – now this wasn't an argument, he was just checking – 'The guy is just walking down the street, why is the music so big?' I said, 'He is not walking down the street, he is meeting his destiny. He is going to meet his destiny.' This is when Jeff is walking down the street and he ends up having the arm wrestle, you know.

SG: Yeah I remember.

DC: By the way, my elbow really hurts from an arm wrestle I just had. I had a millennial arm wrestle with a friend, and, as we were starting to

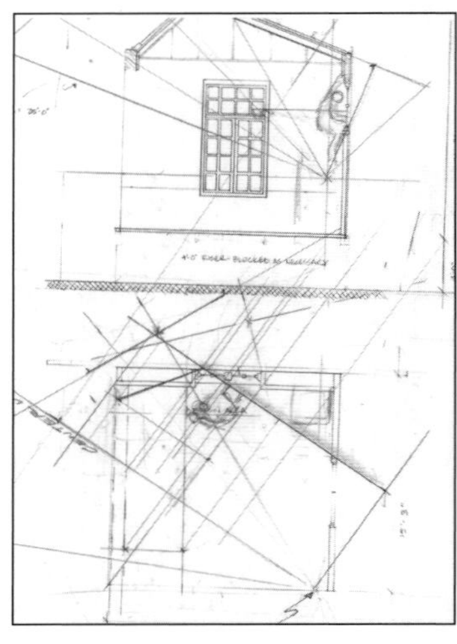

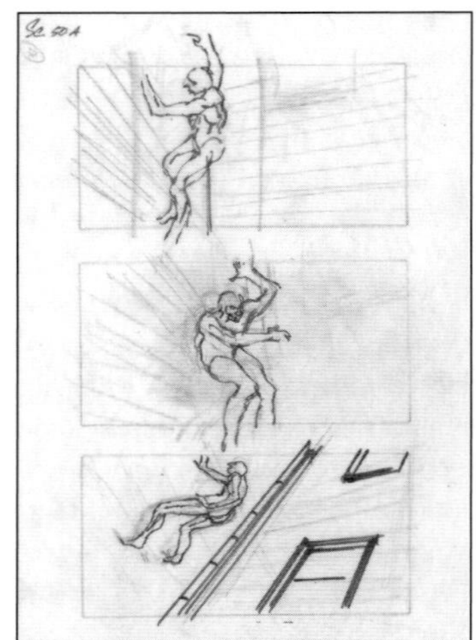

This page. Left: Storyboard in the preparation of this classic special effect, a cube turned completely around on its own axis while the furniture stayed fixed to the floor. Below left: The magnificent designs of Harold Michelson, a former collaborator with Alfred Hitchcock, prepared the journey of Brundlefly up the walls, onto the ceiling and into his loft. Below: Six special makeup storyboards by Stephan Dupuis, depicting the progressive mutation of Seth Brundle.

Opposite page. Centre: a page from Howard Shore's score for The Fly, in keeping with Cronenberg's wish that it should be 'an opera'. Surrounding images: frames of charcoal sketches by Harold Michelson.

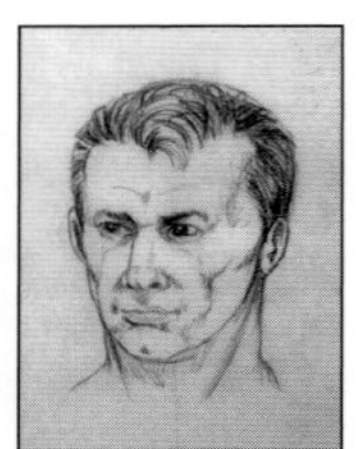

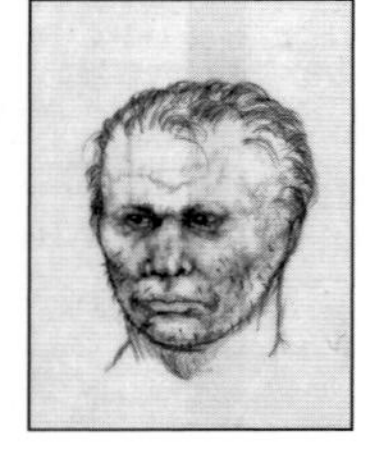

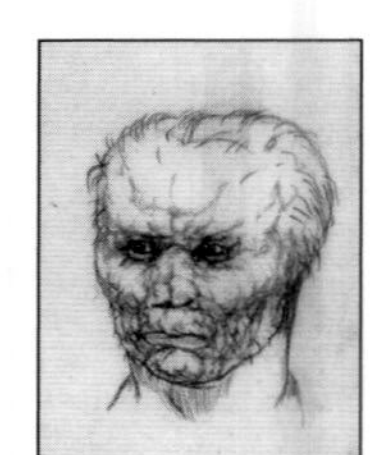

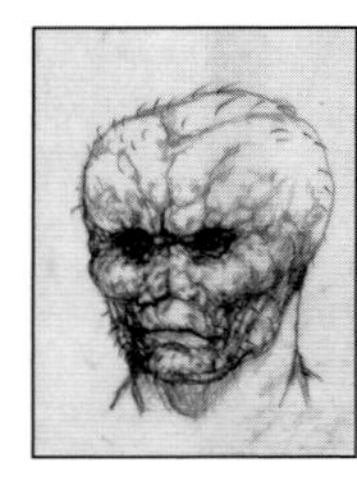

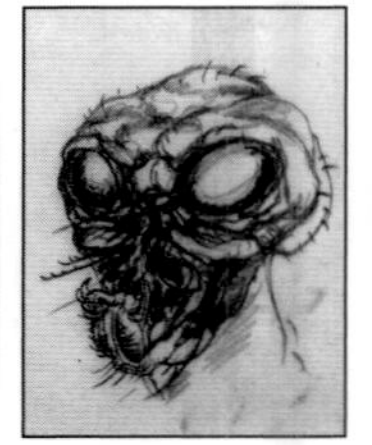

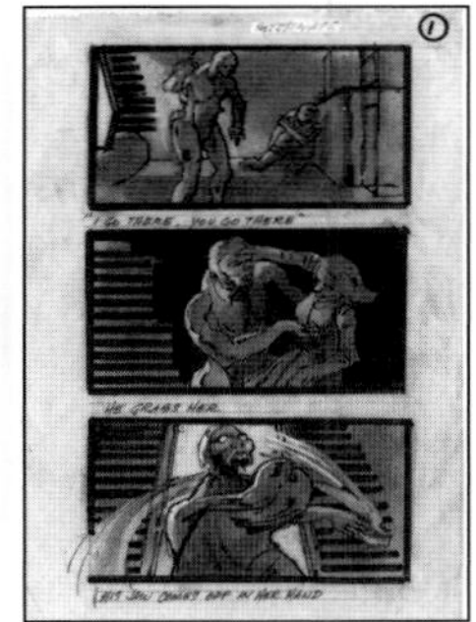

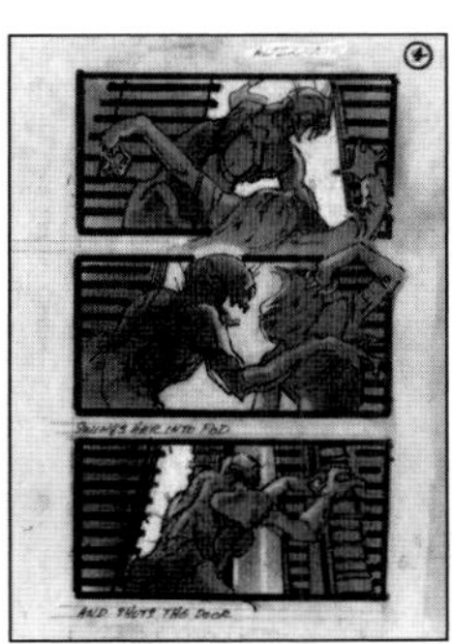

Prod: THE FLY II OM3 Title: THE SOMP TRANSPOSED SCORE

STATHIS EYES CLOSE — STATHIS ON GROUND — c/u SETH

♩=120 :00

Fl. 1 / Flutes (Picc.) 2	
Oboes 1 2	a2
B♭ Cl. 1	
B♭ Cl. 2	Col Cl. 1
Clarinets Bs. Cl. 3	cresc.
Contra-bass Cl. 4 in B♭	
Bassoon	
Contra-bassoon	
F Horns 1·2	1·2 – Con Sord. — to open
Horns 3·4	
B♭ Trumpets 1 2	Straight Mutes — to open
Trombones 1·2	sfz
Trombones Bs. 3·4 Tuba	sfz
Timp.	Gliss.
Lg. Sus. Cym. / B. Dr. + Tam Tam / Percussion	sfz — Sus. Cym.
Violins I Div. a3	senza vib.
Violins II Div. a3	senza vib.
Violas Div. a3	senza vib.
Cello	Solo
Bass	

① ② ③

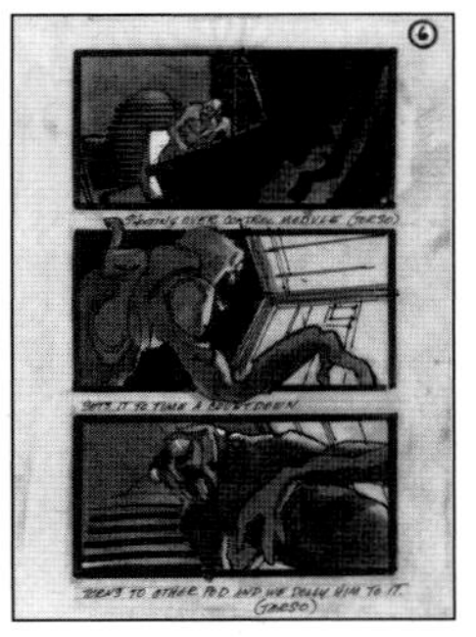

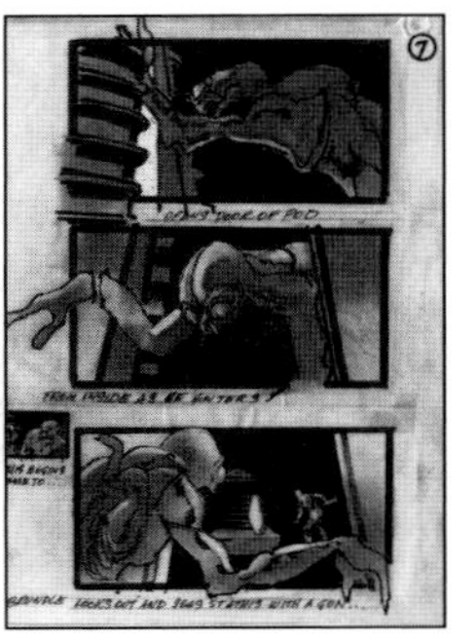

do it, I heard this ripping sound in my elbow like canvas [imitates the sound of ripping canvas]. It's still killing me. Anyway, we all fought like *The Fly* at that moment.

But we had arguments because Mel was mixing a movie, I think it was *Spaceballs*, and that's why he was in England, otherwise he wouldn't have been there. So he was in another studio. And he got a little nervous because he was having money problems with *Spaceballs*, I think his own money was in it and it was going over budget. He started to think that we should have a video and rock 'n' roll song, like a pop song, that was connected with the movie. And I didn't want to do that because I saw it as an opera, and the music was working really well. We actually went to the extent of getting a song called 'Help Me' recorded by Bryan Ferry, who had been the lead singer of Roxy Music. Lionel Rogers was the producer, who is a very well-known, very strong, successful producer. In fact I even liked the song, it was a good song. I visited them when they were shooting the video of it and stuff. But it didn't work in the movie, and they were trying every-which-way to find a place to put it in the movie. Stuart wanted to put it over the end credits: after this big emotional thing you suddenly get this pop song. So I showed him and I said, 'Here's how it would look,' he saw that it was wrong. We ended up putting it in the scene in the bar, mixed down like it was coming from a jukebox.

So we had some ferocious arguments about sound and stuff. Once again I knew what was right, you know, and of course the movie made some money and so everybody was happy.

SG: I think the scene of Brundle coming out of the telepod is a really good example of the importance of birth in your movies. In *The Fly*, and in this sequence especially, it's very clear. Seth Brundle is coming to life in an egg-shaped machine. In *Dead Ringers*, of course, the two twins are obstetricians. You play the part of an obstetrician too. Or *The Brood*, of course. I could give so many examples, not to speak of *Naked Lunch*. Why is this theme so important for you?

DC: It's funny, because when you say that, I find myself resisting and I say, 'No, no, it's not birth here. It's transformation.' And maybe it's transcendence. Birth is an important event for many reasons, and most of them obvious. But maybe it's really *rebirth* we're talking about, and transformation. Change that is so substantial that it's almost equivalent to being reborn. I think really that's what I'm more interested in than just birth itself, as a start. Of course birth is the beginning of everything, but a rebirth is a more complex thing. You're not starting from scratch. You're not starting from zero. I remember when I was thinking of my own children and thinking of the second one and the third one, thinking, 'My God, we have to teach them everything.' Whoever it is, we have to teach them everything again. It is overwhelming to think that. But if it's a rebirth, a transformation, a rebirth is not the same thing. So much of what was there before is still there, and that's a fascinating thing to me, because we're constantly regenerating ourselves. Reinventing ourselves. To me, I think it's what I'm more interested in. Of course in *The Fly*, where I delivered on screen, but with a mask, the fly baby in the dream sequence, it's not really a birth, it's an invention. So I'm almost more interested in not just the biological fact of birth, but the creative fact of human rebirth. The idea that we are reinventing ourselves, or reinventing something, reinventing the world. The first thing I was going to say was, 'No, no, I'm not interested in birth particularly at all.' Of course, when you add up the evidence, you have a good case. But I think it's really more than that.

SG: I think Goya said, 'The sleep of reason breeds monsters.' So in a lot of your movies, whether it's birth or rebirth, the result is almost always what could be called a monster.

DC: Yeah, but I think that monstrosity is a relative thing. And times have changed since Goya in ways that would certainly astonish him. What might be considered monstrous in one era

becomes the normality of the next era. It happens even physically. Humans, physically, would have been monstrosities put amongst the original hominians. So I think we would love to have stability and we would love to have absolutes, but we have to invent them because they don't really exist. There are no absolutes. So I think I'm fascinated by the creativity of what it is to be human. Of human existence. It's constantly creative in ways that we're not even aware of. I mean not normally aware of. In the sense of reality. In the sense of what we consider to be normality, reality. All of those things are constantly shifting and changing . . . It's monstrous but it's exciting too. I don't always see them as negative. I'm not talking about the Frankenstein monster in that sense.

SG: **The metaphor of the monster is something that is easier for the audience to follow, the monster being, as you said, an idea or a concept, so it is easier to show a monster like a 200-pound fly than perhaps to thrill them by pure ideas. In Italian the word *mostrare*, or *montrer* in French, is to show or to display. Which could mean, perhaps, that everything in show business is monstrous by nature. Or the monster is always the centerpiece of any show. Would you agree with that idea ?**

DC: This is an interesting question, because when I think about literature and the influence on me . . . I have to go back to what I was saying before. When I think of how literature has influenced my film-making, and I think it's not a direct thing, it's a subtle thing. There is an obsession I have with metaphor. How do you . . . you can't do it literally. Eisenstein tried the experiments of doing literal equivalents of metaphors. People stood up and roared like a lion, then he would cut to a lion standing up and roaring. It was silly. It was ludicrous. It took people out of the movie. It didn't work. Yet metaphor is really the bedrock of all prose, of all literature. How do you do metaphor in film? For me, I realise that it's the creation of imagery, monstrous imagery, so that if you talk about, as you did, pure ideas, pure ideas are invisible. You don't have anything to photograph. This is, of course, something you can do in literature, but you can't do on the screen in the same way. I have to *make the word be flesh*, and then photograph the flesh because I can't photograph the word. That's how it feels to me. So I'm always looking for metaphor, and I have to create it myself, and usually then my plots generate it. It doesn't have to be monstrous in the sci-fi sense, the horror film sense, but it could be, for example, the surgical instruments in *Dead Ringers*. Which are feasible. They're physically feasible. And yet they are monstrous also. It doesn't have to be a 200-pound fly. It can be surgical instruments. So I need that. Rather, I seek that out. The alternative would be, I suppose, to deliver it in speech, in the words people speak to each other, and I do do some of that as well. But I think I'm looking for the metaphor. That leads me to a certain monstrousness, I suppose. I think that's really why I invent those things.

SG: I was thinking of the actual rebirth of Brundle. It's clearly a shot of an egg with this mist, all very mysterious. And then – and I think it's very important perhaps in most of your movies – he's coming out as Apollo, the Greek god. He's absolutely perfect. An angel. In the following part of the movie, he will believe himself to be an angel or a god. Then he will completely fall into animality, monstrosity, nevertheless the two concepts and the two images co-exist in that section of the film. You seem to say, or show, that perhaps this kind of sub-human experiment is both something god-like and animal-like.

DC: You can see we even have an ape in this scene. You have an ape and a god and an insect as well. Everything's covered. I really find it difficult to make judgements. This might be the Canadian part of me, I'm not sure. Or the Jewish part, I'm also not sure. I can see all the sides of all the arguments simultaneously. And I can see all the good parts and the bad parts of everything simultaneously. If one were to live one's life there, one would be paralysed. You would not be able to act. So I see the necessity to make value judgements in life. Turn left instead of turning right. Go straight instead of turning backwards. But I find that I don't want to believe in these as absolute goods or bads. So in my art, that's where I can express this non-judgemental thing. For example, as Brundle begins to deteriorate and become hideous, he speaks for me. He says, 'I'm not sure that this is a bad thing. I'm not sure that this [is not a] more godlike [creature] that I'm turning into. Maybe the other is a mere superficial, aesthetic thing. This creature I'm becoming – as parts of my body become irrelevant, and I put them in this little museum, to remind myself of where I was – on the surface might be ugly and hideous and horrible, [but] a deterioration is in fact a recreation.' Here we have a rebirth. A transformation into something that, if I change my sense of aesthetics, and I change my sense of morality, I can see that what I'm becoming is a superior thing, or at least an equally good thing. So that's the play that's going on in the movie. He's by force of will not accepting himself at face value, because the face is too hideous to accept at face value.

SG: Nevertheless, most of the experiments in your movies, especially *The Fly*, are failures in the end.

DC: I think they're both failures and successes. I don't think of them as failures. I think that what I'm presenting to the audience, at first I say, 'Oh, my God!' Now we look at this [and] we say, 'This is a failure. This is a mistake. This is hopeless.' Then I try to become the devil's advocate and say maybe not. Let's look at it a little further. How bad is it really? To me, I suppose that's the ultimate end to all human experimentation. Or the human experiment. That we're doomed to failure by our own very strange standards, but is it really a failure? I'm not really sure that it is. And I think of that as our reality experiment. That we create our own understanding of reality. That what we see is a creation. And it can be constantly transformed. It is being constantly transformed and changed. I mean, one of the reasons

I think most historical films fail is I don't think those people were the same as us at all. Not remotely the same. I think they were absolutely alien creatures. I don't think they saw the same things that we see. That they smelled the same things . . . Everything was different. And to do a historical film that would really represent that would be a very exciting thing. Actually, I'm getting excited thinking about it. That would be the only reason to do a historical film for me. To convey how completely alien these people were, because that gives us a measure of how much these people have changed. Because it's not a matter of years. It's a matter of total perception. And understanding of everything. So I'm presenting failures as possible successes and really trying to turn things upside down. It's as Elliot says in *Dead Ringers*, that there should be beauty contests for the insides of bodies. He's saying basically what we consider beauty is not an absolute. It changes. It constantly changes, and we could will it to change. If we all became overnight hideous because of some radioactive cloud, we would have to find beauty somewhere in each other in order to exist. So, gradually, I think our aesthetics by force of will would change. What we considered beautiful we would now have to consider ugly. I think we could do that, and I think we would do that. I think it would happen very quickly.

SG: That's one of my favorite scenes [when Brundle looks at his reflection in the mirror of his bathroom], but for many different reasons. We have a monster and it's clearly a transformation, the looks, the lost organs, but he also looks at himself in a mirror, and there is this idea in his head about being a monster, about being the other . . . So is otherness the ultimate monstrosity? Because in your movies there's always something about the other, the other gender, the other species.

DC: The other is also another possibility. That's the thing. The other is always a potential for you, so I don't really . . . I don't know if I'm evolving into that understanding of it, or if it was always there unconsciously, but I don't think of myself as the other. You talk about Kafka. You say of course he was the other because he was German-speaking. He was Chekoslovakian and he was a Jew, so he was the other twice removed. So on and so on. I don't feel that about myself *per se*. I don't think that's what I'm expressing, at least not on a level that I feel very strongly. Consciously anyway. I think the other is a seductive possibility. A dangerous one perhaps and a scary one, but something you could become. You've seen the example of someone else being that. That means it's a possibility for you. Perhaps it is the next norm. The next absolute. It's an absolute that is not an absolute, but it's perceived as that. So maybe that's really what is attractive to me about that. It's something that really is a possibility. It's like people who were very fascinated reading about degenerates and perverts, what they considered to be degenerates and perverts, and people who live disgusting lives on the edge of society and so on. The fascination, I think really, is that you perceive that in yourself, the possibility of that for you. In fact part of you wants that, wants to express that, wants to live that. So to me, in a way, that's what that otherness is. It's not so simple . . . It's not just a threat, let's say. If you were considering yourself at the moment the norm in society and perceiving . . . and what if you are the other? How do you perceive normal society from your point of view of otherness? Brundle is kind of presenting it as a possible future of humanity for a while, and we think, 'Oh, my God, he's so hideous!' He's deluded. Then we see he has strength. He has certain strengths and his intelligence is different, but it's a real intelligence. So we say maybe he's right. Maybe this is not so hideous. Maybe he's become the future superhuman. So I think that, to me anyway, when you ask me like that, that's where's it's seeming to go. The sense of otherness, which I agree is always there. But I'm not sure there's a real dialectic between otherness and the norm.

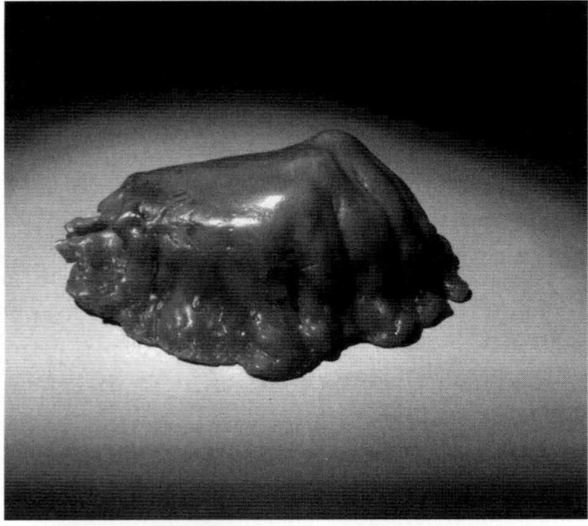

Three models (by Chris Walas – who won the Oscar for his special effects) used for the final transformation. These little works of art hark back to the paintings of Bacon.

SG: Could it be your fascination with insects? . . . In your movies there's always another step in the transformation. Like for a fly, a butterfly, or other insects. Which is not really the case in the human species, but would you say that you are interested in the potential next step?

DC: Yes. I think that we do have those steps, and I think you have to be of a certain age before you recognise them. I look at photos of myself as a young man and I am not that. I have changed. I'm a completely different creature. I don't look like that. My lips are different. My bone structure. Everything is different. I remember being that, dimly. But I'm not that. It's not as obvious a transformation as going from the caterpillar to the butterfly with the pupa's state in the middle, but I think we do go through immense transformations in our own lives. And it's physical, it's everything, it's mental, it's perceptual, it's nervous system, on every level. So if death, if aging, were not really just a deterioration, which I don't think it is, there could be other stages. I don't think that I'm being evasive. This is not a new version of religion where you say after you die you're still alive, because I think that's a joke. It's a necessary and sometimes a cruel joke, but I don't believe it. But I do think we are in control of our own evolution now without even realising it. We've interfered with the normal evolutionary process, which I think is a brilliant understanding of something that's very real, the understanding of evolution. It's very important. But I think that we are in control of it now. We've interfered with all of the normal, natural mechanisms that used to determine what would happen to an animal species. How it would mutate. How it would change. So we are causing our own mutations without being aware of it. And we are evolving and we are changing. I think it happens to an individual in his own lifetime. That's the difference. Because of technology, because of the pressure we have put on ourselves on this planet, everything is compressed. So you can actually feel it now in an individual lifetime, whereas before, when evolution was measured in millions and millions of years, you would not feel it in an individual lifetime. So I do think that that is partly my subject matter, without *being* it. Not in a science fiction way really, although I often use that metaphorically, but in a very real, naturalistic, normal, everyday, mundane kind of way.

SG: **I was showing that sequence of Brundlefly discovering his image in a mirror, and I think it's very important in the context of the movie, but the other scenes [I would show] would be the use of television or television monitors in your films and of course in *Videodrome* . . . Which means that replication or reproduction as an image is central to your aesthetics.**
DC: Well, of course any filmmaker is interested in the problem of imagery and the creation of images. Whether or not that's a major theme or whether it's just a reflection of that. I think you have to get outside yourself to see yourself, obviously. The simplest way to do that is with a mirror. Of course we don't just do that. We do it with many media. With film obviously, and video, with all kinds of image-making devices. But whether that's a major theme or not, it's not exactly an obsession, I think, to see oneself, in the philosophical sense of coming to understand yourself, to have a perspective on yourself. That's important to me thematically, too. But whether it really translates directly to . . . I'm actually not that fond of reflection shots. In fact, when I did *Crash* I deliberately didn't do – I think there was only one shot in the mirror of a car. The idea of doing shots in the rearview mirror, or the side mirrors, of the car is this classic thing to do. And for some reason I didn't want to do those. I don't know whether it's just because I felt it would take me into the realm of imagery that had been done too many times before, or what. So I'm not sure. I can't immediately begin to talk about it naturally. I have to work very hard to make that case.

SG: **I would say that, in a way, reproduction of imagery would exactly fit your definition of rebirth. To reproduce an image is the birth of something new. You don't start from scratch. But what you get in the end, the image, is not the object you have reproduced. This is very constant in your work. When Brundle gets out of the telepod, he's been reproduced but he's not the same.**
DC: If you look at when I started making films, the difference between then and now, and it's not that long, but it's what we were talking about in the span of a lifetime, and even a professional lifetime. The proliferation of imagery and the number of ways that images can be reproduced has increased a thousand times, I think, to now from then. So it's quite different. One is much more aware of it. Digital cameras, computer imagery, images are sent over the Internet, DVD, laser discs, tapes, all of these things didn't exist when I started to make movies. I'm very aware of that, but that image making is not . . . I hope that I'm not really stopping at the level of image only. When you talk about reproduction, that means more than an image. I want three-dimensionality. It's that sculptural thing that I was talking about before. The physical and the tactile. An image is not enough. Even an image in a mirror is not enough to engage. 'Brundlefly', that's something. That's something you can touch. To me the cinema, I feel, is very tactile. It's not just visual. It's sensual in many, many ways. I've even wondered about . . . this is completely not what we're talking about, but the sensuality of thought. How physical is thought? Because it seems on the surface to be very disembodied. But I don't think it is disembodied. You can't have thought without a body, which is why I always return to the idea of the body being the primary fact. The first fact of human existence is the body. So when I think of imagery and metaphor and thought, it seems a very sensual thing to me. It needs to be embodied physically somehow. So just an image in a mirror, for example, does not excite me too much. It's just a beginning.

The Coronation

Dead Ringers

It was with *Dead Ringers* that David Cronenberg would (at last!) find unanimous critical recognition, at least in Europe. Was this a mistake? It is certain that many believed this story of twin brothers to be a 'psychological drama', indeed a character study . . .

But when we look into the sources of the work we find, once again, that it dates back to Cronenberg's youth and to the script synopses he wrote in the seventies such as *Roger Pagan, Gynaecologist* or *Pierce*, where we find references to 'instruments for operating on mutants' in the hands of a serial killer, along with the idea of an insane gynaecologist. It was in reading the newspaper reports of the twin gynaecologists found dead in their devastated luxury New York apartment that Cronenberg, with the help of his friend Norman Snider, was able to filter his old obsessions into the story and fuse them into a perfect film, at once hermetically complete and open to all sorts of narrative hypotheses. (One can read the film from the point of view that there is really only one brother.)

The presence of Peter Suschitzky on camera allowed Cronenberg to create an even more fluid style, especially in the conception of 'invisible' special effects, and towards a formal purity which has about it something of Robert Bresson. In Cronenberg, there are never naturalistic digressions, scenes of transition that allow the audience to breathe. On the contrary, he loads his work with significance and the unspoken, which (though fashionable with many filmmakers who are short on inspiration) is always situated by Cronenberg between the lines of his dialogue, in the confrontation between sense and signification.

In *Dead Ringers*, the viewer is barely able to assimilate one complex idea before being obliged to analyse the next one. There is, in this journey to the very heart of an impossible duality, something breathlessly exhausting, the dizzying ineluctability of tragic destiny, and, as with *The Fly*, the air of an opera. And, perhaps as never before, the filmmaker gives the most polemical representation of the regions of the body: the woman's vagina (metamorphosed according to a logic that does not exist in nature), the depths of the human organism, the mysteries of birth and reproduction, the sadism inherent in all sexual relations, the paradox of the born actor in every human being, the impossibility of living alone, or of living with others . . .

Dead Ringers is, in itself, so 'fantastic' that its author did not feel the need to sprinkle it with violent and shocking images; the film itself and its situations are sufficient to evoke mental images that are sometimes hard to admit to, transfixing us with their inherent power. Is it for this reason that, once again, there was a degree of feminist backlash against the film, with Cronenberg standing accused of the worst intentions? Probably. Certain attacks are almost a tribute to his talent. And one could undoubtedly leave the film untouched, depending on how one interprets the narrative.

But the ironic and desperate performance of Jeremy Irons is central to the film. And Cronenberg, who had long been suspected of having no interest in actors, now became one of the directors actors would turn to when they wanted

Above: The Mantle protractor: an obstetric instrument invented by the Mantle twins.

to stretch their talents. *Dead Ringers* is one of the purest of Cronenberg's films; its action takes place in no particular place or time; this is what makes it closest to a modern tragedy, almost mythological in its dimension, laden with a dark, difficult secret, hidden under the existential malaise of the Mantle brothers.

SG: **There's something that comes [across] very often in your movies: a Hollywood movie is where the happy ending is the proof that everything works fine for everybody. In *Dead Ringers*, there is a phrase that comes very often: 'It doesn't work that way.' In a way, I think it could define most of your movies. You show that it doesn't work that way, or that it doesn't work so easily. It's not the way it works.**

DC: Finding out the way it works is a hopeless task, of course, but one that I feel art is devoting itself to. Finding out how it works at that moment, which might not be how it works later, because even biology is changing constantly. Really there are very few absolutes, and if you're looking for absolute truth, it's a joke because it will only be absolute for a moment and then it will shift, but it's a constant. So that's another of the crazy ideas of Samuel Beckett and Giacometti, understanding together that they were both despairing of their art, feeling what they were creating was useless, would say nothing, was meaningless, and yet they had to say it. They had to still pursue their art even in the face of that meaninglessness, that nothingness. That's modernity. It's not now, but I think it still holds true. Even in Hollywood you can have now an ending that's not a happy ending and it's still false. So Hollywood has found a way to give you not a happy ending that is still not the way it works. As the Hollywood Godzilla stomps over the landscape of world cinema, I think Hollywood's never been more dominant than it is now. And it's not just in its success at the box office. It's in the success of the language as well. We now have wonderful French, Italian and German filmmakers all making films in English because they can't make films in their own language, they can't make films with their own film stars, because English is the new *lingua franca*. This is the irony. So it becomes more and more difficult, but I suppose the struggle is part of what makes it attractive. If it were easy then I'm sure I wouldn't want to attempt it anymore.

SG: **Nevertheless, let me stress this – in *Dead Ringers*, for example, one of the Mantle twins say there should be beauty pageants for organs.**

DC: For the insides of the human body.

SG: **Which means that at least the representation of organic things has a certain interest to you.**

DC: Absolutely it does. Because I meant what he said. It's astonishing to me that you could have a beautiful woman, who everyone would agree is a beautiful woman or many people would agree, yet [they] would be disgusted by X-rays of her body. Or if they were watching surgery on her body would be repulsed. The inside of her body is not beautiful. We don't have a total human aesthetics because we have not dealt with the interior of our bodies, and our understanding of organs. So I'm being playful and flippant, but also serious, when I say why not have a beauty contest for the most beautiful kidney, the most perfectly formed stomach, the most exquisite liver? Why not? Why don't we have this? It might seem obvious to some people. I don't think it's obvious. I find it unusual. I think it's strange. And it indicates how we are not really totally integrated with ourselves yet, physically. The body is still a mystery which, in some ways, it will always be. One of the things that I'm doing in my movies, which works for me but not necessarily for other people, is I'm trying to change the audience's aesthetics. In the course of the 90 minutes or however long the movie is, I want them to start with a normal revulsion that they have and, by the end of the movie, see some kind of beauty, or some possibility of beauty, in things that they thought were repulsive to begin with. That's my own project in a way. It's a project of aesthetics. It's transforming human aesthetics.

I suppose if you're going to be a creator, one of the things you're going to create is creatures. So many things to me – I feel as though I invented twins, for example. So even in a movie like *Dead Ringers*, where you do not exactly see monsters in the same way, except for maybe the grown-up Siamese twins in the dream sequence, I felt that we could imagine a world where twins didn't really exist. They were an imagined possibility. Just like we could have imagined then three or four exact replicas, but you could never have three or four exact replicas. You can now because of cloning, but you couldn't then. Even there I feel that I invented my twins as impossible creatures. And once again, I think it's the return to the flesh. The body. Real creation involves the physical, the fleshly, and the living, the organic. So it's very natural for me to want to do that – to invent new creatures. It's almost what happens anyway on earth. After all this time there are so many undiscovered species that keep showing up. And of course, because they're constantly mutating and changing . . . I mean, everybody focuses on the ecological disaster, the disappearance of species, but in fact there are new species being developed all the time also that we're not even aware of. So I feel as though I'm contributing to the propagation of new species on the earth. And some of the things I'm inventing, who knows, they might someday exist for everybody.

SG: That small creature we see at the gas station first [in *eXistenZ*] seems also to be connected with *Dead Ringers*, is he not?
DC: Yes, he's a twin. Two people, two creatures, two minds who cannot get physically far away from each other. They're like the original Siamese twins.

SG: Obviously, since you had some musical training, played some classical guitar, your mother was a musician, music would have been important in your life.
DC: Music has been important in my life. It's interesting, because I feel quite ignorant when it comes to the classics. I listened to a lot of rock 'n' roll as a kid, but I don't like using rock 'n' roll in my movies. I've only really done it twice, with *Fast Company*, which had an original kind of rock score. That's not a film that's seen very often. The other time is in *Dead Ringers*. There's one fifties rock song, a kind of soft ballad. That's it. It's interesting for me to watch a filmmaker like Martin Scorsese, for example, who is mostly interested in that . . . he doesn't like composed scores very much, and he would prefer to put together a score made up of source music, what we call source music, period music, but I don't want to do that because I can't control the response of the audience. Of course you can't anyway, but people have a very specific attachment to old rock 'n' roll, let's say. They remember where they were when that song came out and the emotion that it called forth, and it might not be what you have happening in the movie. It might be quite different because it might have a very bad association for them. So I'd rather create music that's unique to the film, and maybe to my other films, to bring them into this world that I'm creating. Because it is an alternate reality that I'm creating, I'd rather not remind them of their old reality. So I can imagine making a film where that would work, but so far I haven't, except for those two exceptions. I haven't used music that has been out there that other people react to. Even with classical music, I don't use Bach or Beethoven in my movies as some people do, for the same reasons really.

SG: How do you usually work with Howard Shore?
DC: Well.

SG: Because this is always something very mysterious, the collaboration between a director and . . .
DC: It is mysterious, it is mysterious. Well, not everybody works this way, because often people

The two young twins who portray the brothers Bev and Elly at the age when we first see them.

pigeonhole a composer: John Williams for a big, epic action movie . . . So if you are that kind of person you say: I want the cinematographer who did this because he's good at that, I want the composer who did this . . . But the other way of working, which is more the European way, or at least what I consider to be the artist's way, is that you form relationships with artists and cinematographers, and you collaborate on each project. You trust them, and you know that your sensibilities match, and that's how you do it. Once I've written them, I send my scripts to four or five people: Carol Spier, Peter Suschitzky, Ron Sanders, my editor, and to Howard. They are my first readers. So Howard would have read that early, I even talk to him about it before we do it, we talk a lot. Howard is from Toronto and we knew each other when we were very young. *The Brood* was the second movie that he ever did music for. It was the first movie that I had original music for, because *Shivers* and *Rabid* had canned music because we couldn't afford original music. So except for *The Dead Zone*, which for various reasons Howard didn't do, he has done every film. So he reads the script and he thinks about the score a year, two years, in advance. It's a pretty common way of working, except that I involve him very early, which is not always common. He often visits the set, we talk about who we are casting, he's very involved. Once I have a rough cut that's worth showing, I show it to him. Not to time it or anything, because it's far from being frozen, but he looks at it and he starts to think about it. Then he starts to write some themes or whatever, he sends me some stuff on tape or minidisk – we haven't done that yet, but we will. We start to talk about instrumentation and what the tone and feel of the score are going to be. It's an ongoing process, and at a certain point when I've frozen the movie, in other words when it's edited in its final form, then we get very serious about where the music should start and where it should stop, very precisely. Although at that point he hasn't composed the music, but he has already started to think about how he will record it, and what the themes are, and so on. I usually am there when he is recording the music, and that's when I really hear it for the first time, and he tells me what the cues are for. And I might be saying, 'Gosh, I was hoping to get this out of it but I'm not hearing it here.' So there is still time to rethink it and re-compose, and we often shift stuff around. For example, the opening credit music to *Crash*, which is with six electric guitars, was not intended to be the opening music. It was intended to be somewhere else, where it still is, but I said, 'No, I really want that for the opening music.' So we either got rid of what he was thinking of for the opening music, or we put it somewhere. So we mix stuff up, we match it around, we change it. On *Naked Lunch* we had Ornette Coleman playing, he was improvising and he was in London. I was suggesting things in the mix, and Howard is not there for the whole sound mix, but he's there for a lot of it. He has Suzana Peric, a woman who is always at the mix representing Howard. And then if there are problems we phone. I remember layering four elements in *Naked Lunch* that were never meant to be played with each other, but I found if we played them on top of each other it gave this great sort of dissonance thing. Anyway, I do this sort of thing and then I play it for Howard, and he either hates it or he loves it, or he likes it and he thinks he can do it better. It's a very organic relationship. And we have had moments, right from the very beginning, where I feel one of the cues doesn't work and he feels it does. And it's that subjective moment where the relationship is very important because . . . It has to be my word, I can't do something that I think is wrong because Howard thinks it is right. It's just the way it is if you are the director. But we try very hard to understand one another and, as I say, it's really beyond words. I mean Howard loves to talk in a very cerebral way, in a very intellectual way. But ultimately you are listening to sounds that have associations for you, so it's a very interesting game and it never gets boring. It's always quite tricky and interesting.

SG: The music in your movies was always very different. With *Naked Lunch*, for example, this mixing of Moroccan music and free jazz: did it have a message other than a period message? What do you want to express in the choice of a musical score, in the direction you give your composer?

DC: I have many interesting discussions with Howard about music, because he can be very intellectual and very cerebral about his music as well. I enjoy that a lot. We really try to do much more than the standard, I must say again, Hollywood use of music, which is usually to underscore, literally, what is already on the screen. If it's a sad scene the music is sad. If it's an action scene the music is exciting. The standard way of using music in Hollywood is to tell the audience how to feel, just in case what's going on on the screen doesn't tell them how to feel. Of course, I try to avoid telling the audience how to feel. That means the music must have a different function from this sort of standard. I'm asking Howard to find oblique levels of emotion and reference, some of them abstract. Some of them emotional. And to attack the scene from different angles and planes. They're not just to simply give the standard kind of *we'll make it more sad, we'll make it more funny*. Sometimes that doesn't work and sometimes he and I have arguments, civilised arguments, because there's nothing more subjective than sound. I think sound is much more subjective than anything visual. So if you think that a music cue doesn't work and someone else thinks that the music cue does work, it's impossible to find a rapprochement. There's no way to come together. You could discuss it forever and still feel the same way. So sometimes we change things around, and we try different things until we find something that settles. Part of the reason for this process is because we try to make it not an obvious thing that we're doing. The music must

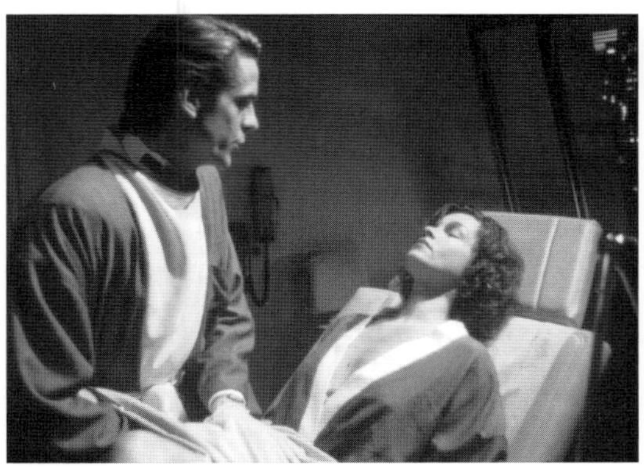

Left: Elliot Mantle (Jeremy Irons) auscultates Claire Niveau (Geneviéve Bujold) in his office. He discovers she has a trifurcate uterus. Right: Jeremy Irons dances with his twin brother (or his cinematic stand-in). The perfectionist English actor wanted each twin to be a distinctly separate character.

bring something else to the scene and to the movie, so that if it were not there the scene would be quite different. If we can't do that then we'd rather not have music. So that's how abstract we get. That's what we really want music to bring to the film. So with Ornette, there's a wildness and an improvisation which is period in some ways, but not in other ways. In fact, Burroughs didn't listen to jazz like Ornette Coleman, he would listen to Stan Kenton or swing. He didn't listen to that music. It has a period feel for us now, but it's not really accurate in terms of what Burroughs would have listened to himself. It was that wildness, that unpredictability, that was mixed with Howard's more stately, kind of composed strains that we liked. We didn't start that way. At one point in *Naked Lunch* we were actually layering. We put three cues that were never meant to be together on top of each other, and it worked beautifully. But it was a surprise to us.

SG: **You are very lucky to have this collaboration. I remember Scorsese saying that when he first saw *Scorpio Rising*, he discovered that you could make a film with source music, etc., and it changed a lot of things, but now it has become such a cliché.**
DC: Everybody does it.

SG: **That's all you have in movies or, as you say, the kind of Spielberg score.**
DC: Yeah, it's interesting because I saw *Scorpio Rising* as one of the original underground films. A lot of people were doing that, not just Kenneth Anger. Because the films weren't commercial, you could just steal music from anywhere and put it on and nobody cared. So you got a lot of rock 'n' roll and other stolen movie music. But the only movie where I primarily made use of rock 'n' roll was *Fast Company*. But that was original rock 'n' roll, composed for our movie by members of the group called Toto, which was very big at the time.

SG: **But that was appropriate for the subject matter.**
DC: Yeah, because that is what those guys listened to, that and some country and western. So the only time I ever used rock 'n' roll other than that was in *Dead Ringers*, 'In the Still of the Night' by the Five Satins.

SG: **Ah yes, when they dance.**
DC: Otherwise, it's my conceit to want music that doesn't have associations other than my movies. The problem with source music for me is the fact that people have very strong associations with it. And as you get older – we baby-boomers,

I'm actually not a baby-boomer, I was born before them – you can't actually control and predict what associations people will have with certain songs. Of course, you can depend on nostalgia, but that's a very weak, sentimental thing. It's not enough to say we listened to that when we were kids. So I want to control that, and that's why I'm very, very wary of using source music.

SG: You're absolutely right, because I remember the first time I saw *Scorpio Rising*, I was a bit upset and I knew it was because of the music. At the time, for me that kind of music just represented the utmost stupidity. I had absolutely no nostalgia, because I saw *Scorpio Rising* at the end of the sixties, and I had a great disdain for that kind of music. I only listened to jazz. And of course now I can appreciate it, because on top of it Anger is playing on words, and completely reversing the meaning of the words, and the effect is quite nice. But it's true that source music is a double-edged sword.

DC: Definitely. And unfortunately – though I should say that Scorsese certainly is not guilty of this – it fits very well with the Hollywood button-pushing process. You don't have to work very hard, because you have a built-in reaction response already: you just press that button, you get that reaction, and everybody is happy. That's too simple for me and not complex enough. It doesn't affect me like music which you really control for the very specific moment in the film. So I have never regretted it [not using source music], and yes of course, every movie has it now: every American movie has rock 'n' roll songs in it.

And the pressure for me to do likewise was never more than when I was working on *The Fly*, although it was always in the background. In *Videodrome*, for example, the question was, 'Why not have Debbie Harry do a song?' And I said, 'Well, because she's not Debbie Harry in the movie.' And that really destroys that illusion, I didn't want her to be Blondie, I wanted her to be that character. I didn't even want her to be Debbie Harry. So that's why I felt that way about music.

SG: I found some very funny short texts in the archives – I haven't read all of them yet, but one was about the psycho gynaecologist. So some [of those ideas] go right back to the beginning of the seventies.

DC: The archives has that?

SG: Yeah.

DC: I guess I didn't look in those . . . I just wanted to get rid of those boxes.

SG: It's very interesting, because most of your ideas – maybe you're not even aware of them – have always been there in one form or another. Of course it is interesting to see how they have evolved, but you were right, the idea of a psychotic gynaecologist . . .

DC: . . . preceded the actual Marcus twins, one of whom actually was a psychotic gynaecologist.

SG: I think, in the first version of the story, he's trying to control a serial killer. It's really quite complex.

DC: Oh I don't even remember that . . .

SG: But there are dual characters, because this gynaecologist is trying to control the serial killer.

DC: Yeah, so that's like *Silence of the Lambs* . . .

SG: Yeah.

DC: . . . two psychotics. Well, I remember when I saw Fellini's film, *Variety Lights*, I thought, all of Fellini is in that movie: the proportions are different, there's the neo-realist Fellini, then there's the sort of extravagant fantasist Fellini. And I remember thinking, when you look at the movie in retrospect – you wouldn't know it if you only saw that movie when it came out – you can see all of Fellini there. All his preoccupations, all his obsessions, all the things that delighted him and fascinated him were all there in one form or another. So it really doesn't surprise me that that should be.

It's interesting, because there is the

Hollywood ideal of the talented hack, you know. We say hack, they say a guy who can direct any kind of movie, a good all-round professional. It's the non-*auteur* theory: it's making a virtue of having no personality on screen, of being a very good journeyman who can do anything from comedies to action to Westerns.

SG: **I think Frankenheimer wrote this: 'I have no personality as a director because I think that's morally wrong. A movie director should be able to do any style.'**
DC: I was thinking of him.

SG: **But he seems to be proud of it.**
DC: Well, you might as well be proud of what you are. But that's the ideal, although personally I think he has a very definite personality. But it's not our archetype of the artist, that's all. It's certainly not the sensitive romantic period of the artist where the artist's personality was very important.

SG: **It's not that I have mixed feelings about *Dead Ringers*, its a film that I love, but I remember that I was somewhat sceptical of the reaction which greeted its release, especially in France. *Dead Ringers* is definitely a Cronenberg movie, not specifically different from the others, but when it came out, suddenly a lot of people who previously despised your earlier movies, or didn't even go to see them, loved it – I don't know why, perhaps it has something to do with what we were talking about yesterday, with B-movies taking over the mainstream. Suddenly your content and your style became not only accessible, but acceptable for the cultural elite. And suddenly, at least in France, there was something like a consensus that *Dead Ringers* was a masterpiece. And a lot of people were saying that's strange for the guy who directed *The Fly*, they didn't know *Shivers* or the other films. How do you react to that?**
DC: Well it's ironic, because in a way *The Fly*, *The Dead Zone* and *Dead Ringers* are the same movie.

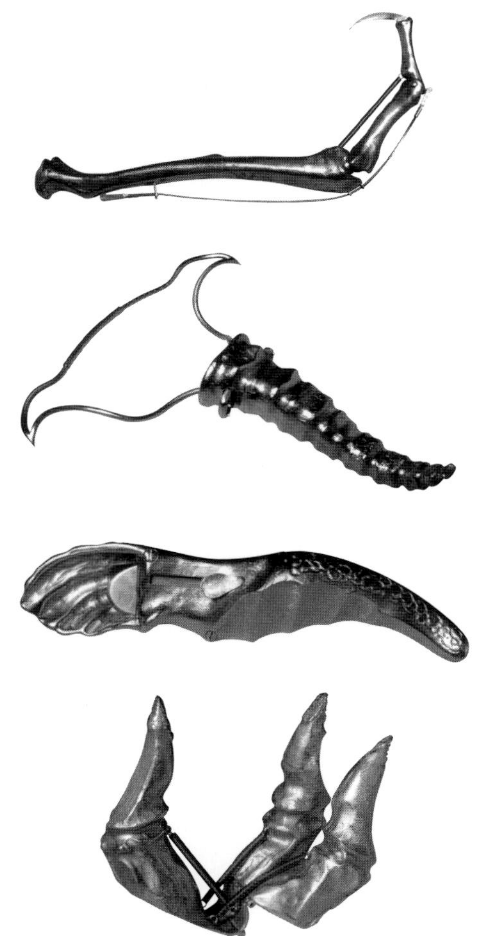

Instruments for operating on mutants: The concept of imaginary operating tools, which comes from an old project, was realised by Peter Grundy, Alicia Keywan and David Dyder.

They are all the same: the lead character dies in the arms of the other lead character, and that's the end of the movie. I guess it takes a while to be perceived, I wonder if the people who were charmed by *Dead Ringers* would look differently at *The Fly* or the other movies. I don't really know. Part of it has to do with a prejudice about genre. *Dead Ringers* is not a horror film, nor is it a sci-fi film, although it does have certain aspects of both of those. But to the normal, average person, it's a sort of strange but naturalistic drama based on a true story – maybe that element helps them to accept it as well. It's nonetheless a common experience for filmmakers and writers: they have one work [which has an inexplicable popular appeal]. I mean, how many people were interested in *Lolita*, but would never have known about *Pale Fire* or any of the many other books that he [Nabokov] wrote?

SG: Actually I was thinking of Nabokov too.
DC: And there are other writers that you could mention that have one book which suddenly, for some reason, catches a certain kind of public imagination. Of all the writers in North America to become a talking point for the entire continent, you would never have guessed that it would be Nabokov, never. Who would ever have thought that the man who wrote *Pale Fire* would be front-page news and a best-selling author?

SG: It was not his fault really.
DC: It was not his fault.

SG: When Girodias published it [*Lolita*] in Paris . . .
DC: He thought it was a good . . .

SG: Softcore porn . . .
DC: He knew that it was more than a dirty book, but it fitted in well with the series.

SG: Yes of course.
DC: I have the edition upstairs. So as I say, it was not my fault, I was just doing my normal thing, and for some reason it was allowed to be legitimised – probably because the film was situated outside the horror/sci-fi genre ghetto.

SG: But could you feel the difference of appreciation?
DC: Yes, yes, although interestingly enough, and this is another reason why critics drive me insane, some of the critics who loved *The Fly* – serious critics, I think maybe David Denby is one of them, he now writes for *The New Yorker* – detested *Dead Ringers*, or the reverse. There was someone who was the other way round. In any case it's like you can't win. Anyway, some critics did not get the movie at all. The problem in North America with *Dead Ringers* was the politics, sexual politics, which was hitting very hard – the whole feminist approach to things. It took very intelligent feminists, which there certainly were, to see that the movie was not a misogynist statement or something like that. You know, politics is death to art, any kind of politics is death to art. Art isn't always death to politics, but the reverse definitely applies. As soon as you approach art from a wholly political standpoint, then it's just propaganda, in as much as you're only looking for things that promote your politics. And once again, it's a different kind of button-pushing, as soon as it's gynaecology and it's showing gynaecologists mistreating women who are in their control, then there's an outraged reaction which totally ignores all the other facets of the film.

SG: Talking of politics and sexual politics reminds me of a fax I received from a critic in New York. We're friends now, but at the time we didn't know each other very well. Anyway, I was going to New York and someone told me I should go and sleep at her place. So she sent a very serious fax explaining that she was living in a shared apartment with lesbian co-tenants, and they wouldn't be happy with the idea of a guy in their apartment. She thought that it might be a good idea if I sent a resumé stating my political views. It's much the same as saying my friends don't like Jews, so if you could say something . . .
DC: Make sure that they know that you are not happy being Jewish, and you wish you were not, then maybe they can accept you.

SG: And it was the first time I became aware of the fact that sometimes, in America, you have to be sorry just for being a male.
DC: And white and everything else . . .
SG: . . . which is not my fault after all.

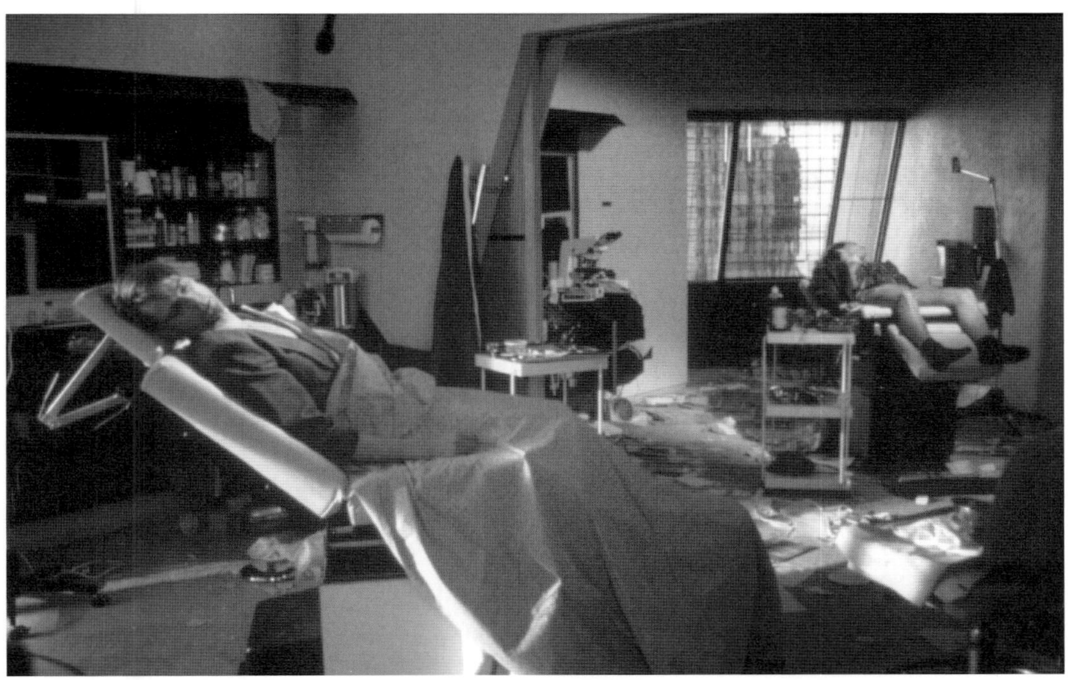

Double vision: Using a system both simple and extremely sophisticated (memorising camera movements via computer), Cronenberg and Suschitzky resolved the problem of twins being played by the same actor – with a fluidity of mise en scéne rarely attained in any film.

DC: It is your fault, you could have a sex [change] operation. Absolutely, to be a middle-class white male in America is guilt, it's like you're guilty. You should feel guilt for the Blacks, for the lesbians, whatever. It's very nuts, America is a very crazy place.

SG: **Yes, because there wasn't anything like that type of reaction [to *Dead Ringers*] in France or Germany.**

DC: I feel that sexual politics and feminism come from a valid place. You can look at the history of Western culture and say yes, women have been short-changed. I think I understand most of the reasons, the sexual reasons, and now we're at a stage where we're intelligent enough and sophisticated enough to see this and to change things. That's understandable, and to that extent I am a feminist. But then, as with any political movement, you get the lunatic fringe like Andrea Dworkin. Do you know this Andrea Dworkin?

SG: **Of course.**

DC: She says all active heterosexual sex is rape, that's it. Well, you know, Andrea, we can't all be lesbians. I'm sorry, I mean I'm sure it would be great, but heck. So that's the extreme, I think Andrea Dworkin is the most extreme and, unfortunately, she has influenced Canadian law, if you can believe that. She hooked up with Catherine MacKinnon, who is a lawyer, and they were involved in framing our sexual harassment laws. They were rejected in the US, but they managed to have influence here in Canada. So now sexual harassment can be a look, a word, a phrase, a glance out of place. If it were really applied rigorously, it would be like a weird sexual police state – very bizarre.

SG: **Yesterday we were talking of your reaction**

to Fulford, and you were saying that you still resent what he did, which I totally understand, but in a way it's the same kind of process. Suddenly you are accused, indicted, insulted for something that, after all, is just yourself and you have no reason to feel guilty about. Today I was reading in the paper about this so-called pædophile . . .
DC: Oh yeah, him . . .

SG: **And the Supreme Court said something very true: [we have to uphold] the privacy of thought or even fantasies, [otherwise] that would really be the thought-police.**
DC: Well, there are people who want that. But it's even worse, because somebody like Andrea Dworkin says, 'I know what your thoughts and fantasies are, even if you don't, and I will punish you for them even if you aren't aware of them.' And she would, so that's the extreme fringe. But the proposed law is that if you sketched something that looked like a child with a cock in its mouth, you could be arrested for having done that sketch. Whereas, of course, if you think about doing that sketch without actually doing it, then unless somebody knows what's going on in your brain, they can't arrest you for it. But that's how extreme we're getting.

SG: **I know that we've talked about this before, and I know that you have been really affected by all these attacks. How do you deal with it finally?**
DC: Well it's a very Buddhist, Zen, existentialist attempt to keep things in proportion, but I feel the scars you know. I do feel it. And the ultimate victory for all of these people would be if I censored myself, and worried about it in my work. I can't ignore what's happening in society, nor do I want to, but I seek out . . . I have got this book upstairs called *Bad Girls and Sick Boys* which she [the author of the book] says was inspired by *Videodrome* and by me in general. And she's a feminist, but she's smart and she understands how perverse and complex the human heart is, and how complex human sexuality is. And she's not politicising, so I can read that. You know, you look for allies against people like Dworkin, who is quite crazy, but there are others in her camp who aren't that crazy. You look for allies and try to be calm and to focus solely on what you're doing. You try to strip away all this other stuff, at least when you're doing your work.

For example, I noticed that most of these student directors I met recently were obviously interested in being Michael Bay – you know, the director of *Armageddon* and *The Rock* – they're not interested anymore in being Fellini or Bergman. But what they don't realise is how vulnerable you become when you are out in public and you are an artist of some kind, or even a craftsman, everybody gets a shot at you. And when we were talking about the Internet, I was saying that it is possible, if you're in my position, to encounter knocks against you by accident. I'll be on the Internet, in the middle of reading a review of some other movie, and I'll come across something like, 'not like that lousy re-make of *The Fly*.' And I'm thinking, 'Leave me alone ! What did I ever do to you?' I'm innocently reading something about some other movie. So the irony and the paradox is that, as an artist, you want to be as sensitive to everything as you can. You want all your pores to be open, you want to close nothing out. But at the same time, if you do that you are leaving yourself open to the attacks, and the insults, and everything that you automatically get as soon as you have a public. So it is odd. It's not quite the same as having stalkers because you're Madonna, but it happens to everybody. I mean everybody who is remotely successful. Obviously you have had a few attacks. I'm sure you have sustained a few.

SG: **Oh yes. For strange reasons, you know. To just take one example: I wrote a book about this very controversial movie by Emir Kusturica.**
DC: Which one was it ? *Underground*?

SG: **Yes. And at the time there were a couple of high-profile intellectuals who decided that**

Kusturica was an accomplice of Milosevic, you know, a murderer. But it was very easy to prove that neither of them had seen the movie, the first article was published even before the first screening of the movie. So I wrote a couple of articles and went on TV talk-shows and, after a couple of days, I started receiving faxes and mail accusing me of being a nazi. So it happens.

DC: Well, especially if you write about an overtly political subject, you are going to get lots of crazy people coming after you who don't understand the slightest thing about it. I mean, subtlety and complexity are not part of politics.

SG: **I know it's not what a work of art should be, but have you ever been tempted – not to respond directly to those people, but to put a moral ethic or a political statement in one of your movies which would reply to those attacks?**

DC: No, because it would . . . I suppose just by continuing to do what I do, that is my statement: 'I will ignore your criticisms because I don't think they're valid.' I don't want to give them that importance, that's why I don't write letters to the editor. I mean, history is full of artists who have spent a lot of time counterattacking: pamphlets, in the papers, on television now. I don't want to spend my time and energy doing that. To me, they would have the victory at that point. When it is a serious thing, a political thing, like some things which are happening right now in Canada, for example, then I think you have to go public and you have to spend some time and energy. At the moment I'm doing a PEN benefit, you know, the writers' thing. But otherwise, you would spend all your time answering your critics, responding, writing things back and forth. I feel that I should just be doing my work instead, and not wasting my time and energy. It's a question of conserving energy. I look at the issue historically and there are couple of wonderful examples, but I can't think of them right now, of writers who really exhausted themselves with their battles, when they would have been much better off just trying to work. If the fight is necessary, because somebody is trying to put you in jail, that's different. Then of course you have to defend yourself. For example, Woody Allen was someone who obviously never wanted to go public, but when he felt he was being attacked, and it was a legal thing and so on, then he had to spend a lot of time going public and talking about his divorce and all that stuff. I'm sure he was horrified to do it, but he was forced to react in that situation, he was forced to do it.

Otherwise I do it in interviews. The interview process has really become part of the release of a film, and therefore it has really become part of the making of a film, and that is my forum for venting. Of course it's imperfect, because if it isn't what your interviewer is interested in then it doesn't get published. At the same time, releasing a film like *eXistenZ*, I did literally hundreds and hundreds of interviews in many countries and cities. So they do provide me with the opportunity to counterattack, and often the writers are interested in that. So those are the two reactions, the ways I react.

The Cinema
as Literature
Naked Lunch, M. Butterfly

With *Naked Lunch* and *M. Butterfly*, Cronenberg entered into the cycle of literary adaptations that would end with *Crash*. If *Naked Lunch* is a tribute to one of his two main sources of inspiration, *M. Butterfly* is a more paradoxical project: how, from a script based by an author on his own successful play, did he manage to explore his favourite themes in a film that many critics do not hesitate to call Cronenberg's best?

The strangest thing about these two films is surely that *Naked Lunch* has very little in common with the novel by William Burroughs. Appropriation of the title was not the only strange thing about this enterprise: fanatically faithful to the biographical details of the greatest American writer of the post-war period, Cronenberg imagined a fantastic genre film (an exotic spy drama in the style of von Sternberg, crossed with the wilder kind of science fiction) and projected it onto a mythical artistic figure (the cynical junky is transformed into an improbable Orpheus figure that recalls Jean Cocteau) to arrive at one of the strangest products in cinema history. Lack of space means I cannot go into detail about its subtle beauty and bursts of morbidity. Cronenberg achieved literally the only hallucinatory literary biopic.

But what links these two works that seem so different is the interest Cronenberg shows in what he once spoke of to me as 'philosophical homosexuality'. In *M. Butterfly*, a man comes to understand (perhaps) that the ideal woman may in reality be a man. In *Naked Lunch*, a writer adopts the cover of homosexuality because, like Cocteau's Orpheus, he has fallen in love with death. This is once again a descent into the pure virtuality of love, the 'new idea in Europe' that the reader of C. S. Lewis's *Allegory of Love* would have been struck by. It also continues to reflect the artist in his modern dilemma, for if Bill Lee is an artist who only ostensibly 'writes reports' for an information agency, Gallimard, the mediocre French spy in Peking, constructs an ideal woman made out of aspects of the martyred women in Italian opera. The artist, even in his romantic strategies, presents himself via a mask, and looks into a world that doubtless exists only in order for him to make us discover its secret. But isn't the actual secret its lack of reality, the unreality of the beings who people it, and the relations they establish in order to live together? These two films go even further into the fundamental enigma of Cronenberg's work. In the style of the great American novelists, he never ceases to tear away the veils of his characters only to reveal other veils, just as, in *Videodrome*, the gallery of screens through which Max Renn runs leads him to a final screen, another veil, which is the trickiest of them all. Or like the masks that Cronenberg's characters often wear (and which he wears himself in *The Fly*) which hide even more enigmatic faces. These two adaptations, beyond the aesthetic pleasure they give us, further reinforce the strategy of doubt which is one of the most prominent traits of his work, and which can be conceived of not only as a radical critique of modern society, but also as an elegy for the modernity in art.

Above: The Bugwriter (a typewriter that is actually an insect), created by Cronenberg and CWI (the special effects company of Chris Walas) and Stephan Dupuis. Opposite: The Demiurge: David Cronenberg expresses rage at the talking cockroach, in front of the camera of Peter Suschitzky.

SG: This is obviously a very Cronenbergian scene [from *Naked Lunch*, with Peter Weller and Judy Davis]. We find all the elements: the literary ambition; the writing machine; the sex element, of course, which even contaminates inanimate objects. The fantastic and gory creature that shares in this couple's situation.
DC: As I recall, it was almost a joke that we should do *NL*. It was so perfect when I talked to Jeremy Thomas about doing *NL*. It was almost comedy rather than a serious thought. And then it just became real. I just stood there and it became a real thing. But I kept avoiding writing the script for a long, long time, because I think I was afraid of how difficult it would be, or that it would be impossible, and I didn't want to know that it was impossible. I think you find that in script writing in fact, I'm feeling that right now, because I've just finished my movie *eXistenZ* – and I'm now faced with writing another movie. In my head there's something wonderful, but when you actually come to grips with having to realise it . . . Now, not on the paper but on the computer screen, it's really the same process. There are many fears that await you. I'm sure you know them as a writer. And one of the great fears is that there will be nothing there. That there will be something there, but it won't be very interesting.

It might be very mundane. It might be very uninspiring. And so you hold onto the potential of it, the possibility of it, for a long, long time, before you come to grips with the reality of it. And certainly *NL* was like that. I feel that, and certainly part of what *NL* was about was the reality that one creates. What it is is an animal, almost, a thing that you bring into existence.

SG: You know, there's a very famous French novel called *La Disparition*, and nobody noticed it at the beginning, but the writer, who was very skilful, had suppressed the letter 'e', which is the most common letter in French. So would you be tempted by this sort of exercise, in terms of imagery?
DC: We know the exercise of using only the 50mm lens, let's say, as a kind of a monk-like purification ritual: 'You shall only use one lens,' or, 'You shall limit yourself to one film stock.' I'm not sure that that really translates to the kind of thing I'm thinking of, but I can see that one could descend into that kind of strangeness. It's not what I'm talking about, but it's always lurking there, always.

SG: I'm thinking of William Burroughs. He started with literary exercises which were very elaborate and complicated, then evolved much more simply. But it's obvious that he was using techniques that came from cinema, the art of modern times. So wouldn't it be systematic to use those kinds of techniques? The editing techniques Burroughs used?
DC: His most famous technique was the cut-up. And I love what was behind the cut-up, which was not a cinematic thing. It was quite a strange, conceptual thing, that if our minds are being controlled by these giant insects that live on another planet, which at one point he really believed – he was doing a very particular kind of drug at that point – then the only way we can break out of being totally controlled is by randomness. It's just chance what you write. You just write, then you shuffle everything. That can't be controlled by anybody else, because you're not controlling it. So even if your mind is controlled, randomness is a kind of freedom. But of course, you were giving up structure and a conceptualised meaning, because that is also random. Now you might fool the giant insects, but are you able to communicate anything to other humans? I don't know.

In the films I make, there is that kind of randomness. In a sense, I feel that I'm almost making documentaries. I'm setting up with the actors, the sets, the locations. Yes, we have the dialogue. And I'm thinking about how to shoot it. And I don't have the storyboards. So I'm hoping that, filtering through my nervous system and through my cameraman, and other people who are collaborating with me on the set, there will come some kind of coherence, visually and in terms of space. Because the way you cut up space is one of the first things that really confronted me as a filmmaker, dealing with space. Moving people through space, and the camera dancing with those people and cutting that space into cubes. I felt like I suddenly understood cubism in a completely different way at that point. That was what really made me sweat on the set: how do I do this with some control, and some meaning?

Likewise in the editing room. There are random things that happen. There are juxtapositions that happen. I've even a case where, while we were shooting, someone put some of the footage together to make a teaser trailer. And I saw some juxtapositions in that teaser trailer that were very striking to me. This was someone that was not familiar with the material. He took it as a cookie jar of wonderful things that he could use in any possible way, unrestrained by my concepts, maybe had not even read the script, and put together some images side by side that I would not have thought to put together. And that is illuminating, even if I don't use them exactly that way, it can be quite revealing to me. So there is randomness, there is this kind of cut-up, of editing technique that is not completely random, but there is randomness involved. I could go back and re-edit all of my films and come up with completely different versions of them. And at this distance I probably would. If I were to edit any one of those two films [*Naked Lunch*, *M. Butterfly*], all the rushes, forgetting what I did, because I basically do forget – I'm looking at these and I'm saying, 'That's interesting. I don't remember this at all.' In a small sense I do, but I don't remember the moment for most of those shots. I would come up with something quite different. So there is that randomness that exists.

For me, the script works from the inside out, not from the outside in, so it's true that, although every once and a while there is a film that we've done with an image, it's much more likely it begins with a concept or character who is actually a conceptualisation – is not a physical idea of a character, it's a concept of a character, and might even be the name of the character, but it's not something you could storyboard. How would you storyboard that? So for me, a storyboard is really a useless thing and not a desirable thing. Really, in a way, an impossible thing. It only works when you're doing a sequence for special effects, where everyone has to agree on, 'We'll only see the Fly from the waist up. We will never see it completely, floor to ceiling.' That sort of thing. Special effects people feel insecure, so they want you to sign off on a storyboard. But that's usually a very small sequence, and it's a very minor thing. So the imagery tends to come later for me. And if it works, it should come from the inside out. I'm very inspired by the space. By the locations that we find. By the faces of the actors. By the costumes we develop for them. By the lighting that my cameraman does. All these things. It becomes a very plastic thing, the development of the imagery, rather than a conceptual thing. It might be what you're feeling is different. But, as I say, there is the history of every shot. The use of that particular lens. You use a wide-angle, a 25mm. You're thinking of all the shots that were shot low, wide, that kind of thing, and you have to divest yourself of that. You have to forget about that. Because it can paralyse you. It can be completely paralysing to you.

SG: Talking of ideas and concepts, I could give you two examples of this contamination. The first one would be the Talking Asshole monologue in *NL*, and the second one would be this dialogue in *Crash*, the very graphic and crude dialogue between husband and wife. It seems obvious that the text, at least the dialogue in those two scenes, is central. So perhaps, did you have the intention of doing that when you adapted *NL* or *Crash*?

DC: No. Once again, when I started both of those, it was with great fear and the constant feeling that it could fall apart at any moment. And then, at some point, it would become very solid and real, and I would know, almost without being aware of when that happened, that these were movies after all. That they were not just some fantasy of a movie, some potential of a movie that actually would never realise itself. There was a moment I remember in *NL*, most of the dialogue was really invented by me with the spirit of Burroughs certainly flowing through me. It was a real case of possession. I had never experienced that before, since it wasn't the same with *Crash*. I was really possessed by the spirit of Burroughs, and the rhythms of his dialogue, which is very unlike his background. We're both North American, but we couldn't have come from more different backgrounds. But the rhythms were there. Suddenly there was music. The Burroughsian Music. And it was at this certain point that I realised there were these beautiful setpieces that would almost not need to be changed at all, but could be taken from the novels and worked so perfectly in a particular context, a different context in the movie than in the book. So it didn't begin with that at all. Likewise in *Crash*, I had no idea how I would deal with it,

Above: William Lee (Peter Weller) injects his wife with a little bugkilling powder. Below: The soft machine: What better illustration of the Burroughsian expression than when this typewriter is transformed into quivering flesh?

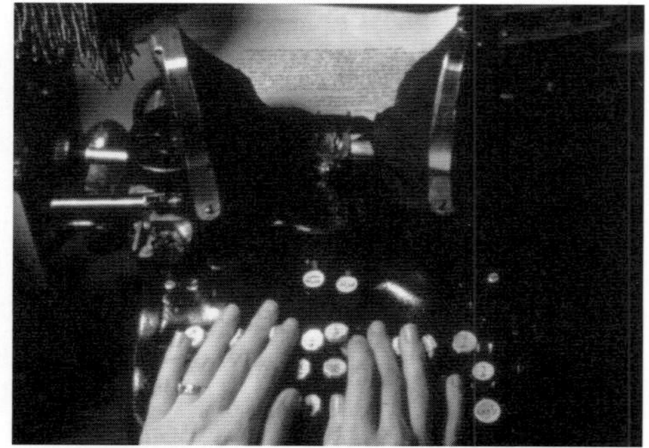

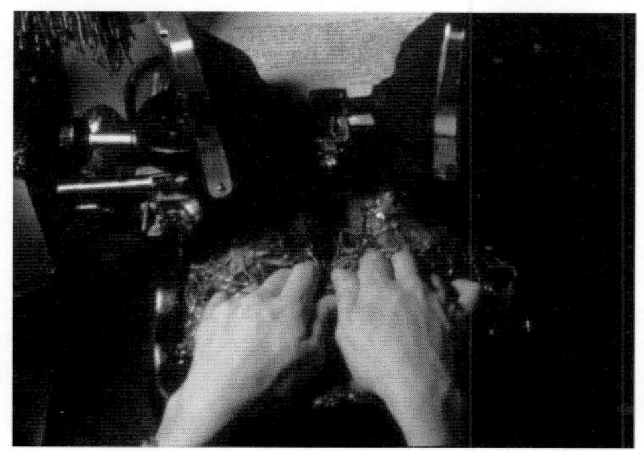

because the dialogue in *Crash* is not very realistic at all. Burroughs is very realistic and idiomatic, even when he's doing these routines, it has a real street flow. You could hear someone saying that stuff. Not all of Ballard's writing is like that. *Crash* is quite unique like that, so it's a very medical, clinical, strange dialogue that's not realistic, I had no idea if that would work on film. [Or] If I wanted that to work. But I found that most of the dialogue in *Crash* came directly from the book, to my surprise. Because, when I thought of the book, I didn't think there was much dialogue in it, and I realised that in fact there was quite a lot. So that movie, after many years of actually worrying, of being afraid to approach the novel as screenwriting material, once I did, it fell onto the page very easily for me, and I was very surprised by that. But I had no preconceived idea of what would happen.

Cronenberg wanted his film to deal with a drug that never existed, to avoid all documentary connotations. And so Lee uses cockroach exterminating powder, the 'black meat' (the flesh of giant sea creatures from Brazil), and finally Mugwump jism.

SG: **What is fascinating about these two examples is that each of them appears as an ultimate homage to literature . . . I remember the first time I saw *Crash* in Cannes, I could feel – and I was not the only one, in this very big theatre – that the words had been printed on the screen. Maybe it's got something to do with sex, one could even say pornography. I know we'll have a long discussion about that, but maybe that's why you've always been very interested by sex. By something that I wouldn't define as pornography, of course, but something that's at the limit of what's never been shown or heard before.**

DC: That's funny, because I think that comes out of my desire to distil an essence, that makes me sort of a hopeless alchemist or something. Because on the one hand, I know that life is very complex. That's one of the wonderful things about life. It's very complex and very difficult to simplify. On the other hand, it's of the essence of art to simplify and still give the illusion of complexity. That art cannot be as complex as life and still work as art. I think it almost comes as that. If sex is your subject, or sexuality, then you are trying to distil it, and come to some essential feeling about what the power of it is, and the weakness of it is, and the futility of it is, and all those other things. I think that that's what really leads me to that point on the screen, rather than a desire to shock, or go beyond what is happening on television right now. I don't mean here, but in general, the things on television that you see. With *Geraldo* and all these talk shows, it's unbelievable. A few years ago it would be an impossibility, and it's almost a joke. And yet somehow they're never really talking about sex at all, even though you're talking about the father who raped his daughter, and the boyfriend who came in and then had sex with the mother, and they're all talking about it, but they're not really ever talking about it. They're not really ever dealing with it. It's almost as if they didn't really experience it. So it's almost as though I have to experience it for them, for it to have some reality. That's the feeling I have. And I feel that I want to do that with everything I deal with on screen. Not just sex, of course, but sex is a potent . . . for me, cinema was sex for so many years, it was one of the few places where the erotic was accessible to a young Canadian boy.

SG: **With all these trials, *Lolita*, *The Naked Lunch*, Joyce, it seems the great writers of this century were involved in what the judges were saying was pornography. Don't you feel it's got something to do with modernity?**

DC: Yes. If you were going to simplify, and find

Top: Fadela, the servant-witch, portrayed by Monique Mercure. Above: Fadela hits the 'sex blob' with her riding crop. The creature is born from the sexual desire of the sentient writing machine.

some essential thing, then you're going to be stripping away all of the falsehoods and social façades, and you are going to come to some truths. However much we may think that all truth is relative, I think there's a sense in which that is also true. To speak the truth is not how society functions. Society exists on pretence, on structures, on repression. I mean in the Freudian formula, civilisation is repression. Whatever anyone might think about Freud, this is still a crystal-hard understanding that in order for civilisation and civility to exist, there must be repression, there must be structures that conceal. And yet if you're an artist, a serious one, then you have the desire to strip those things away. Not just to play around [with] the façade, which is what most cinema is at any given time as well. And you are then in danger of telling the truth, of going behind the façade, of breaking the agreement of civility and of civilisation. That is not forgiven very easily. It's true that what you see on television now every day, like *Jerry Springer* and *Geraldo* and all these talk shows, it comes in a strange form rather than coming in a TV series about sex, although there's a lot of that as well. It comes in the form of talk shows, as supposed reality TV, with big quotes around 'reality'. All of these people would have been put in jail not very long ago. You'd have Jerry Springer and Geraldo in jail with James Joyce and William Burroughs. It would be quite an interesting group. So the understanding about what is acceptable, about what is allowed to be revealed, has changed, changes, but I still find that with *Crash* – it's so strange. The book was already 25 years old when I made the movie. The movie was not really very explicit. It was verbally explicit, but nothing like you hear people talking on sex shows all the time, and yet somehow the form of the movie so touched a nerve. As if to say: You think that you are not puritanical. You think that you are telling the truth. You think that everybody is now speaking very realistically and truthfully about their sex and sexuality. But they're not really, there's still a façade. A subtle one. There's a code, and the movie somehow broke with the code. It decoded what was encoded and was not acceptable. If you look at the movie shot by shot and analyse it word by word, there's nothing that you couldn't find on television every single day in North America, so I think therefore it's inevitable. There cannot be a society that is always truthful. It's impossible. So there will always be hidden, taboo things, even if it's only in the form that those things are communicated that is taboo. Perhaps the information in a sort of clinical way is not taboo, but somehow the way of conveying it will be. So I think there will always be taboos, and it's always in the nature of art to dive into that, and wrestle with that and not accept the dark corners. That's where you want to go. It's an instinct.

Troilism: William Lee and Joan Frost (Judy Davis), 'twin sister' of the woman killed during a 'literary' orgy.

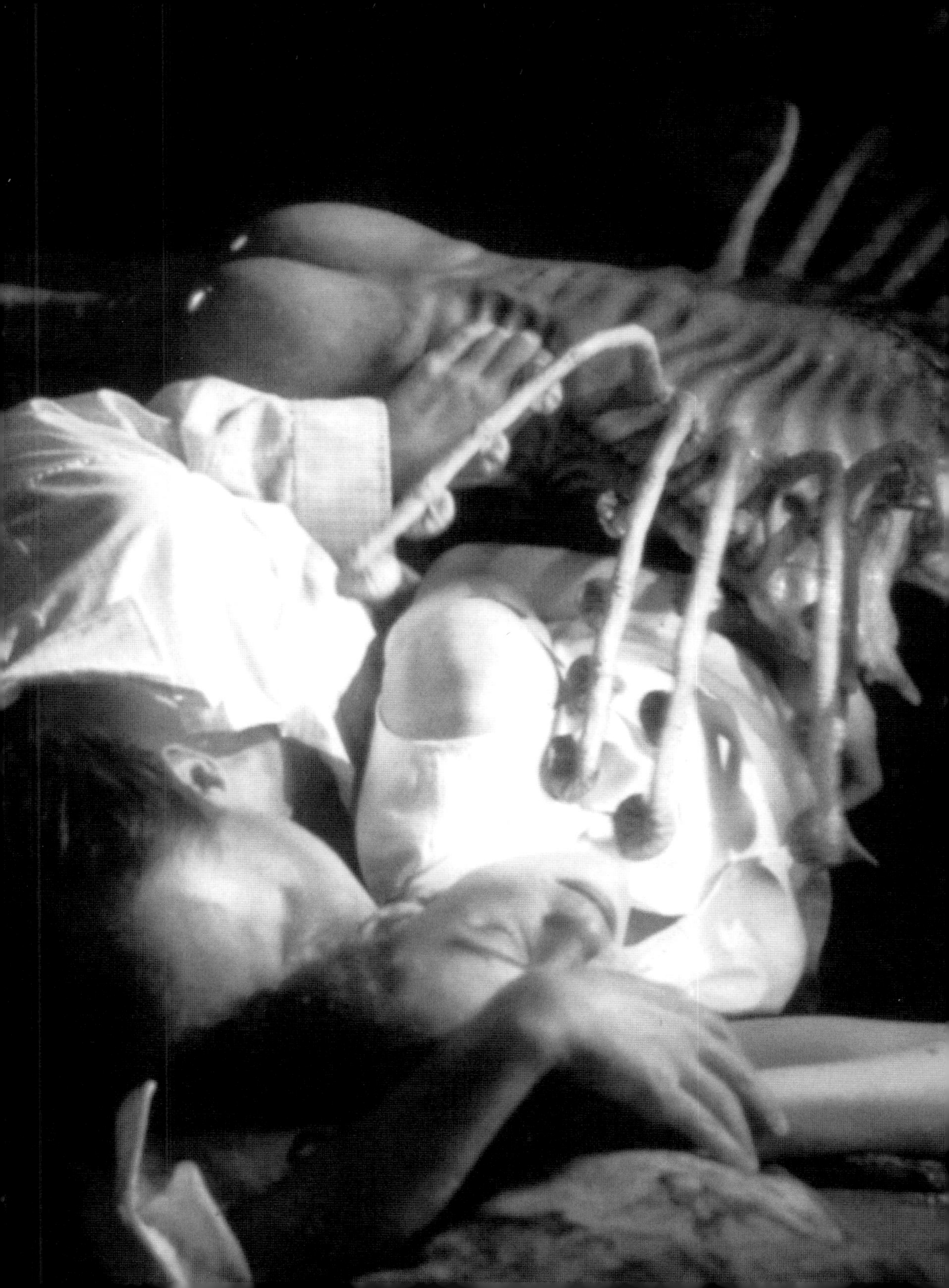

Opposite: The bestiary of Interzone: Peter Weller converses with a Mugwump. Above: The Burroughs gang; from left to right: William Seward Burroughs (author of the original work), David Cronenberg (screenwriter and director) and Peter Weller (who plays William Lee, the pen name adopted by Burroughs for his first novel, Junky).

SG: I think I've told you this before: a girl that is very close to me, the first time she saw *NL*, she cried at the death of the typing machine. Of course it's very cute, but at least it proved that you as an artist were able to create a universe where characters, however fantastic they are, have an existence of their own.

DC: That's a beautiful story. I love that. That is the ultimate compliment to the creative act. That you actually have brought something to life in a way, as so many characters from, let's say, Shakespeare are alive to people in a way beyond their body. Now this is another interesting thing. I mean, what about this life beyond the body? Because there is one. Where we feel that Falstaff, for example, big, heavy, boisterous, very vital character from Shakespeare, seems very alive in a very physical way, except that he has no body. He's embodied by a series of actors over many centuries, so he has a kind of a physical life beyond the human life. At that point you feel that you have almost created life. Not quite.

SG: I've been wanting to ask you this for a long time: in a way, you're maybe one of the most original directors in respect to love, because love is a theme in most of your movies, but you're not treating what is usually called love in the same way as others. Is that something to do with what we've already seen? Different levels of reality? Are two lovers on different levels even when they fall in love with each other?

DC: I think my understanding of love is . . . I think it feels very deep and very profound and very real, but it's not courtly love. I remember reading C. S. Lewis's book, *The Allegory of Love*, which is basically a book of literary criticism, but it was stunning to me. I mean, this was a major book for me because it really discussed how what we consider to be love, romantic love, certainly what I grew up with in the forties and fifties and sixties, that it was an invention, a poetic invention around the year 1100 in a part of France, and it became reality. It started as a literary convention, based on the whole feudal sys-

Opposite page: Metamorphoses – Original storyboards by Stephan Dupuis, depicting different stages of transformation for the 'Cloquet creature' (the monster that originates from the character played by Julian Sands). Bottom: sketch by Dupuis of the metamorphosis from wasted junky into deviant Mugwump.

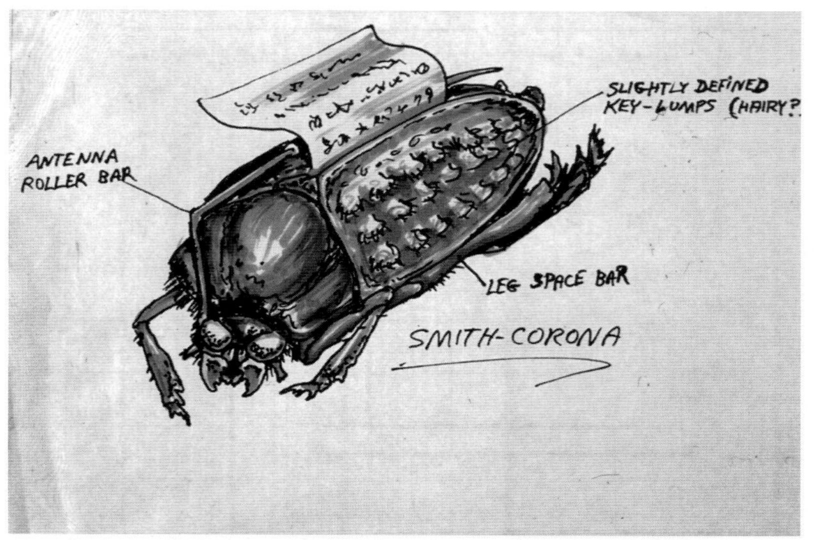

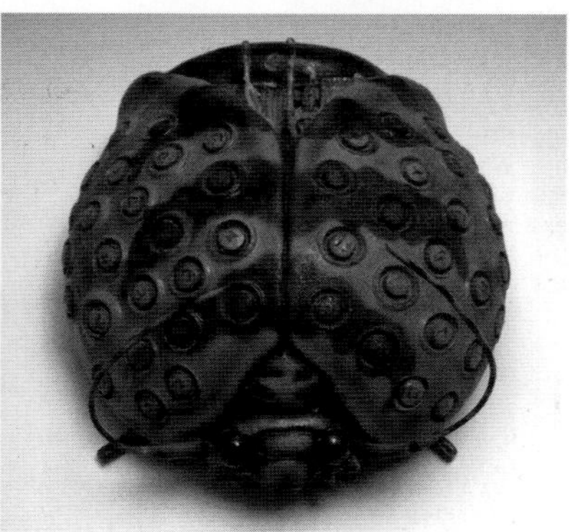

This page: The Insect Machines: Preparatory sketches and models for the various writing-insect machines of Naked Lunch (by Stephan Depuis and Chris Walas). Bottom: Bugwriter – the final prototype of the 'writing cockroach' machine.

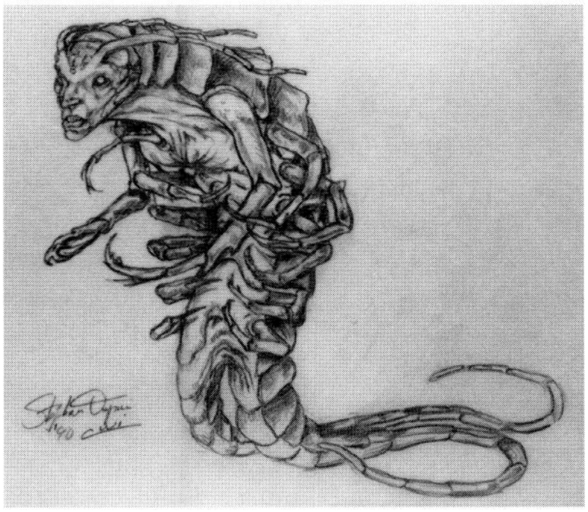

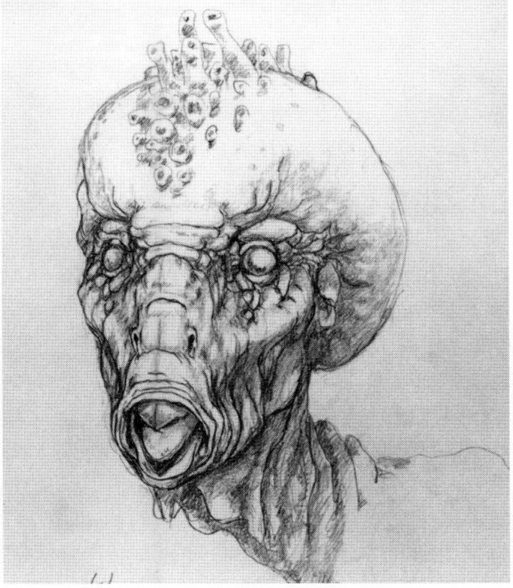

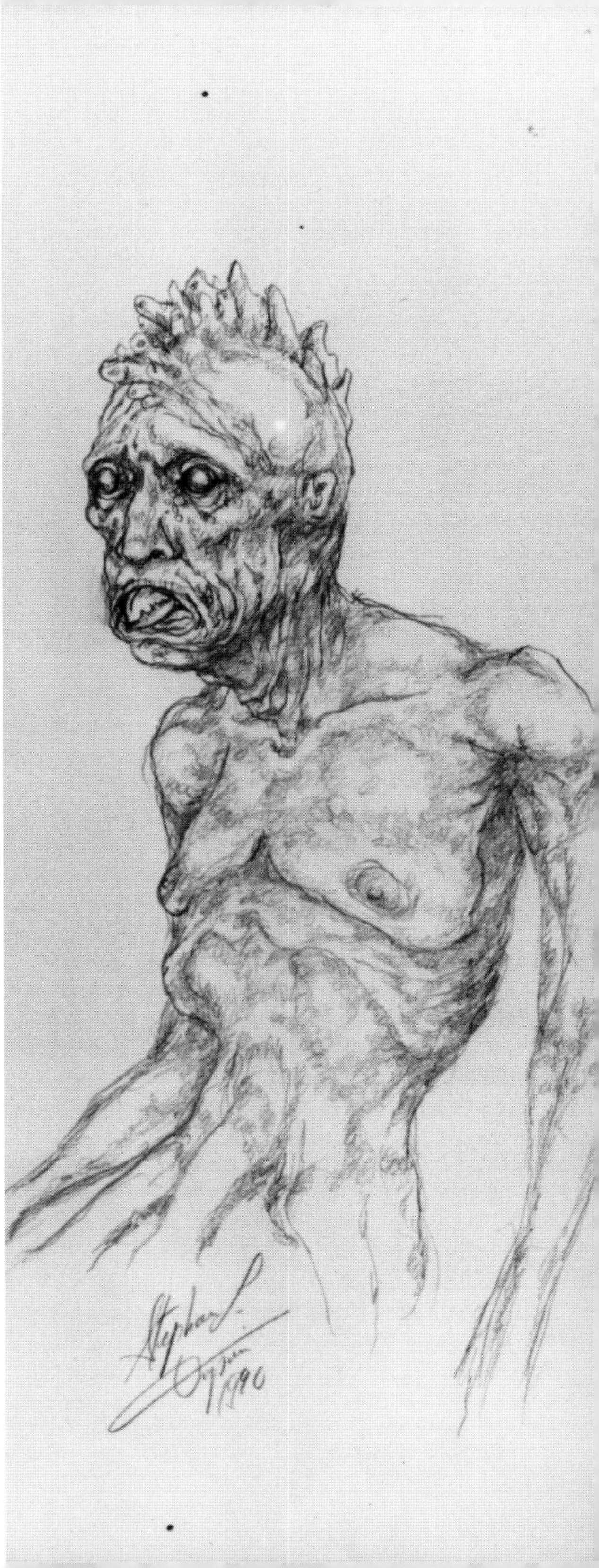

Opposite page: Set by Carol Spier, designed by James McAteer – the walkway of Interzone. To realise the passage from the reality of New York to the hallucinatory Interzone, Cronenberg instructed his production designer to recreate the same structures but to 'dress them up' differently.

This page: Psychological Landscape – William Lee (Peter Weller) in the room that overlooks the Casbah of Interzone. Following the Gulf Crisis (1991), the insurers refused to let exteriors be shot in Tangiers. Carol Spier recreated, on two large platforms, the Tangiers Casbah and the other exteriors, giving the film a more dreamlike feel. The view from the window is a photo of Tangiers.

Top: Peter Weller gets connected in his room in Interzone. Above: A Mugwump at work (Chris Walas, Inc.).

tem of the knight kneeling before the royal lady, and became the reality for millions of people, but it was an invention. And he has wonderful proof that, before that, that kind of love didn't exist because no one believed that it existed. They didn't actually feel it. So that was really quite stunning to me, because it connected with my already developing sense that many things that we are given through society as absolutes, as reality, are not real. They're variable and they're open to change and transformation. In a way, that freed me intellectually, to let my concept of what love is and [is] not float. It's very convenient to use those old forms to express love, or talk to other people about love, and it's something that's still common currency in popular entertainment, this whole idea of courtly love that began in the twelfth century. So my understanding of love is something that I'm exploring in my films, and it has nothing to do with the old idea of courtly love. It has more to do with biochemistry and physics and then, of course, it's evolving from there. I feel it. I have children. I understand. I feel all of those things, but I don't put that structure around them that many people do. I'm sure that that's what you're sensing in my films. I hate movies that just push all those courtly love buttons and expect to get a response, and of course often they do. They get a response from people because it's built into the nervous system until you change your nervous system. I don't really want to talk about *Shakespeare in Love*, but that movie really annoyed me. Not only is it deconstructionist film-making, but it's also just *Romeo and Juliet* again. Really it's no more. It's in fact quite a bit less, and part of the reason is it's courtly love again. It's expecting an audience response that's based on these old, out-moded forms.

SG: **I've tried to translate a verse by René Char, one of our greatest poets. It's very awkward, but I guess you will understand the general meaning. He wrote, 'the poem,' but I guess we could say the work of art, 'is the realised love of a lust that remained lust.' Would you agree with that?**
DC: Read that again.

SG: **You know, love realised. The realisation of love, or of a lust that has remained a lust. Pure lust. I think he stresses the difference between lust and love, but this is his definition of a work of art. The poem, as he says.**
DC: That's very pretty, so I could agree with it because it's aesthetically pleasing. Whether I really understand it . . .

SG: **Because in a way a movie is 'realised', but what's beneath it is a lust, or a drive maybe . . .**
DC: It depends what you mean by lust too. For some people that means pure carnal, physical . . .

SG: **No, let's say lust as in Freud.**
DC: Then I could agree, but in English, lust has

that other meaning. Because there's a real passion, and you can feel it particularly when your film is attacked. Or when it's mutilated by censors. The feeling that you get at that point is like a child, is like protecting it. But it's very physical, the reaction you have to that. Very physical. You would do great violence to someone who would do that to your film. So you can feel the power, the connection that you have. It's not a trivial thing. It's a very potent thing, I think, for any artwork. It's not understood by people who change your movie. 'We'll just cut some up because of the television.' They don't understand what an atrocity that feels like to you. It's perhaps out of proportion to other atrocities, but at that moment it feels like an atrocity to you.

SG: **I think there's something very close to that in the dialogue of *The Fly*, when there's all this talk about wanting to eat babies, cannibalise them, which is of course a form of longing or lust. Sometimes, very often in your movies, there are very violent and graphic scenes. Sometimes I really have the feeling they are pure scenes of love.**

DC: I knew you were going to say that, and I agree with you. It would be very difficult for most people to accept that or understand that, but I think you're right. It's a desire to fuse with, to absorb, to somehow cut beneath the surface of. I think that this is once again an understanding of love that doesn't fit into the normal, very rigid kind of structure that people have seemed to accept, in the West anyway. Because there are many forms of it, and many ways of it being expressed, that are a lot deeper and more potent than the standard ones. It's interesting, because in society now we are allowing the expression of things that a few years ago were not allowed. There's a lot of scarring, tattooing, mutilation, piercing. A lot of wife-swapping even among very middle class people and so on, but no one would want to think of these as love. They think of these as sorts of sexual delights or explorations. They don't even want necessarily to call them perversion, maybe a little bit. But if you were to suggest that they were new forms of expressing love and experiencing love, people would probably get more upset. They would rather think of them as sort of superficial, sexual madness, a momentary kind of thing, rather than what you're talking about. But I think you're right though. That's exactly what it is. The old understanding of love is gradually being eaten away from the inside.

SG: **If we accept the fact that, basically, love is a misunderstanding between two persons – sometimes, and most of the time, a very complex form of complete misunderstanding – then sometimes the reaction of the audience can be the misunderstanding of a misunderstanding, which drives us always to the same point: that censorship is an absurdity.**

DC: Censorship is an absurdity. It's only understandable as an expression of power, repression. That's what it is, and in that sense it makes sense. Censorship only makes sense if it's really someone trying to repress and suppress someone else, in terms of adjusting society, to make society acceptable. I have had this experience a couple of times myself, talking to people who wanted to censor my films, and it's impossible. I would lie. I would have to lie to make things simple for them to understand. And I would say things to manipulate them. If I actually told them what was going on in the film, they had no way of understanding it. No way of understanding it whatsoever, so it's a very bizarre situation. In a way, of course, the filmmaker is trying to engage in a kind of complex love relationship with his audience. And of course the possibility, in fact the inevitability, of misunderstanding is inevitable. So what you're there to do is to manipulate the misunderstanding, so that somehow the end result is the same as if there had been understanding. I don't expect anyone to really understand my films the way I've emitted them. Of course, there are elements of my own films that I don't understand, in an articulate

and conscious way, myself. So it is a strange kind of constant adjustment and circling and feeling out. And it is like a marriage, a good, complex marriage, where it's not a free flow of absolute bits of information. It's not that at all. It's much more like what you're saying. It's constant shaping and molding of constant misunderstanding.

SG: In one of your movies, *M. Butterfly*, Song seduces Gallimard first as a diva and then as a Peking opera singer. But both times she's driving him toward something totally deceitful, knowingly or not. Are not all types of seduction – even, in this case, with the help of an opera, a work of art – the same kind of tactics ?

DC: Yes, I think they are. It's a performance that is perhaps a façade in front of a façade in front of a façade. It's very hard, to me, for two people to meet who absolutely know who they are, so they

Top left: The Domain of the Mugwumps – Hans (Robert Silverman, an old collaborator of Cronenberg's – The Brood, Scanners, eXistenZ . . .), the dealer of Mugwump jism. Left: Cloquet (the Swiss dandy played by Julian Sands) devours Lee's little friend, Kiki (Joseph Scorsiani). Below: The Mugwumps, enchained, dispense the precious fluid that enslaves the junkies. Opposite: A Mugwump in chains, at the ultimate stage of his alienation and addiction – *'the algebra of need'*, to quote Burroughs.

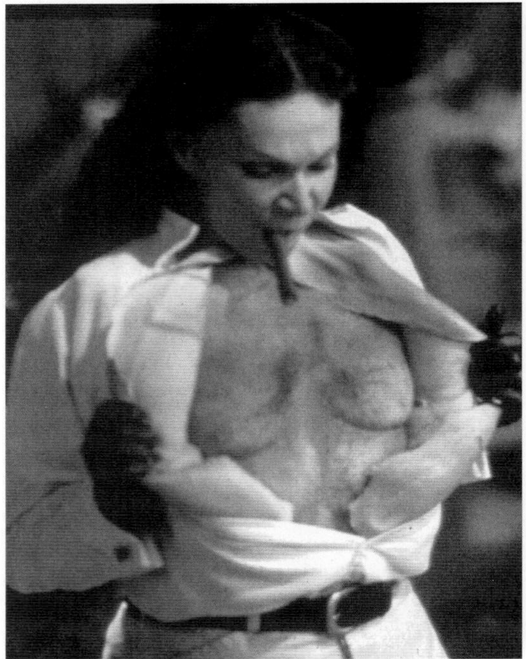

The Metamorphoses: Fadela (Monique Mercure) at the pupa stage; in the Cronenberg universe, inspired by entomology, there are multiple transitions between the lava stage and the 'imaginal' stage.

are always performing or playing some role. Especially the older you get, the more settled you usually get in your role. But of course, Gallimard is deceitful as well. He pretends to be something that he is not. So they're both playing the same game. And, in a way, they both really don't want to ever say that it's a game. That sort of spoils it. So there is some game-playing involved, but it's more than game-playing.

SG: There's something that always surprised me, and frightens me a little bit. When Descartes wrote *Le Discours de la Méthode*, the first sentence he wrote in Latin was, '*Larvatus prodeo*,' which means, 'I wear a mask.' And it was supposed to be a scientific and philosophical book. No one knows exactly what he meant. So a creator always wears a mask?

DC: Yeah. More than one. It's good if you have more than one. I feel constantly that I could not speak the truth even if I knew what it was. It would be too destructive and too coruscating and too corrosive, and so it has to be shaped, and it has to modelled, and it has to be structured, and it has to be . . . devolved in a way – not to make it more acceptable . . .

SG: It's always nice to see a connection between two artists. Even if you've just confessed to me that you've never seen Cocteau's *Orphee*, it's almost a visual pun to show those mirrors. There are a lot of things in common between this movie and *Naked Lunch*, although they are quite subtle, and I must say it's an American critic, Bill Krohn, who really discovered it and wrote a brilliant article about it. What about those kind of influences, whether they come from cinema or literature or visual arts? Even if they are totally unconscious. Even if they come from things you are not aware of.

DC: That's interesting, because you really then have to be careful about your definition of the word 'influence'. I think about reading about evolution, and people who still don't want to believe in evolution say, 'How could something as wonderful as the eye be developed in just those several hundred thousand years?' It seems impossible from just an amoeba to the eye. There must be God. And it's been proven, it's been shown, by using computer simulations now, that not only was the eye developed once for everyone, it's been developed about ten or twenty times. The squid has an eye that developed in a completely different way to the human eye. The insect eye developed completely separate from the human eye, all to the same purpose, which is to perceive light and motion and to allow the creature to function visually. But they were all developed separately. In fact, the squid's eye is apparently a much better design than the human eye, the mammalian eye. It just evolved along a different path. So you can't really say that the development of the squid's eye, the insect's eye, the human eye, influenced each other. They all

In the skin of Fadela, Dr. Benway (Roy Scheider) stands revealed, a recurring figure in the Burroughsian mythos. Cronenberg faithfully captured the essence of the master's words (but without the wordplay that implied the character was a heroin addict).

came from the contextual pressures on these organisms to respond to light in increasingly sophisticated ways. I think you wouldn't talk about an influence in that sense. It's conceivable, then, that what I'm saying is Cocteau, Burroughs, and I, and of course others, we're all developing our own eyes along separate evolutionary paths, so it's not necessarily an influence. It could be that under the pressures of society, and how we perceive life, and the antennae that we have to sense things, that we've all come to the same place, but really by separate routes. That is not an influence in the normal way. That we were all influenced though by the same context, you understand what I mean.

SG: ***Orphee* was released in 1959, the same year *The Naked Lunch* was published in Paris. Of course Cocteau was gay, as was Burroughs, and Cocteau used morphine a lot and even wrote a book about it. So when you're speaking of antennae, I can understand what you mean because I am absolutely sure Cocteau and Burroughs never met. But perhaps they were a little bit on the same level of reality. What is also interesting is that a myth as ancient as the one of Orpheus has been beautifully treated in three great movies : Cocteau's *Orphee*, which is directly linked, Hitchcock's *Vertigo*, which is also two women, one of them dies, comes back to life, etc., and of course *Naked Lunch*. So maybe there's something in a myth when it's as potent as that . . . I don't want to sound Jungian, but there's something very strong.**

DC: You could sound Jungian if you wanted to. You look much more Freudian though, I think.

It's a mysterious thing. I don't know about the presence of these eternal myths, I think Jung is suggesting that we're almost born with these embedded in our nervous systems. Of course the cultures have them embedded in them, it's true. It's interesting that my movie of *Naked Lunch* is quite different from Burroughs' book, in terms of his relationship with his wife, and the constant recurrence of his wife in his attempt to rescue her, and so on. I was taking that from Burroughs' life, not from his art. That even complicates further. If I were to be influenced then, by Burroughs, it was really by his biography, not by his art. So it can be a complex question. Fortunately, thank God, as an artist, I don't have to worry about that. You do it as you feel it. It's interesting for me to discuss it after the fact, of course, but it's not something that you're feeling when you're working. As long as you feel that you've plugged into the proper sockets, and you're getting the energy, it doesn't really matter what those sockets are until afterwards. Then you have to deal with what you've created.

SG: In *M. Butterfly*, you have the feeling Gallimard is always projecting an image, and he tries to become a fake reproduction of his ideal.
DC: That's like Brundle. It's a fusion of oneself and the other, and certainly Gallimard tries to do that, to become both things in himself, to fuse himself. That is a real transformation in a way: to think it's a butterfly and it's a fly, both [are] insects, both undergo transformations, and certainly he's monitoring his transformation in a series of mirrors and reflecting surfaces in *M. Butterfly*. But once again, it seems to me very much about transformation. Maybe it's a fusion as well. Maybe it's an evolution. But it's a transformation. It's a willed transformation in both cases. The Chinese performer is also willing a magical transformation of himself into some divine, idealised woman.

SG: Someone who would prefer illusion to . . .
DC: Yeah, that's right. Joyce Wadler wrote a book called *Dangerous Liaisons*. I met her . . . I read that book and I was interested to talk to her about it. I read it after I made the movie.

SG: *M. Butterfly* is considered a little bit apart from your work, and I think it's absolutely unfair. So would you say that there's a monster born in *M. Butterfly*? Some kind of monster?
DC: Sure. It's very parallel really to *The Fly*. You have the Gallimard character, who by the end of the movie is just as monstrous as Seth Brundle, and for the same reason. He has fused himself with the other. He has fused himself with something, in fact, that is his own creation, to create a kind of composite character. So he has embodied both of them when he cannot have his lover, he becomes her and himself at the same time to create this weird hybrid creature, and in effect commit suicide – and does commit suicide, as [does] Seth Brundle. So there's a real similarity, and I think it would be quite strange to sort of set that movie aside from my other movies. I mean on a very superficial level, yes, you can see why. But it's a very superficial level. Anybody who thinks about it twice, I think you can see a lot of the connection.

SG: On top of that, I would say that there are two monsters, because of that very beautiful scene in the police van when Song reveals to Gallimard, not to the public – which is very important – her masculinity, her real self. She becomes in his eyes, you can see it on screen – the idea becoming flesh – a monster.
DC: Yes, that's right. It causes horror. Because she hopes by revealing herself she will be revealing her true beauty, which is what she thinks he's wanted all along, and discovers in fact that it's repulsive to him, and that he abhors it. It was the illusion that Song willed, her creation, that Gallimard was obsessed with, not with any other reality. I could imagine a version of that story where Song fused with her own cover. This also connects with the Burroughsian idea of an agent fusing with his cover. That Song believed herself to be a woman, perhaps had a transsexual operation, which would be the equivalent in a way of going into the telepod. To fuse with her cover, to become what she was pretending to be and

live out of that. You would have a couple of monsters then in the movie at that point.

SG: The confrontation between these two monsters is also interesting, because in a way it's two cultures, two different universes that confront. Would you say in a certain way that the real hero or protagonist in *M. Butterfly* is not at all this young French diplomat, but in fact this Chinese woman-man?

DC: Yeah, I think you could make a real case for it. That the sort of controlling energy of the movie, the sort of hard centre of the movie, is the character that John Lone plays. That the Gallimard character is the kind of satellite character that goes around her. You would get into an interesting discussion about what one means by the main character in the centre of a film. I think that she is the planet that Gallimard is circling around. She holds the truth. She has a much stronger understanding of what she is, what she wants to be. The illusions that she's creating and what she wants out of life. It seems that her love is actually the true love and that Gallimard's is kind of an illusory love. For her to gain his love, she would have to change into something else, another creature entirely who, perhaps if she had had those operations and those transformations, would no longer love Gallimard. So she is the central paradox in the movie really. So in that sense I think you're right, and it's a really interesting perspective to see the movie from.

SG: In a way, of course, she's also the director because she's creating fictions during the whole movie.

DC: She's the director. Inside the movie she is definitely the director, no question. She controls the lighting and the costumes and the *mise en scène*, and she does that because, if she does not do that, she cannot maintain the illusion. Yes, that's a lovely point. She's definitely the director in the movie.

SG: If we invert things, would you say that a good director should be an agent?

DC: A good director is an agent. It's a question of . . . you almost cannot tell the truth if you are not an agent. Now I'm not sure what I mean by that, but I think I know what I mean by that. I think that bluntness and straightforward honesty cannot actually convey the truth, which is too subtle and too difficult, and perhaps too frightening. So for an audience you must be deceptive. You must use the costumes and lighting and everything to make things absorbable. So in order to be truthful you have to be deceptive. I think that's absolutely true, because the truth is not a stone you can pick up and look at and throw through somebody's window. It's a much more subtle and transforming thing that's constantly changing. So if you are going to be the agent of some kind of truth, you are the agent immediately. You have to be.

SG: *M. Butterfly* seems to be quite far from the play, and then it totally becomes your film. I don't know exactly what part you took in the writing of the screenplay, but it's very mysterious. Some people I know in Paris, a couple of them at the *Cahiers*, really think *M. Butterfly* is your masterpiece. One of them, in the last issue, put *eXistenZ* as the best film of the decade, and one of them put *M. Butterfly*. But when you take a screenplay which seems to be quite apart from you – of course, it's not that far apart from you, otherwise you wouldn't have made it in the first place – what kind of choices do you make?

DC: Well it's funny, because in a way it felt to me like *Dead Ringers*: in that I heard about the play, and then I heard about what the play was based on, the real story and the real guy, and I read about that – this was before I was thinking of doing it and it reminded me very much of stumbling across the story of the Marcus twins and then realising that there had been a novel and many big articles written about them and so on. So it felt like that process. Of course, the difference was that the book *Twins*, that was about the

Marcus twins, actually sold very well, but wasn't really in people's consciousness the way *M. Butterfly* was. And it came about at a time when I tried something . . . Ironically, if there was ever a film of mine that you could call a sellout, it was *M. Butterfly*, but I don't think of it that way. But it was the process which went like this – well I suppose, in a way, *The Dead Zone* was like that too. I had finished *Naked Lunch*, and I realised that it was taking three years between films. And I thought, if I'm going to write a film – I don't have them all lined up like airplanes on a landing field ready to take off, like some directors do. If you have other people writing for you, and you are sort of a producer-director like Spielberg or any of those guys, they have many ready to go at any given moment. Whenever they're ready to make a film, there's a film there that's well-developed by writers, they have rewrites, they have actors interested and so on, I don't do that. So after *Naked Lunch*, I knew, if I were going to start from scratch, it would be three or four years before I made my next film.

I said to my agent, 'Look around and see what's around, you know my taste, and see if there is anything interesting.' And the most interesting thing by far was *M. Butterfly*, and there was a script which had been written for it by David Hwang, who wrote the play. I hadn't by that time seen the play, so I actually read the script first and then I saw a production of the play in LA. And then I thought about it, and of course I had to convince David Geffen that I was the right director for it. He wanted Peter Weir, Peter Weir had turned it down because he was tired, he had just made *Green Card* or something – that's the story I heard anyway. So I wasn't really on his list, and I can understand that. Because when I went to talk to Geffen, he said that he really didn't understand why I would want to make the film, that it never occurred to him that I would be interested. And I said, as I had already met David Hwang, 'Funny, because the writer of the play said that I was the most obvious choice to direct this movie.' And Geffen was strong enough to take that, he didn't take it as a criticism or anything. He said, 'Well I guess he knows better than I do.'

I had talked to David, because I didn't want to start getting involved in it unless we had an understanding. I had very good relationships with all the writers I was involved with. I didn't want to make changes, and then have him denouncing the movie afterwards as being a betrayal of the play or something. And I told him what I thought was wrong with the play, and there were many things which I thought were wrong with the play. In particular, I thought the politics of the play were wrong, I said I thought it was much too propagandistic. I said, 'Yes, there is the mythology of the geisha, but there's also the mythology of the samurai.' I mean, Western mythology of the East is not all that the East is passive like a geisha girl. I said, 'It's much more complex than that, and karate, and samurai, and ninja warriors and stuff . . .' I said, 'The stereotypes you're talking about are quite old and things have gotten more complex now.' And there's a lot about what people think of the East that seems to them more powerful, more sophisticated, more refined: the philosophies and the art of war, and all of that kind of thing. Even in Hollywood the art of war is very big. 'So it's not all the East is submissive and female, and the West is aggressive and male,' I said, 'and that's what your politics are in this play. And I don't believe them, I think it's a distortion of the truth, which is more complex. So, as propaganda, your play is fine, but as what I would be interested in doing in a movie, it's not fine. I want to do something new with it, I want to take it somewhere else and focus on other things that mean more to me, and that are not so obviously political and propagandistic. And if you don't want to do this, then I won't do it. If you think what I'm saying is horrible, and you don't want to be involved, then I will walk away, because I don't want to make you upset basically.'

And he understood what I was saying. I don't know if he 100 percent agreed with it, but the idea that we would go somewhere else with it, and not just try to do the best movie version of the play, did intrigue him, and he rewrote it. And all I did was make it shorter. He did a rewrite based on what we talked about, and then I – on my computer, literally – just subtracted some scenes that I thought were redundant: just tightened it a bit. I mean, I didn't add any dialogue, I might have on the set a little bit once or twice or something, but basically it was his screenplay. So this was a case where there was no question of me taking a screenwriting credit, I didn't deserve one.

So in that sense it was like *The Dead Zone*, because it was written to my specification more in the approved Hollywood manner, you know. I can see directors and producers feeling as though they almost wrote the screenplay, because you can get very detailed in your directions to a writer about what you want, and what you don't want, and how the character should feel and so on, but still you're not writing it. And if they sat down by themselves, most of those directors and producers couldn't write a word.

Still, it's a very close involvement, so it really does reflect what I found intriguing about the actual situation. And it brought it much closer to the themes that I find interesting: the themes of transformation and fantasy becoming real, and identity, and a whole bunch of other stuff which I had explored before in different ways. It seemed to me a different context to discuss a lot of the same themes. In a way, the world of China was as fantastic to me as the world of Interzone, except that it existed already, I just had to shoot it. And it was, of course, the first movie really that I've shot out of Canada. Even so, most of it was shot here in Toronto. But the few weeks of it that we shot in China, and in Budapest, and one or two days in Paris, that was serious location shooting of a kind I have never done before.

SG: Of course you're aware that perhaps the main achievement of the movie was not to make this couple a gay couple, which meant that the meaning of the relationship was universal – both heterosexual and homosexual. But if you had made the choice of showing a homosexual couple, I'm not saying it wouldn't have been interesting, but most of the complexity and the mystery of the movie and of their relationship would have been destroyed.

DC: No, I agree, because that's what intrigued me about it.

SG: But a lot of gay friends of mine told me the same thing.

DC: Did they? Well that pleases me, because in fact the criticism that I get most about the movie is from straight guys, who say, 'Oh, how could he not know? How could he not know if he's actually fucking this creature?' And I'm saying, 'You're a fool if you think it was not possible.' Of course it was possible, and, of course, maybe the actual guy was a repressed homosexual who needed this fantasy in order to express his homosexuality, but this was at two removes from the real story already: it was a movie of a play about that. I'm also saying, 'It's interesting that you're so sure that all of these mechanical things are obvious, because they're not obvious.' And then you are dependent on the sexual experiences of the person who is talking to you, as to how far you can go in telling them that they have to experience a few more things before they understand that such a deception, especially when it is a kind of mutually-willed deception, is very possible, very possible. It probably happens more often than people like to think.

SG: I'm sure it happens all the time. Suddenly, after ten years, you discover your wife or your husband or your companion is a bastard, a monster.

DC: Yes exactly, not what you thought, not what they appeared to be.

SG: Usually you don't fall in love with someone because he or she is a monster, and then one day you discover he or she really is a monster.

DC: And always was.

SG: **Yeah.**

DC: Was when you met them, but you couldn't see it for various reasons: sometimes because of deliberate deception, sometimes because of your own refusal to accept it. I agree, but the people who can't relate to the movie, they are literalists, you know, and I think, unfortunately, *The Crying Game* put them even more in that frame of mind.

SG: **Of course.**

DC: Because it is a literalist movie. I mean, only when the audience sees the guy's cock do they realise that he's a guy and then they feel betrayed, and it's all very straightforward really. But it's not subtle in certain ways, and it provided a context that encouraged people to say, 'Well it's obvious John Lone is not a woman,' and so on.

SG: **Lacan wrote that love was, strictly speaking, impossible – it was the impossible. But he said that love was based on a sentiment – the translation is, 'Basically I don't want to know.' And it's true. I mean, love is a choice where you mainly choose not to know what is obvious.**

DC: Yeah . . .

SG: **Suddenly a girl is beautiful, and wonderful. Maybe you have seen her for five years, but you have never found her beautiful, and suddenly she is. And all the rest you don't want to know. Lacan is saying that you don't want to know reality, you always choose to live in a symbolic world. And that's why *M. Butterfly* is really a very beautiful movie. Suddenly Gallimard finds the perfect woman, so even if there was a chance for him to know, or discover, he doesn't want to know or discover. He will do everything he can to keep the embodiment of the perfect woman.**

DC: It's amazing though, Serge, how many people – men, it's always men – approach it from a totally macho point of view. I mean, it's almost a threat to them to suggest that a man could fall in love with another man, thinking that it's a woman. So they have to therefore ridicule the movie, and say that the whole premise is ridiculous. And they cannot enter that realm, the symbolic realm or the metaphorical realm, or even the realm of psychological truth that's in the movie. That immediately stops them. The reason they like *The Crying Game* is because it is a woman, basically it is a woman with a cock, so they can accept that sort of up till the moment of sex, because they are fooled too. So it's a sort of macho test, if you can accept this movie then you have failed the test of machismo.

SG: **In French and English, the same word has two different meanings, and it has to do with a major theme of *M. Butterfly*: déception in French is 'disappointment' . . .**

DC: What's the word for 'deception'?

SG: **'Tromperie'. So it's very funny, because if you could have a mutant language combining French and English, to be disappointed would be to realise that you have been deceived, but to be deceived would be to suddenly realise that you didn't want to know in the first place.**

DC: Because then you would be disappointed.

SG: **Because after all, we are not scientists. We are not trying to unravel layers, to discover truth. If that were so we could never feel anything.**

DC: No, because what kind of truth would we look for ? Biological truth? No, it would be impossible to exist, all your circuits would burn out.

Well, the reception of *M. Butterfly* very much disappointed me, I have to say. I knew just from a marketing strategy point of view : the Directors Guild of Canada has a morning session, and you go and you speak about the film that you are working on. And I said at the time, 'I'm very worried about *The Crying Game*.' And at the back was a woman from Warner Brothers, who stood up and said, '*The Crying Game* is just a little film, it won't be a problem.' And I said, 'No, I think it is going to be a problem.' And sure enough, it became more and more popular and won

Oscars. You know, I got lucky with *The Fly* and with *Scanners* when they were released. I think maybe even *Dead Ringers* was the Number One film for a week or something. I think I have had three Number Ones, but I'm not 100 percent sure of that. I'd have to check, it's not something I'm obsessed with. It's just a question of what other films are around. So I've had some luck, and then I've had these disappointments, where the timing of my film has been very negative for the success of the film. *Farewell My Concubine* was about a gay couple in the Peking Opera – now how many films do you see about this sort of thing? So those two or three films were often reviewed together, with *M. Butterfly* being considered the least of the films. It's just odd, because the level I was attacking the subject on was quite different from those other ones. But people couldn't see it, because the strength of these other two films was very strictly about gay, deceptive females, in drag, all of that stuff.

SG: **When we started this series of interviews, we were talking of all these Hollywood films which work like machines. We have an expression in French, 'You're not chewing food for the audience.' In the case of *M. Butterfly*, however, you could also have chosen to push one or two buttons here and there. I can really see how a Hollywood director would have shot exactly the same script. I mean, you have to show, once in a while, because of course people feel a bit lost. It's the opposite of a Hollywood movie, where if you are a bit puzzled at some point, at the end you really know where you are. At the end of *M. Butterfly*, it's even worse than at the beginning.**

DC: Well, I wouldn't have problems in including some of those buttons, if it didn't unbalance or destroy the subtlety or the mystery in other parts. And you know, in the horror films, I have certainly done my share of having things jump at you from the side of the frame so [that] you jump. These are also classic Hollywood filmmaking moments, and I know how to do them, and I have done them. And when they work to the film's advantage – as they do for example in *The Fly*, the man leaving his fingernail marks on your hand – then I don't have any qualms about using them. They're in the nature of the flow of the movie, and it feels legitimate, and not like a betrayal or a sellout or anything like that. But movies like *M. Butterfly* for me are all subtlety, all subtlety. The politics are mixed in, but it should nonetheless be subtle, which is what I didn't like about the play: the politics were very unsubtle, they were very politically correct. And as I say, David Hwang was very congenial and happy to play, and I feel that he likes the movie, I think he was very happy with the movie.

But I was disappointed that it got no critical support. This is when critics say that they have no power, for certain films – I mean, maybe with *Armageddon* it doesn't matter, but with certain films critical support matters. And I remember after the first weekend, we were dead. Even before, because they knew that this was a movie which needed critical support. The previews, as usual with me, were not great. In this case they weren't horrible, but they were not great. If I had gotten a couple of major critics in the US to support the film . . . They [the distributors] directly said to me that there was no critical support for the film. So they basically cut their losses. They released it, but not with much enthusiasm, and not with much advertising, and they were right in as much as there wasn't much critical support. So that was it. And I was disappointed, and remained so. You don't forget these things.

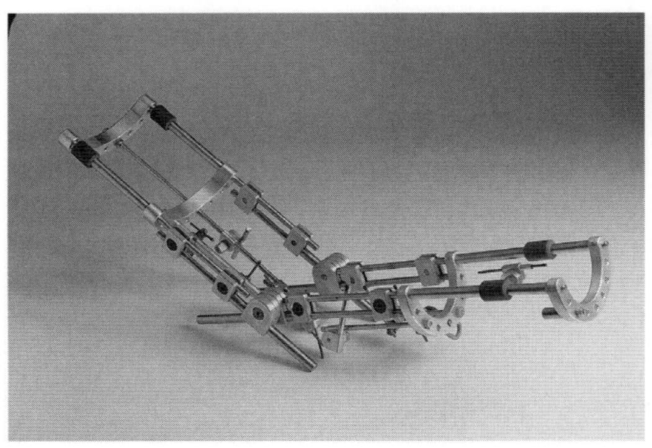

Ever More

experimental

Crash

Crash by J. G. Ballard was the book event of the seventies, a kind of punk text where the author, in his preface, stated his intention to invent a new form of pornography. Who other than Cronenberg, with his passion for motor sports, marginal sexuality and the 'man-machine fusion', would have been able to handle such a project?

But after the two commercial failures of *Naked Lunch* and *M. Butterfly*, the greater opportunities to finance the film which might have come earlier in his career had disappeared. So it was with very limited means that he began this new adventure: an intensive casting process that attracted no big names; some replicas of old cars, some wrecked cars; special effects that were, for the most part, confined to stunts; simple shooting equipment; some well-executed special makeup, and a musical score by his old colleague Howard Shore – recorded in a small studio without a symphony orchestra, but with several guitars and some samplings of industrial noise. It was almost an independent film.

The script was fairly faithful to the original text, yet Cronenberg metamorphosed *Crash* into one of the most important films of the decade, a descent into the psychopathology of sexual fascination, with no linear narrative, plot twists or gory effects – an organically pure and irreducible fantasy. Francis Ford Coppola's award of a special prize to the film at the Cannes Festival sparked an outcry among the 'moral majority' (although the sexual imagery in the film was no more extreme than anything seen on television throughout the West after eleven at night), and even led to the film being banned in certain parts of London, where its release was delayed. It must be said that, during a scene where James Spader and Deborah Unger are lying on a bed (in a room that recalls that in *Videodrome*), discussing the acts they would like to perform with Vaughan (Elias Koteas), using words that are not crude but, on the contrary, clinical, one might have the Sadeian sensation that the phrases are inscribing themselves on the very 'flesh' of the screen (the word made flesh or the flesh made word?).

When Sandra Tucker, Cronenberg's assistant and producer, told me that the director had arranged a screening of Jean-Luc Godard's *Weekend* before the first day's shooting, it confirmed something that had, until then, been a mere intuition: Cronenberg, avant-gardist though he is, is more and more in search of a form of modernist classicism, so to speak. He needs also to recapture the lost era of North American cinema in relation to what was happening in Europe during his youth, like all the generation of filmmakers who came from the film schools of the United States, but who, for the most part, seem rather keener on rapidly attaining financial recognition or status.

Crash will probably have no descendants. Cronenberg is not one of those who create schools or movements – even if his influence has become increasingly important for aspiring young filmmakers and, above all, in art schools. For, in the purest sense of the term, he is an *auteur* and not a master, great or small, of a genre or a style. One day I showed a videotape of *Crash* to a friend of mine, a noted contemporary painter. Underlining the points the film had in common with certain recent artworks, he said simply, 'It is contemporary art as we would like it to be.'

Above: *Metal prosthetics created by Stephan Dupuis: in his most experimental latter-day film, Cronenberg observes the limits of desire in our time with a frankness far removed from the Hollywood narrative.* **Opposite:** *Elias Koteas, favourite actor of Atom Egoyan, 'the other Toronto cineaste', incarnates Vaughan as a fantasist obsessed with accidents and inhabiting the legend of James Dean as a kind of game.*

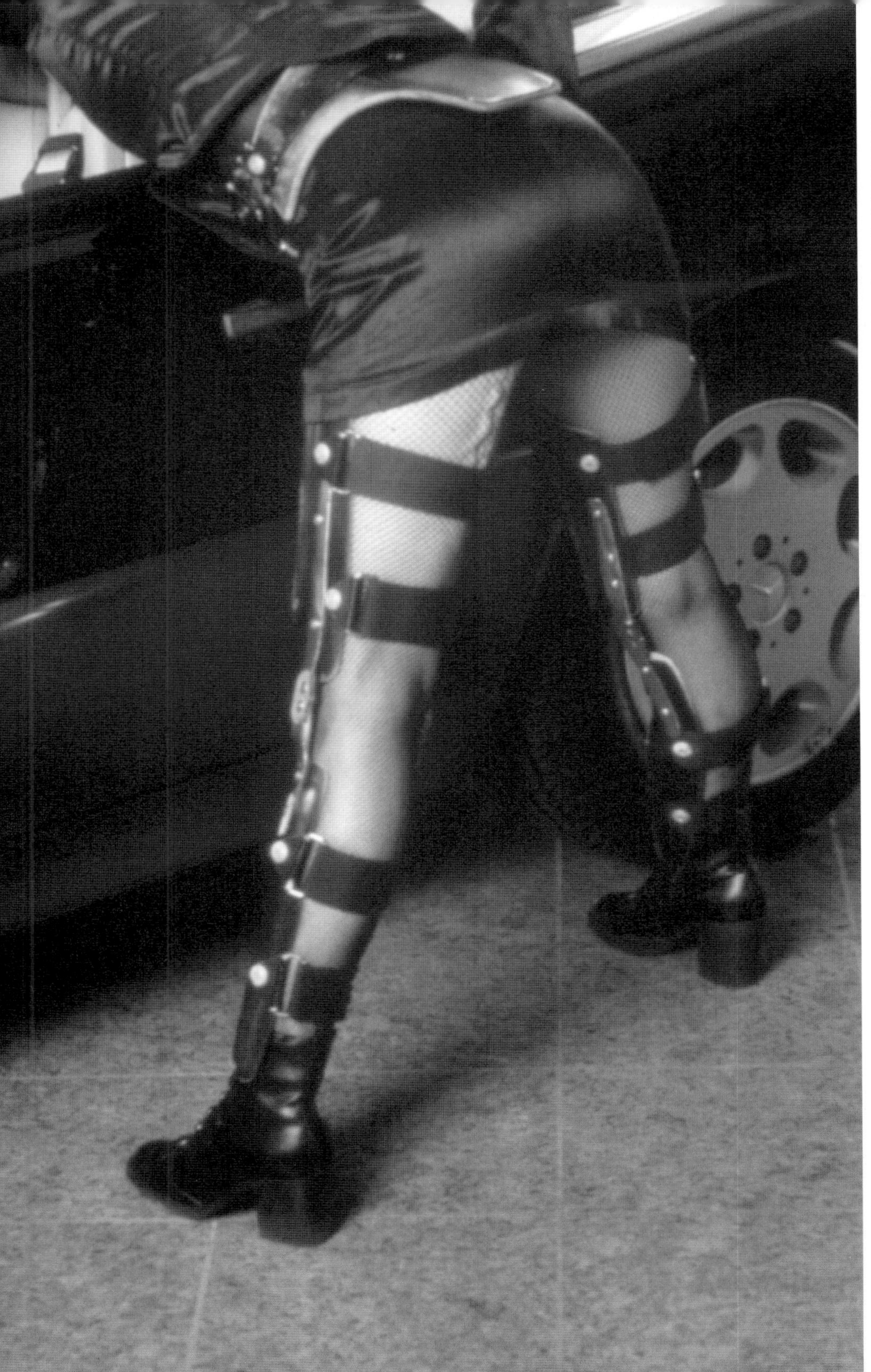

Opposite page: James Spader (as J. G. Ballard), a producer of television commercials who discovers, in the aftermath of an accident, troubling connections between sensual pleasure and death. Deborah Unger (Catherine Ballard), a woman on the edge of frigidity, who gives way to her husband's pathological fantasies in order to revive their conjugal life. Holly Hunter (Dr. Remington), who Ballard has made a widow during the accident, relives the perfect moment when the petite mort ('little death') and death itself become amazingly one.

This page: Rosanna Arquette (Gabrielle), handicapped after an accident, has discovered new instruments of sensuality. She provokes the discovery of a new eroticism when her 'new flesh' melds with the surgical steel of her prostheses.

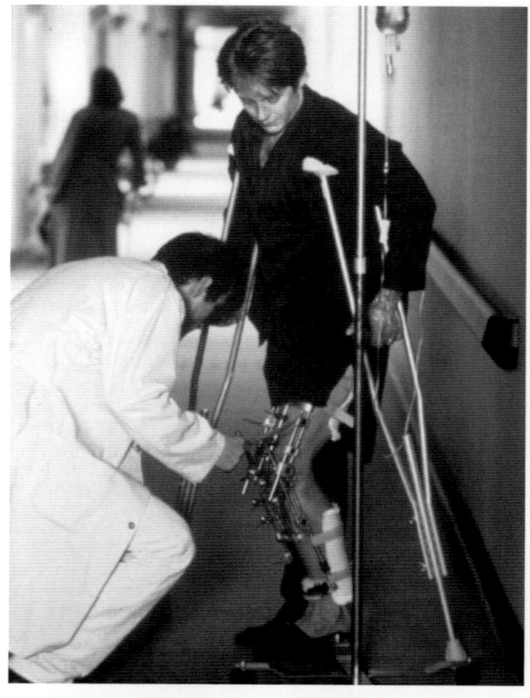

SG: So then there was *Crash*. When we discussed it in the past, you told me how the book had been important for you.

DC: No, it hadn't been. It was different with *Crash*. Here's the story. This is different from *Naked Lunch*, obviously. I had not read J. G. Ballard, and the first time I heard of *Crash* was once again ten years before I made [the film]. And I got a letter from a critic who I had done an interview with – I can't remember her name, I think I met her in Philadelphia or Chicago maybe, when I was on the road for some movie, it might even have been as far back as *Scanners*. And she said that I should really make a movie of *Crash*, this J. G. Ballard novel. And that was the first that I had heard of Ballard or *Crash*, I have to admit. I might have heard of Ballard as a science fiction writer. And I think she might have sent me a copy of it, and I didn't read it. And then Jeremy Thomas started to talk to me about *Crash*, and he said he knew Ballard and that I should . . . He might have even talked to me about that before we did *Naked Lunch* together.

And then I started to read *Crash*. And I read about half of it, and I put it away because it was disturbing and I just, I don't know, I just couldn't finish the book. And I said to Jeremy, 'I can't read this, I can't make this,' and so we forgot about it. And then at a certain point I picked up the book again, I don't remember why, and I read the other half, and then I read it again. And at that time, I felt that it was obviously an extraordinary book, but not one that you like, which didn't bother me. You don't like it exactly, it's not a likeable book, but not that that matters. And then one day, I was talking to Jeremy about something completely different and I said, 'You know, I think we should make *Crash*.'

Top: Vaughan kneels before Ballard – out of respect for his mutilated flesh, or fascination with the beauty of cold metal? Left: An urban freeway in Toronto: The film incessantly sets down the metaphor that circulation of traffic = circulation of the blood. The pulsating traffic rhythms of this strange story led Howard Shore to create a musical score mixing metallic instruments (layers of electric guitars) and industrial noises with an extraordinary techno-lyricism.

And it was like what happened with *Naked Lunch*, I surprised myself saying that. That had happened with *The Dead Zone* too, I was sure that it was finished with, and that I didn't want it, and when it came back up again I just sort of spontaneously said, 'Yes, I think I would like to do it.' So, obviously, the book sits there for a while, and then suddenly it establishes itself in your nervous system somehow as a legitimate thing, and with enough force to make it possible to make it into a movie, because you . . . It needs to occupy a very deep part of you for me, it can't be a superficial thing. You have to have passion for it and it has to have meaning. You know that you are going to spend a few years fighting for it, trying to make it work, and if it's not really deeply embedded in you, then you won't have the energy or the desire and the passion to carry it through. So I guess I have to wait until it settles to that point, and then suddenly it becomes obvious that you must do it.

Jeremy said, 'OK, let's do it.' And I procrastinated for a couple of years before I sat down to write the script, I think I was afraid to write the script, thinking about *Naked Lunch* and how long it had taken me to write that. Because of course, *Naked Lunch* was quite a different . . . Well, I didn't know, I hadn't read anything else by Ballard when I wrote the script. I had read some interviews with him and so on, but I had only read the [one] book. But Jeremy did introduce me to Ballard, as he had done with Burroughs. And of course I got along very well with Ballard, he is a delightful man, and a lovely guy, and obviously quite different from Burroughs, he is a much more conventional man in terms of his day-to-day life.

And when I started to write the book – that's a good Freudian slip – when I started to write the screenplay, to my surprise, it went very quickly. I thought that I would have to do what I had done with Burroughs: to bring in other writings, to bring in I didn't know what. Somehow I didn't think that the book was going to be enough, but it went a completely different way. With *Naked Lunch*, it was expanding into other areas of Burroughs, and Jane Bowles and Paul Bowles, and with this it contracted to this sort of dark, black hole, it was so dense that it distilled beautifully. I really was using the dialogue from the book, which, when you first read it, seems very artificial. It doesn't seem like movie dialogue, but then it somehow was perfect: you didn't want naturalistic dialogue because it was not a naturalistic movie. So suddenly I was using the dialogue, I was using bits and pieces of the descriptions that Ballard wrote to describe the various cars. They are all embedded in the screenplay, in a way he wrote half the screenplay, really. And it had much more of a narrative shape than I ever suspected. When I read it, it didn't ever seem that it had a coherent narrative, but it did. So once I had accepted that I was writing it, it was a very short, compact screenplay, as the book is, and it went very easily, and I really made only two changes. One was the beginning and one was the end. I added the scene at the end, which does not exist in the book, and I changed some details at the beginning.

And then, when I made the movie, I shot all of the script, but I did throw away a couple of scenes that do exist in the book that seemed to be redundant in the movie: a scene in a lingerie store with her [Deborah Kara Unger's] assistant whom she is sort of flirting with, and so on.

So it was once again yet another kind of writing experience. I mean, it seems to me, as many screenplays as I have written, each one has been a totally different experience, which is good and bad. It's good in that you are not going to get bored by the process, but it's bad in that I never know how it's going to work: whether it's going to go quickly, whether it's going to take a long time, whether it's going to be joyful or whether it's going to be mainly painful, it's always different. And as I get older and things change, it becomes different because it's also three or four years between screenplays, and sometimes more. And so I sometimes can't even remember how to type.

SG: *Crash* is your most radical movie, and I have always wondered if you knew it when you started the project.

DC: Yes, it was obvious. I mean we all knew, and the actors knew, everybody knew. You can't read that screenplay and not know. What I didn't, of course, quite know was how potent all of this stuff still was, because the book was over twenty years old when I started to make the movie. And one might have felt that the existence of Ballard and all his other writings – *The Atrocity Exhibition*, and everything else he had written about, there's a lot of material on Ballard and he has written a lot of books . . . I thought that doing a movie that accurately, which was as radical as the book, would not have produced such a radical result, just because his sensibility had been around so long. And many things had changed, there had been a lot of atrocities out in the open since he wrote that book, sexual and otherwise. And I thought that people would be more sophisticated now.

SG: We were discussing that the other day, how things that were obvious in the sixties have suddenly become the object of scandal now. And at the same time, I remember six months ago I saw a TV programme about an S&M restaurant in New York, where you actually get whipped at your table. And this is completely acceptable. But perhaps, if *Crash* had been made in the more or less underground climate of the sixties, it would have been accepted as a part of this cultural movement. But then, suddenly, in the nineties a lot of people react . . .

DC: Well you know, it's mysterious on many levels . . . I mean, it's gratifying in a way, because you don't want your picture to be taken as some kind of antique gesture to the past, that is kind of cute, but that's all. But on the other hand . . . Maybe it has to do with the place of cinema, because you can see an S&M restaurant on TV or even in movies, but as a joke or played humorously. It's almost an indication of how conservative film has gotten. Because of the Hollywood influence, and because of the big money and the corporate takeovers of all the film studios, film has become a medium of reaction. And so if you throw something in the middle of it that is only slightly radical, I think, the radicalness of it is accentuated by the fact that you are throwing it into the middle of this medium. I mean, books that are written now are incredibly [radical], much worse by far, and they don't get banned, they don't cause much of a stir.

SG: For example, a book like *American Psycho* would have had no chance of being published in the 1950s.

DC: That's correct, that's correct.

SG: When you think that *Lolita* was banned then . . . I mean, people were reading Sade, but 'sous le manteau', as we say, you couldn't find it in bookstores.

DC: Well, I really felt that it had to do more with cinema than with what the movie was saying. It's true the movie is saying some hard things, which obviously struck a nerve in many people. But, in terms of what you see on the screen, I could turn on this TV set and see way more extreme stuff any night, without even accessing the porno channels. So it's odd. But then I take it as a compliment, because obviously the tone of the movie draws people in, puts them in a certain mindset where they are vulnerable to the message the movie is giving, which is about sex and death, and not really so much about violence, but about the physicalness of us and our existence. And it makes people very insecure and threatens them. And I suppose that is an indication of the fact that the movie works. Even though, as I say, there's not one still that you could take out of the movie that really is shocking, compared with a lot of other things that are around.

SG: I don't know if I told you, but I was asked by the French cultural services in London, the week *Crash* was released in England, to go to

the French Cultural Centre to present *Crash*. And there were a lot of people – in particular, the president of the British board of censors – and I didn't want to make a speech. So I did something which is exactly what we have been talking about. I asked a girl to read the English translation of that famous page of *Madame Bovary*, which started the censorship trial.
DC: Which page is that? When she dies at the end?

SG: **No, no, no, you should re-read it because it's . . .**
DC: I just read it very recently

SG: **OK, so you remember: it's when Emma goes in the cab with the young guy, and Flaubert describes very precisely what they will not see. So you have really a very cinematic mental image: they get in the cab, shut the blind, and then Flaubert writes that it's a pity because they won't see the cathedral, etc. At no time does he describe what's happening in the cab, of course they are making it, but there's not even one word. If you associate certain words together, you can have a fair idea of what's happening, and the driver has a certain reaction. But you know, when the French censors read that page they found it pornographic, and that's why eventually the trial stopped. Because at one time they – maybe in the nineteenth century they were a bit more intelligent – suddenly discovered . . .**
DC: That there was nothing there.

SG: **No, and the whole trial started because really they had projected [their own perceptions onto the page].**
DC: Well, there was another thing about *Madame Bovary*. I've just been reading this book called *Bad Girls and Sick Boys*. The woman who wrote this book mentions that they were also very disturbed by the description of the dead Madame Bovary, where her mouth was just this round black hole that this fluid came out of. They found that so disturbing, because he was describing a corpse and not her soul escaping. I also found that very interesting, that that should be so offensive and so disturbing and so threatening, that passage of description which is very powerful. It's almost religious censorship at that point, not sexual.

SG: **It's obvious that it's in the censor's mind, everything is there, but usually it's always as pointless as the British censors' reaction to *Crash*. I mean, even in England they have soft porn on TV, even in very popular programmes. I think everything that's inventive, as Flaubert was in his time, as *Crash* was, produces this reaction: people say, 'There must be something wrong.'**
DC: And what is pathetic about that are the attempts to find the reasons for censoring. I remember seeing this guy named John Bull, if you can believe it, like the symbolic character for Britain. This guy was on the council for Westminster, obviously not a very well-educated man, but he was talking about 'road rage'. He was sure that people would see this movie and then they would commit more road rage: they would jump out of their cars and beat each other. And then he went on to admit that he kind of liked the movie, I mean, he was as simple and straightforward as any man in Westminster – he wasn't such an elite whatever – but he started thinking that he had to protect other people who were not like him, who were lesser than him. He was just grasping desperately at things, to find a way. And it got very ridiculous, with one guy writing about how sex with cripples was disgusting. And he thought he had everybody on his side, he was writing for a very conservative paper, and then of course he got many letters from the disabled, who were very upset when he said that. And then they started to make Rosanna Arquette's character a heroic figure, because she is crippled and disabled, but she is still fully sexual and she is going to enjoy sex. Then they had radio discussions with the

disabled, who were talking about sex . . .

SG: Yeah, they told me they organised a special screening for disabled people.
DC: Yeah, they did in England.

SG: And they loved it.
DC: Yes, that's right.

SG: And most of them said it was the first movie where they were treated as . . .
DC: . . . sexual beings, which they are but no one wants to admit to that. Yeah, I mean there was an article in the paper where a woman said that if you're disabled and you want to have sex, you have to first of all have a good sense of humour, because funny things will happen and you have to be physically pretty flexible. And went on and on in great detail, saying that the depiction in the movie was quite accurate. But I mean, even that was silly – of course, I'm happy to have allies wherever I can find them. But it was interesting to see the politics shift: this guy thinking that he was going to get everybody on his side, and then suddenly he made a politically incorrect statement, even though he was trying to use political correctness to beat me.

SG: But the other radical aspect of the movie is, as they say in university, the narrative strategy, which verges on the non-narrative.
DC: I think it's because you have recognised stars: you have [James] Spader, you have Holly Hunter, you have Rosanna Arquette. These are recognisable people who have been in Hollywood movies, they are acknowledged industry people, even though people don't understand how radical Spader and Holly Hunter and Rosanna really are. But they have all had movies, you know. And the movie begins like a sort of normal movie, looks pretty good, and it has these actors. And then suddenly they are saying and doing these things, it's not progressing the way a normal movie does, and the characters don't work like real characters from a Hollywood movie. I think that's part of it, it's that people are sucked into thinking that maybe they are going to see a 'real' movie in that Hollywood sense, and then it's not a 'real' movie. It's some weird art thing, but it keeps looking like a movie, and these actors are still the same. You know the way people were saying they couldn't believe an Oscar winner like Holly Hunter would allow herself to blah, blah. So they feel betrayed, and tricked, and deceived, and caught in something ugly.

I did a show here with a woman who used to be one of those airplane reporters, she would report on traffic from an airplane, now she's got her own talk-show. She saw the movie with her sixteen year-old son, who was horrified, and they both walked out. She told me it was like looking in the toilet. Mind you, I knew she hated it, she told me she did, but I said I'd do the show anyway. But I was going to say, doctors tell you that you have to look in the toilet if you want to know what's going on inside, so it's not such a horrible thing. But it was that kind of thing, I mean she was just repulsed completely and had no way of connecting with the movie.

And of course, I had to fight to keep the movie the way it was because some people got nervous and wanted to add a voice-over, the traditional cop-out. And I was saying, 'A voice-over of what? I mean, do you want someone to read from the novel? Have you read the novel?' Of course, he had read the novel, but he somehow felt that you could explain the movie so people would get it. The first reaction from Bob Shay at New Line was, 'I don't know how people are going to be able to access this movie.' That was his word, and that had to do, of course, with the structure and everything else. But to me they are not separate things, the film is an integral whole. If it's working then it's all an organic whole, you can't separate the lungs from the muscles, etc. They all have to work together, or you have nothing. So I was very happy with the movie, and I knew that it was

Above: : Ballard (James Spader) and Dr. Remington (Holly Hunter) rediscover their erotic functions in the car, the traditional venue for first love among North American adolescents. Left: Deborah Unger never looks at her husband as she disrobes and continues to search for her next orgasm. The phrase that opens and closes the film encapsulates her contemporary frustration: 'Maybe the next one, baby!'

the way that it should be, and that it had to be like that, and whatever was going to happen would happen.

SG: **It's very funny, but it's the first time I noticed that you have never used a voice-over in one of your movies.**
DC: No.

SG: **That's very interesting, because only last night I was reading this Kubrick biography. In the beginning, there was always someone around him, a producer friend, who said to him that because he wasn't very good with actors, and the movie was a little too complicated, he should add a voice-over. And he would. Because he would prefer to add a voice-over . . .**
DC: Than to change the other things.

SG: **Yeah. But it's true that a lot of critics say that, except with very specific movies, the voice-over is always, I wouldn't say a sellout, but . . .**
DC: It's a cop-out.

SG: **Yeah.**
DC: It does work in some movies, it worked in *Badlands*, for example, and there are other movies where you almost don't even notice that it's there.

David Cronenberg filming Crash, in the cold and damp of the Ontario winter. Rohmer might have called the work a 'winter's tale', as Peter Suschitzky complemented the harrowing tone with a drained twilight feel.

SG: **Well in *Taxi Driver* it works.**
DC: Yeah, I didn't even remember that there was a voice-over, but of course there is.

SG: **It starts from the beginning.**
DC: Yeah. And it is interesting that it should be *Taxi Driver*, which is not based on a novel. Because mostly voice-over is used to compensate for what film can't do, which is that inner voice, being inside the head of a person.

SG: **But there was a lot of *film noir* with voice-overs.**
DC: Yeah.

SG: **In the 1940s and 1950s, so it is a kind of genre literature...**
DC: And even *Sunset Boulevard* has a voice-over from a dead person, which *American Beauty* does too. So that's a cheat, but it's kind of an entertaining cheat that people accept. 'So there I was lying dead in the pool,' you know. I avoid it but I don't know why. I do know that I think of it as a cop-out, and when Bob Shay said, 'I'm going to suggest something to you that you're going to hate,' I said, 'You're going to say voice-over.' And he said, 'Yes, that's right.' It's like a reflex whenever you have done an adaptation of a novel. He was familiar with the novel, and he knew that the novel was as difficult, but he somehow hoped that I could explain the movie. *Blade Runner* is a classic case of a horrible voice-over that kind of ruined a movie. There were other things that ruined it too, that's a very flawed movie, but that was a big flaw that wasn't originally intended. It's kind of entertaining, because you can hear that Harrison Ford is hating to do this voice-over, you can hear it in his voice. And yet I love that inner-voice so much. Maybe it's because I love what you can do in a novel that I have too much respect for it to try and cheat it into a movie. I won't say that I would never use, it though. If I found it coming naturally, I would use it.

SG: **But you know, it's exactly like the legend about Hitchcock's total control of the movie. The *Nouvelle Vague* used only voice-overs in**

the beginning, but they only used them because they had no money and a 16mm camera without sound . . .
DC: If you look at my first two feature-length films, *Stereo* and *Crimes of the Future*, they have voice-overs for exactly the same reason. But in my first two 16mm movies, I was finally able to use an Auricon which allowed me to do sync sound. So *Stereo* and *Crimes of the Future* are two movies on which I actually did use voice-overs.

SG: **That reminds me of one of the first Godard movies, a short, *Charlotte et son jules*. He had Belmondo, who at the time was a wonderful actor, and there is dialogue, but when you hear the voice of Belmondo's character, it's Godard. Because he did the shoot and there was no direct sound, and Belmondo went away . . . It's always funny when you hear people theorise about his use of sound in that movie, when it really was an accident of circumstance.**
DC: Or physically necessary, but not even desired. Well, as an artist, it's a good strategy to make a triumph out of something that initially was a disaster. If you can carry it off, it's a good trick.

SG: **Maybe that was behind the *auteur* theory. I really don't know if a lot of artists are looking for positive disasters.**
DC: But it finds them anyway, so you might as well make it your strength. It's easier to say, 'I want it this way,' than to say, 'I hate this but there's nothing I can do about it.'

SG: **Was *Crash*, for you, a way of doing something you would have done, let's say, in the 1970s, but that you couldn't afford to do when you were a young, unknown filmmaker?**
DC: No. Because I wouldn't have thought of it in terms of money, because there are more car crashes in *Scanners*, probably. That's pretty action-heavy . . .

SG: **But I'm talking of the radical narrative, or**

Vaughan (Elias Koteas), high priest of contemporary mythmaking, reconstructs the fatal accident of James Dean. Colin Seagrave (Peter MacNeill) and Vaughan, behind the wheel of the legendary Porsche, in a staged version of the famous accident. Seagrave, the stuntman, dreams of a beautiful death.

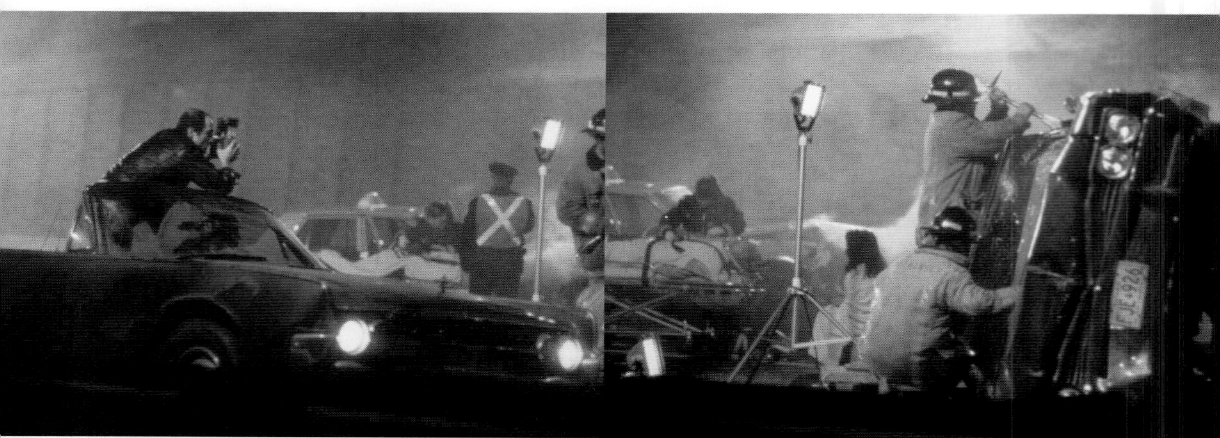

The multiple pile-up sequence: Inspired by road travel and Jean-Luc Godard's Weekend, the scene is a piece of pure lyrical cinematography.

non-narrative, of *Crash*.
DC: I don't think so. I mean, in the 1970s I was struggling to survive and I was also learning my own craft. And the plot, for example, of *Rabid* is quite complex. It was very difficult to sort out because you have all these things: there was the city and the military, etc. So I was learning how to do all those things, and each time I did it, of course, it was the first time for me to do it. So no, I don't think I ever – certainly I wasn't thinking about *Crash*. No, I don't think so. I never had that feeling.

SG: You say that *The Fly* was ultimately an opera, but the same could be true of *Crash*.
DC: Except that it doesn't have operatic music. But in what sense do you mean that?

SG: The rhythm is very musical, and there are recurrent musical phrases. Of course it's a metaphor, but it could very well be a contemporary opera or an oratorio.
DC: It would make a nice opera, I think.

SG: And it's as extreme as certain operas.
DC: Also it's true that the plot structure of most operas is quite strange, I mean it [*Crash*] really is quite strange and truncated and compressed. Yeah, operas are quite odd narratively, because they have other demands made on them. But they are even odd in terms of character studies: they are not really character studies, and yet they are but they aren't, you know.

SG: *Tosca* is, for example – I know it was inspired by a French play, but it couldn't survive without music and rhythms.
DC: Yeah, there's not much there [otherwise] . . .

SG: You said somewhere in an interview, 'All my movies are autobiographical.'
DC: I don't know if I can remember what I meant by that. I think it all comes from your life experience. I didn't mean it in the classical sense of these are incidents that happened to me in my life. But it filters through my sensibility, my nervous system, my visual sense. All of that comes only from my life experiences. That includes seeing other movies, of course. That includes reading books. So even if I'm inspired by something that I've read, I consider that autobiographical in that sense. I'm just really trying to say that the idea of personal film-making is to me inevitable. I think [it is] for anybody. It's difficult, in other words, to talk about true autobiographical film-making as opposed to

false, or personal films as opposed to distant films. Yet at the same time it's true, that with certain filmmakers you really get a sense of that actual person. Somehow through the course of their work, there's always an identifiable feel about it. With some very good professional filmmakers who are still journeyman filmmakers, you don't get that feeling. There's a kind of impersonal something there. So I'm not sure where that leaves us. In a sense, I think even a Hollywood journeyman filmmaker should . . . you know, it's the old *auteur* question. And it's still debatable. Is Joel Schumacher an *auteur*? I don't know. It's an argument.

SG: **But since we've already said that, for you, truth comes from the body, or returns to the body at one stage, I'm not going to ask you what has been asked of Bill Clinton, of course – but would you say that, in a way, you have lived some kind of experiences in your life, bodily experiences, that could be related to your movies? I won't be more indiscreet than that.**

DC: Yeah . . . Yes, I think so, but it's the experiences most people have. It's sex, of course, but it's also food. It's eating. It's defecation. It's problems with your ears, and the wax in your ears, and it's not being able to see, and having to wear glasses, and supplement your senses with the telephone, and having athlete's foot or an ingrown toenail. It's nothing necessarily more exotic than the normal life that people live of the body. The difference is, I think, that I'm very aware of it, and I find metaphorical value in it. Whereas for most people it's just an annoyance, perhaps something they have to deal with, brushing their teeth or whatever, to get to the real stuff of the day, which is their work, their business, their whatever it is that they do. To me it's the other way around. The body stuff is the real stuff. It's the real process of existing and living, and the other stuff is a diversion, it's a distraction from what's happening with your body, including of course death, and the advancement towards mortality, which is the thing that we ultimately are trying to evade in every possible way. Avoid thinking about it. And evade the reality of it. Maybe that's really what I think I meant, when I talked about my films being autobiographical. Of course, I cannot perceive of a filmmaker who is not working to make his films out of that kind of centred thing. It's just different. It's not necessarily inferior. It's just another kind of film-making.

SG: **Antonin Artaud said in one of his texts: 'I, in my body, know all.'**

DC: Yes, I like that. It's wonderful.

SG: **I'm sure you've been asked this question**

Top: Women together – the film was premiered at the Cannes Film Festival, before a jury presided over by Francis Coppola, and won a special prize for its 'audacity'. As the result of a campaign started by the tabloid press, Crash was subjected to a total ban from certain areas of London for a year.

many, many times: What is the real connection between David Cronenberg, the very civilised individual one can see in everyday life, and his work? There seems to be such a great distance. I'm not saying that people expect to see Frankenstein, or a vampire, but almost.

DC: Or they expect me to be obsessed with the grotesque and the ugly and the repulsive and all that, which I'm not. I mean, I know people who are, and they're not me. I have such a direct connection with what my films are, but it is a connection and it does seem to come out of me, but it's not me. This is the eternal mystery of art, as far as I can see. It's of you, but it's not you. It's not identical with you. It's not the same thing as you. I find there's any number of examples . . . Mozart was not like his music. People would be surprised to meet Mozart, having only heard his music. And I think it's just one of the mysteries of what art is. There is a part of it that seems to come from someplace else. Physically it doesn't come from someplace else . . . We have antennae that are sensitised to different things. What we take into our bodies and our nervous systems is so vast, and there's a surplus that spills over from us. The reason it goes into the art is that it can't be incorporated into the life. That's really the way I feel, for me anyway. It's the spill-over, somehow, of something that has to go somewhere. In my case it goes in my art, but it's not in my life. It's not in my life that way at all.

Opposite page: The end of Vaughan: Vaughan is thrown from a Lincoln Continental (resembling that in which President Kennedy died), in the course of his self-inflicted death.

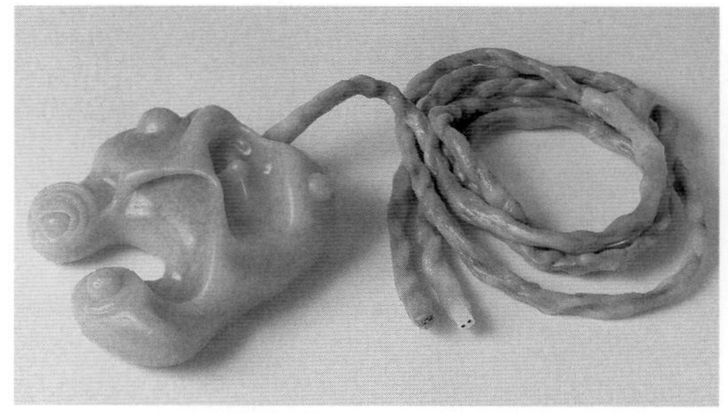

The Creator
and his creations
eXistenZ

Cronenberg always defines himself as an existential filmmaker. With *eXistenZ*, we undoubtedly approach a clearer notion of this concept. The film may seem almost as theoretical as a design sketch, but it is no less wonderfully modern. This is because it endlessly sets up a series of hyphotheses, only to destroy each one as it goes along.

Allegra Geller (the magnificent Jennifer Jason Lee, who Cronenberg fought for to have among his cast) is the incarnation of the supreme state of the artist: one who literally creates other worlds. In the improbable future that Cronenberg paints (a hypertechnological civilisation which is, paradoxically, depicted in a rural setting), she is a mystical figure, a 'goddess', who builds alternative universes thanks to an organic console with which she has an autoerotic relationship, echoing certain pages of Burroughs. She has to battle against a terrorist organisation, the 'realists', who take it upon themselves to forbid any form of fantasy or delirium, in order to return definitively to 'reality'. But where is this reality? In whose head, exactly, is this intrigue taking place?

In the guise of a modest science fiction tale, Cronenberg launches an offensive on all rational narrative, so much so that the creator is no more than a character, and we discover, to our astonishment, that if the story has no end, it also – and this is a lot rarer – has no beginning! Just as the phrase, 'Be afraid, be very afraid!' has been quoted hundreds of times since it was first heard in *The Fly*, 'Are we still in the game?' risks becoming a cult movie catch-phrase. The filmmaker has often said that the central idea for the film came to him while interviewing Salman Rushdie (the writer who was living in a different time and space from the mullahs who condemned him to death), who had paid him a compliment in an article where he described the death of Princess Diana as a kind of remake of *Crash*!

We are already, without always knowing it, characters from *eXistenZ*, just as we have since discovered that we were living in *Videodrome*. Even if he denies it, Cronenberg well knows, deep down, that all true artists are prophets. (This is what Ian Holm, as Frost in *Naked Lunch*, says of Bill Lee, that imaginary William Burroughs who is more 'real' than the real one.) Imperceptibly, reality has begun to resemble his films. But *eXistenZ* is also, like all Cronenberg's work, a profoundly refined reflection on the cinema where each shot, even the most seemingly banal, seizes us with its intelligence and beauty. (I am thinking of the flight of Allegra and Pikul in the Land Rover through the nocturnal forest that calls to mind Hitchcock's *North by Northwest*, or the line of workers moving mechanically to the Trout Farm workshop at the Chinese Restaurant which evokes Fritz Lang's *Metropolis*.)

Cronenberg's presence at the peripheries of Hollywood raises the question, 'Is cinema a popular art-form?' If this is the case, can we hope for authentic artists to transgress the norm and shun repetitive mediocrity? The fact that Cronenberg has done this for 30 years would seem to give us some kind of hope. Even if it is always the result of a misunderstanding, his notoriety, while no guarantee, has preserved him up to now. His vitality, his mordant but uncondescending irony, and his fantastic imagination gain Cronenberg new admirers with each new generation, all of them astonished to discover, on late-night television, on

Above: *Game-Pod connected to an UmbyCord, created by Stephan Dupuis. The console of the organic game is part animal and part machine, plugging directly into the nervous system.* **Left:** *David Cronenberg prepares to depart on a new voyage into a cinema that can only be defined as 'existentialist'.*

video and, when possible, at the cinema, films that are so modern and so deviant that they seem to come from elsewhere. Just as Max Renn learns that the Videodrome broadcast does not come from the Far East, but from Pittsburgh . . . next door!

SG: The central character in *eXistenZ* is someone who designs and creates illusions, virtual games.
DC: I think there are some very direct references. Allegra Geller, the character that Jennifer Jason Leigh plays, is a filmmaker, an artist, in a new medium that I'm creating for the film. But she does represent the artist, although the film does go through several spirals.

SG: I mean she gets lost in the fiction.
DC: Well, in the end we're not sure whether she really is the artist after all. It's interesting. As a director, as a creative person, you sometimes wonder if you are really the artist after all. Is that where it comes from? I mean, with somebody like Mozart the feeling was that he was just a conduit for some cosmic musicologist, music creator. When we talk about someone who, for no reason, shows talent, we say, 'For no reason this man was able to be a filmmaker.' 'For no reason this man was a wonderful poet.' That's what I think we mean. Where is the agency there? Who is the real agent? Who is the conduit? That's all very mysterious and exciting. And, of course, as one who wants to create and has the urge to create, you are really dealing with that all the time, whether consciously or unconsciously. So I do talk about that in many ways in *eXistenZ*.

SG: Would you say that as a film director, when you compare your first movies with the last one you just finished, you see an evolution and transformation?
DC: I do, and it's very interesting for me. With my new movie, *eXistenZ*, people say it reminds them somewhat of *Videodrome*. I can see that in a superficial way. I'm wondering though, I think I'm not the same person who made those movies, and when I watch the movies that I've made it's shocking really. I mean it's shocking because it's not a question of not remembering what I did, because I can remember the moments on the set and all of those things, but I'm surprised at what I've done. It seems alien to me. It seems quite strange to me. I find it very difficult. Almost impossible to watch my old movies. I never do. I've recently had to do the commentary on laser disc, and now DVD versions of the film. I talk while I see the movie. And even *Crash*, watching it a year later and talking about it, it's almost as though I'm talking about somebody else's movie. It's very strange. So I do feel that distance, and it's increasing rapidly as I get older.

SG: So maybe it's the answer to my previous question about otherness and sameness. We can see your movie that you made three years ago as something 'other'.
DC: Other. Definitely other. And I can see myself as other too, definitely. It's exciting and it's terrifying at the same time. A bit frightening.

SG: Would you agree that this aspect of your films deals with three different things that are closely connected: reflection, as in one's reflection in a mirror, reproduction, and duplication? You have explored all these aspects of what you define as rebirth since the beginning. Would you agree with that?
DC: Well, it's hard for me to see it like that. It's not like Borges and his obsession with reflection and replication. I don't really want to restrict my thinking to that. I guess you could make a case for it, and you'd have to tell me, because I don't think of it in those terms.

SG: Well, what should we say of *eXistenZ*? It's an original screenplay, yet a lot of people have said it was like the second part of *Videodrome*.
DC: A sequel or throwback.

SG: I would say the second part, because it's

not really a sequel and it's not at all a remake. But let's say that we are almost in the same neighbourhood. And yet one can feel that there is all the experience you have gathered since *Videodrome*.
DC: Yeah. Well it does have a fairly radical structure and a style too. I mean, many people talk about how theatrical it looks, certainly at the beginning – of course, there is a stage there. But the difference certainly is the computer, there is no presence of the computer in *Videodrome* because [at the time] there weren't any to speak of. The whole idea of computers, and computer games, and that kind of fantastic world that people spend a lot of time inhabiting as though it was real, that was the major contributor to the structure of *eXistenZ*. Which was considered to be too radical, really, by Miramax who were distributing it. I mean, they were distributing it, but they really wanted me to change it, and I wouldn't change it. That is why it was put into turnaround at MGM by Frank Mancuso, Sr. It was developed there, but they just felt it was too radical. That's kind of interesting, you know. Some people criticise me on the basis that it's just me doing the same old thing again, and yet within Hollywood it was considered too radical a structure. [They were convinced that] people would be confused, they wouldn't understand the whole shifting of reality, and especially they didn't like the whole shifting of the characters, they didn't like the characters to change into other people.

SG: **We have this French academic term to describe the reality within a movie: 'réalité diégétique'. The main difference between *eXistenZ* and a film like *The Matrix* is that when, in *eXistenZ*, a character goes from reality to virtual reality, actually there's no difference. On the other hand, in a movie like *The Matrix* or *The Lawnmower Man*, every time there is a shift between reality and virtual reality, the virtual reality is heavily emphasised. Like in old, very corny fantastic movies, when there was a dream sequence you would hear modern music, and**

The New Cultists: Allegra Geller (Jennifer Jason Leigh), the 'goddess' of virtual environment games, in eXistenZ. Carol Spier and Cronenberg created a world without odour or taste, a land without borders where objects leave no trace of their existence, an ideally impersonal world of concepts and designers.

there would be a blue filter, etc. And this is really radical, it's the strongest basic idea in your script. Of course, when we talk of Hollywood mechanisms, what we're really talking about is the simplest form of audience manipulation: here you are in one world, here you are not, and maybe when you are back in reality it will seem a bit different. And it's true that the narrative strategy of *eXistenZ* is to lose the viewer and to force him to take risks himself.
DC: Well, one critic said something I liked; he said that what was funny about *eXistenZ*, and humorous too, is that it gave people a chance to imagine a whole new world. But if they didn't have much imagination, it was just going to be the same as their own world. So I kind of like that, and it's similar to the idea that now, because everyone has a digital video camera, they will all become fabulous movie makers; but

Allegra penetrates the spinal column of Ted Pikul (Jude Law) with the umbilical cord that plugs in eXistenZ. Virtual Sexuality: 'You have to play the game to figure out why you are playing the game.' Inside the bodies of Allegra and Ted, the void . . . At bottom lies their desire to know a world where communication is possible.

then you think maybe they won't. Maybe they'll just be shooting around the house, and it will be like home movies, only on digital video.

SG: **And you know I'm not Robin Wood, but I would say that . . .**

DC: Is he still around, do you know?

SG: **I don't know. But if it there was such a thing as progressive movies or reactionary movies, I would say that what would be really reactionary would be a movie that ends with 'back to reality': that's really what Hollywood producers try to make, and what the audience expects ; to go on a rollercoaster ride, but then to get off the rollercoaster and back to normal, even if they are a little shaken. A friend of mine in Paris, who is not really a cinema buff, told me before he went to see *eXistenZ* that he had heard that it was a bit disappointing. So I said, 'Why was that?' And he said, 'Because it's a kind of back to reality movie.' And I said, 'No, trust me, just go and see it, and you'll see that it is exactly the opposite.' And so he went to see it, and afterwards he said, 'You're absolutely right.' But I'm sure you've read that somewhere. It just goes to prove that some people project their own perceptions onto anything.**

DC: That's been one of the most consistent things that I have found from people's reactions to all my movies. That's why I really say it's a collaboration: the collaboration is not just with my cinematographer and my production designer, it's also a collaboration with the audience, because they can only go so far. You try to take them someplace, but everyone is to some extent a projector, they do project. They come to the theatre fully loaded with their own films of life. As I was saying about *M. Butterfly*, if you have only had a very straight, limited sexual experience, then the whole premise might appear totally fantastic, and there's no way that you can convince them that it is realistic in any way, or possible. And in some of my other movies, that same limited sexual experience – and I don't mean just physically, but in terms of their minds, and what they will allow themselves to think or imagine – causes them to shut out or to see things that aren't even in the movie. I mean, some of the critics of *Crash* were inventing things: they sounded pretty good, but really they weren't in the movie. So they were so horrified at the whole thought of it that all sorts of spectres leaped up and attacked them, all from their own movie; that was their own movie they were making. It's in the nature of art really. It's just sometimes more spectacularly obvious, and sometimes funny, than it is at other times, but either way, it is inevitable.

SG: When did you realise that you should expel all technological artefacts from the movie? When did that become obvious?

DC: It was pretty much right from the beginning although when I was shooting it I did even more, it's true. But once I had decided that the technology was organic – not in the Geiger way, but in my own way – then I realised that, even when we were designing some creatures, for example the inside of the gamepod, I had originally thought that it might have circuits and chips and things inside, mixed with the organic stuff. So it was a process; some of it was in the writing, because I didn't have computers and I didn't have scenes with high-tech anything, it was all very seedy and tacky. But then when I saw what the gamepod looked like, with the computer chips and stuff inside . . . I also had insect boards, insects on circuit boards, with the nervous systems of the insects functioning as part of the circuit boards. And I really quite like that idea, because I think you could do that actually, and in a way I think it is being done now. But it [these ideas] didn't look good. On the written page it worked very well. You would see a circuit board, but instead of transistors and things stuck to it, you saw actual insects, not live, with little electrodes attached to their legs and to their brains, and so on. It was a nice concept intellectually, but it didn't work visually. And it wasn't simple in a strong way. When we were well into pre-production, I think we might even have been shooting, I told the special effects guys that I wanted to completely change the concept of the gamepod, and that it would in fact be an animal, completely a hybrid mutant animal. But when we did the dissection scene, instead of seeing circuit boards with insects, I got rid of the insects. I said, it's all going to be sort of amphibians and reptiles. So I rewrote Ian Holm's speech, about a gamepod being basically an animal, and so on. That was quite late into shooting, and we had to change not the exterior of the pod, but the interior, and give it a spine and make it an animal. So that came late, and then it was in the discussions in pre-production that I gave out a little list of banned items: that there wouldn't be television sets, that there wouldn't be running shoes, that there wouldn't be patterns on people's clothes.

It's so interesting, because I was just reading an article yesterday about video-taping for the Internet, and one of the things they said is bad is patterns, complex patterns on clothes, because it's more information and it can't be handled. In a sense, what I was thinking in terms of gaming is now in terms of webcasting: keep it simple because of people's slow modems. Once we have high-speed everywhere, then you can have more detail. The same with motion; movement has to be simple.

And there's a lot more cutting, editing, in *eXistenZ*, than there is camera movement. It wasn't an intellectual thing, it was just visceral. It felt to me that I needed to move around, but I didn't want to do big, swooping camera moves, even though there are some video games that do use big, swooping camera moves and stuff. So it's more montage than *mise en scène*, you know. But there are no radios, there are no television sets, there are no telephones except for the one [pink] telephone. I didn't want to make it obvious, but I wanted to strip away what most people think of as technology, to show them the other kinds of technology: the sort of biological technology, and sort of fuse it with that. So that happened in pre-production, it wasn't in the script. I'd have to check the script to see whether in the motel room . . . I think I do mention that there's no television set in the film.

SG: It gives the movie a sort of radical look. You don't know exactly . . .

DC: How it's achieved. Well, for example, even the idea that everything is labelled, is generic: motel says 'Motel', Chinese restaurant says 'Chinese Restaurant', gas station says 'Gas Station', and that was all part of the same *zeitgeist*.

SG: Which you see in modern art, there's a female artist who has done a lot of photographs with labels . . . So once again – you were talking of *Farewell My Concubine* and *The Crying Game* with *M. Butterfly* – then it was *The Matrix*. I have read a lot of articles by people comparing *The Matrix* and *eXistenZ* in the French papers and on the Internet, and very often it's to your advantage, but nevertheless it's kind of annoying.

DC: Well, it's odd. I mean, I knew *The Matrix* was going to be a problem. I hadn't heard about it until a certain point, so I didn't even know it existed for a while. But I did know about *Dark City*, and of course I knew about *Lawnmower Man*. In other words, even my script fell into the category of virtual reality movie, and was judged inadequate by producers in Hollywood. It wasn't an action movie and it wasn't a major.

SG: I talked with the director of *Dark City*, and his movie was meant as an homage to Cronenberg, and Fritz Lang . . .

DC: Oh that's sweet!

SG: No, no, no, really! And there were some good things in *Dark City*, and some very bad things, which was a shame but . . .

DC: I have to say I liked it better than *The Matrix*.

SG: Oh yes, yes.

DC: Because a lot of people were telling me about *The Matrix*, and about how fantastic it looked, and how great the fight scenes were. I had been hearing this, and I was waiting to see it on this TV set in Dolby digital, satellite whatever – and I was so surprised at how bad it was, and how bad it looked, and how juvenile it was, like it was made for eight-year-olds. And I know the Wachowski brothers know my work, and they admire it, so I don't like to say bad stuff about them, but it was . . . Well, *Bound* was at least visually kind of interesting in the early Coen brothers way, very storyboarded kind of *noir*. This had no visual coherence at all, and I thought it was pretty boring. But, if people are going to be comparing things, they should really be comparing *Dark City* and *The Matrix*, because the similarity is there: you have some aliens who are creating this illusion in order to keep the humans happy, that's a very specific comparison.

SG: At least in *Dark City* there's the imagery of the end of the world, an actual end of the world, a totally Dickian universe that stops as in the Middle Ages, when people felt you would go to the end of the world . . . This was quite nice, but in *The Matrix* I cannot find one idea or one image that's a tiny bit interesting . . .

DC: No, no, the strongest image in *The Matrix* is the baby with all the things attached, but even that's very Geigerish, I mean it's mostly derivative. I have to say, I'm envious of the success of *The Matrix*, but when I see the movie I'm a little baffled by its incredible popularity: people see it three or four times. I couldn't, I can't imagine seeing it three or four times. What would sustain you? But it obviously does something for people, they love it. But they were saying, 'We weren't sure that the world was ready for an intellectual action film.' So I saw the movie and I thought, 'I don't see the action, I don't see the intellect. I certainly don't see the intellect.' Just because they refer to classical literature, and they mentioned the White Rabbit [from *Alice in Wonderland*] and a few other things. They think that to be an intellectual you put stuff in the movie, you put intellectual stuff in the movie. And they say, 'Yeah, we put all that stuff in there.' It's very American that way, because America is still basically an anti-intellectual culture, and their understanding of intellect, the average person's understanding of intellect is very juvenile: it's like you read books and you know classical stuff, and that's what being an intellectual is.

On Cronenberg's Interview With Salman Rusdie

SG: **It was very serious, Rushdie's Japanese translator was actually killed.**
DC: Oh, people were killed and wounded and attacked, and Rushdie's life was really in danger, there was no question about that. And it destroyed his life as he was living it then: it destroyed his marriage, and, of course, it really interfered with his relationship with his son. I mean, if you had read in the paper that he had been killed, you wouldn't have been surprised at all.

SG: **And you know, there is something strange, because when you think – I'm talking of France but it's universal – of the kind of books and pamphlets and stuff, and even the general feeling of the public during, let's say, the eighteenth century, now you have the feeling we are going backwards. During the eighteenth century in France, everybody would say 'horrible' things about God and Jesus and Mary, and write them and print them, and usually it was well accepted. There was a lot of hypocrisy, of course, but it was a libertine society. And now I remember, for example, President Chirac – though he wasn't actually president at the time – said, 'Of course we must defend and protect Rushdie, but I must say that I despise people who attack religion.' I mean that's absolutely not the point.**
DC: Not the point at all . . .

SG: **Even if you violently attack one religion or all religions, it's your . . .**
DC: And what does that mean anyway? Would he be upset if someone attacked the religion of the Trobriand islanders? It's a meaningless phrase, it's a politician being political: being afraid to support Rushdie, but figuring that he will soften it by letting everybody know that he really loves religion, and thinks it's an important thing.

SG: **And I'm sure you know the same thing happened with Scorsese's movie [*The Last Temptation of Christ*]. In France, some extreme-right Catholics threw a Molotov cocktail into a theatre and someone died.**
DC: Really ? I didn't know that he died . . .

SG: **Oh yes. So I really don't see why, if anybody wants to make a movie about Jesus, or a similar subject, or a prophet, why he wouldn't be allowed to do so.**
DC: But Serge, you're being naïve, and I don't think of you as a naïve person. From your point of view and mine, culturally and intellectually, we completely understand what we're talking about. But you know, people feel vulnerable, they cling to things desperately. If they are clinging desperately to a religion, anybody who says anything negative about the religion is nibbling away at that life-raft. They take it very personally and very emotionally, it's like an attack on the only thing that will save them. And they are not tolerant, it's not in the nature of religions to be tolerant.

SG: **Yes, but you're talking about simple people, but when Scorsese's movie was supposed to be released in Paris, the Archbishop of Paris said he wanted the film banned, and someone asked him if he had seen it and he said, 'No, that's the point, we don't want to see it.'**
DC: But you see, he is a simple person.

SG: **No, no, no, he's the Archbishop.**
DC: I'm sure he's very Machiavellian . . .

SG: **Oh yes he is.**
DC: . . . but I have upstairs the index of prohibited books, and some of the best writing in the world is on that list. If you are devoted to a structure like the Church, the Catholic Church, why not suppress everything that you feel may possibly be an attack on it? It's a control thing, is it not? 'I'm the Archbishop, it's my Church. What is this guy doing reinterpreting Christ's words? It doesn't matter what he's saying, because I'm the one who should be saying it.' So you see, in a way he is a simple man because he's

just a control freak, just another control freak basically wanting to exercise proprietary rights over the mythology of Christ and the life of Christ. 'If anybody is going to say anything about it, it should be us.' I can see that, it's like protecting a brand name. It's like Nike suing people who make fake Nikes or Rolex . . .

SG: **But don't you feel that one day it will really become like the corporate protection of a brand? . . .**
DC: Yes.

SG: **. . . because one day you'll write, or perhaps even say something in public like, 'This cult is mainly composed of lunatics,' and you'll be sued.**
DC: It's happening already. Sure. I think that's the way things are going. It's all very mysterious, the way this happens, and it does seem to go in strange cycles, but people are watching what they say now, people are being very careful of what they say. I mean, we just had a broadcaster who was fired. She was the anchor for . . .

SG: **I've read the article.**
DC: And the thing is that these people have no sense of humour, and there's none whatsoever in all the minority group stuff. Because this woman was making a joke about how corporations deliberately hire people from minorities in order to seem to be fulfilling their quotas. I mean I saw the direct quote and it was obvious that she was making fun of herself first and foremost. And we've all said that they [the corporations] will hire a lesbian dwarf Black, etc., so that they will have it all covered in one person. These people are so serious: they write in, the Blacks and the lesbians and all. And the militant groups are all up in arms: taking it totally seriously as though she had really said, 'I hate lesbians and they should be killed.' But she wasn't saying anything like that. They just have no sense of humour . . .

SG: **And it would be suicidal for her to say something like that.**
DC: Well yes, of course, and that's another thing: she knows it would be suicidal. She knew immediately she was dead . . . But you know: no sense of humour. Well my friend George Jonas, who is a writer and was the producer of one of my early films and some of the TV things, he just wrote an article that I asked him to write or suggested he write about this proposed censorship of tax funds here. This is the latest thing: that the CAVCO (Canadian Audio-Visual Certification Office), who have invested in most of my movies recently, should have a screening procedure whereby they will not invest funds in movies which are violent, or have violent sexuality, or this or that. We go through this all the time. Then, when we're discussing mechanisms to decide what these are, they say it's not censorship because you can still make the movie, you just can't do it with their funds. And of course my name was immediately mentioned. So George is writing in his usual very funny style, and he is saying, in order for these bureaucrats to discern what is offensive and what is violent and so on, 'David Cronenberg is making a training film' that will show them what is offensive and what is not permissible. And he goes on and on about that. But it's the same old stuff: no sense of humour. And they have bureaucrats responding very directly to Andrea Dworkin in this case, because when you say, 'We will withhold funds from [what is] socially unacceptable,' what does that mean? It will become very broad, and they're talking about a panel of experts, because they know as bureaucrats that they can't make [the decision. And then there is the whole issue of deciding] who these experts should be. It just goes on and on, it's the same bullshit as always. And of course the panel of experts will be filmmakers who are jealous of the guy who is getting the funds. It's so obvious that it can't work. They're like newborns, they proceed as though no one has ever done this before. [They are convinced] that they have stumbled on this brilliant idea and they will make the world safe for propriety, and nobody will ever be offended [again].

I told you about Castlerock, didn't I? I had a

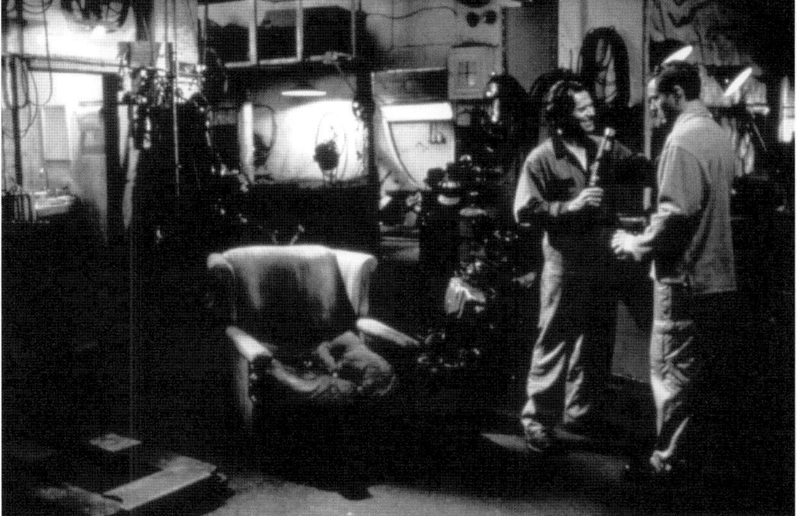

The 'country gas station': The couple are on the run in a Land Rover. Allegra says to Ted: 'Where are we going to find a bioport at this time of night? In the country gas station!' – a merciless parody of Hollywood narrative technique. Nominalism: The mechanic at the gas station (Willem Dafoe) – called 'Gas'.

small role in Michael Apted's film *Extreme Measures,* it was a Gene Hackman movie and I had a scene with Hugh Grant. I just played a lawyer and I was on screen for about five seconds. It was a Castlerock movie. I received a sheet, a packet in the mail, which said that before I came on the set I must sign this, I must agree to this. And it was a whole series of pages about conduct on the film set. And it said, 'You cannot make jokes about,' and then there was a list: 'a person's gender, sex, race, sexual preference, Vietnam era status,' like you couldn't joke about them being a draft dodger, and on and on. And it said, 'You are not allowed on the set until you have signed this.' Well I mean, it would completely silence you, you could say nothing about anything. And jokes are always about those things.

SG: Of course.

DC: That's where the humour is. So you have a completely humourless set. The humour on the set of *Crash* was so sexual, and so out there, which was our way of release. [But according to that Castlerock form] we would all be arrested, and thrown off our own set.

SG: It seems in Canada all the funds for film, public health, farming . . .

DC: It's not just Canada, you have the same thing going on in France.

SG: But it seems to be very brutal here.

DC: That depends on the province. In Ontario,

because we have elected a conservative government and, unfortunately, the same asshole has been elected twice to be premier of Ontario, [we have] hospital cuts and all of that stuff. It's very brutal and quite ruthless, it's sort of a Thatcherist kind of thing. [And it followed] in response to a left-wing government that was here and blew it the other way. They did it the other way, they got us into huge debt but didn't do it intelligently, so this was a reaction against that. The NDP (New Democratic Party) – which is our one remaining viable left-wing party, I think there still is officially a Communist Party, but it might be gone now because you never hear about it – came to power in Ontario at a time when right-wing Thatcherites like Reagan, and Thatcher herself, and even our own Mulrooney, were in government. Suddenly Ontario was all left, so it was like a big experiment. And unfortunately they were inexperienced, because they had never been in power before, and they couldn't believe that they were suddenly in power. And they had a chance and they blew it. So the reaction against that has been vicious: you cut all bottom line, cut the debt, the debt is the only important thing, on the basis that everything else good will flow from that – but, of course, it hasn't. However, the economy is booming and they keep getting re-elected, but it's vicious. But we can make a case for the economic viability of the film industry, because it has been making money for us and so on. So maybe we have a chance to at least help there. But you wouldn't do it on terms of culture and art, that's for sure.

SG: They are considered improper words in North America.
DC: Really, they'll be banned soon.

SG: When Douglas Sirk arrived in Hollywood in the 1940s, he said, 'Hollywood is a very interesting place where, when you say «arty» or «artsy», it means something derogatory; and he was not aware of that in the beginning. At first he didn't speak perfect English, and he thought it was the first name 'Arty'. So he would ask, 'Who's Arty?'
DC: Arty, artsy, yeah, that's right. That continues, they're a little more sophisticated, they might pay some lip service to it but not much, not much.

SG: At the same time, it's absolutely impossible to defend an art form as such. I find it very difficult, because it's true that most Hollywood movies are not works of art, they're industrial products. So there too politics is involved, because suddenly you take sides and you become very simplistic.
DC: That's what I hate about politics, it forces you to simplify to the point where you're not sure if you are even talking about anything real anymore. Because you know that people are complex, society is complex, sexuality is complex, it's all very complex and sophisticated and you can't speak on that level. Who could ever bear to be a politician? You really have to be a schizophrenic cynic to be a good politician, or you have to be Reagan, who I think really believed everything he said – he thought it was all that simple. He was a guy who could get Alzheimer's without anyone noticing the difference.

SG: But nevertheless, when you did that interview with Salman Rushdie it was a political statement.
DC: Well, it was because it had to do with freedom of writers and freedom of expression, which are really the foundation of all my politics. They are all derived from that: that we cannot repress each others' thoughts, and that censorship is a very dangerous tool that should be used in only the most sensitively judicious way, and in a manner that may sometimes shock people when they realise what the implications are. For example: I don't think people seeking to deny the existence of the Holocaust should be suppressed. I think they should be allowed to speak and they have to be countered. People talk to me about neo-nazi websites and stuff, but I feel that, first of all, strategically speaking it's not bad to know who your enemies are, and where they are. [Depriving them of their means

The Demiurge: David Cronenberg contemplates on his monitor the cyclical path of creatures in a cruel universe, fated to fall to the bottom.

of expression] won't make them disappear, they'll just go underground, so even from that very pragmatic point of view, freedom of expression still works – that they should be countered ferociously is part of it, of course. But trying to silence people does not get rid of the thoughts in their heads, and you can't silence thought. So I would sometimes defend the right of people to speak who might surprise some other people. Basically, interviewing Rushdie when he was still under a death threat – and he still is now, though perhaps less so – was saying that I would not be afraid, and that I would not decide not to meet this man who I wanted to meet, and that I would make that meeting public. So in that sense, yes, it was definitely a political statement. I also had read in England the strangest things by John LeCarré and David Cornwell, the writer attacking Rushdie and saying he deserved it, and he brought it on himself, and he must have known what he was doing: all kinds of crazy stuff that I couldn't believe that a writer writing out of the same tradition would betray.

There's a jealousy amongst directors and actors, but I think jealousy amongst writers is the most ferocious. And it must be because of how introspective they are and how isolated they sometimes feel. My experience is that writers, especially fiction writers, are the worst. And English fiction writers are maybe the absolute worst, because they just rip each other to shreds in the most vicious way – it's unbelievable. But you would think that when a man's life was on the line they would stop, but they didn't. It was the same, it just became absorbed as part of the game: the writing game, the jealousy game. It was as though they had no sense of the reality of it.

SG: David, you were telling me that there was a direct connection between the long interview you did with Salman Rushdie and the script of *eXistenZ*. Can you elaborate on that, please?

DC: Well, I had an idea, not very well formed, of doing a movie about an artist who is in Rushdie's position. Not exactly his position, but something that would connect somewhat to *Naked Lunch* and the Burroughsian concept of the things that you create becoming living things that can come back to hurt you, or haunt you, or things you have to deal with. Something you've created, you bring it to the world and then you have to deal with it. Rushdie was a prime example of that. Something that he created then had a life of its own, and called forth responses from people that he seemed to not remotely have expected. He was completely surprised by that. So I was interested to talk to him. To meet him, to talk to him about his situation. And I found the opportunity when a Canadian magazine, *Shift*, agreed with me to do an interview. It actually was their idea to interview Salman Rushdie. They wanted to me to do it on the phone. I said I have to meet him. So I ended up meeting him in London in a hotel. It was all very secretive. There was Scotland Yard. We went there by taxi and I didn't know where we were going. Then I had a long discussion with him about many things. It was an interview in general. One of the things we talked about, actually, was whether or not games could be art. Could there be a game that was also art? We both basically agreed that [there] probably [could] not. Because the idea of art is to lead, to show and reveal something. You do not really want it to be completely interactive in the way that a game is, but there might be some new medium that could make that possible. I was leading, that was my question to him. But as I was sitting and talking to him, I was thinking about the film that I would make that dealt somewhat with his situation. When I came back to work on my script, I thought we would never play the game in the movie. I thought it would be more about an artist who has a fatwa pronounced against him because of his art, and that the movie would really deal with that: with being a creative person who is on the run, who is in hiding, who has no stability, no security. The lead character turned out to be a woman, and as I was writing it, I was so curious about the game that I couldn't stick to my concept of not playing the game. It would have been very cute. It could have been very strong to never play the game, but I couldn't stand it myself. I felt that I really wanted to play that game myself and see where it led. That resulted in a shift in the emphasis of the movie, even though those basic elements are still there. We have a character who is a game designer, that is my artist in the film, who is on the run because of what she's created. But we do get into the

Opposite: A universe of designers: Kiri Vinokur (Sir Ian Holm), a living god giving life to a virtual creature . . . but if everyone in the world is a 'designer', then who has the time to play the games? Above: The 'Trout Farm': Yevgeny Noursih (played by Don McKellar, another Toronto cineaste, with a bad Russian accent), attempts to manipulate Jude Law. The film is a rare cinematic application of the philosophy of Burroughs: 'Nothing is true, everything is permitted.'

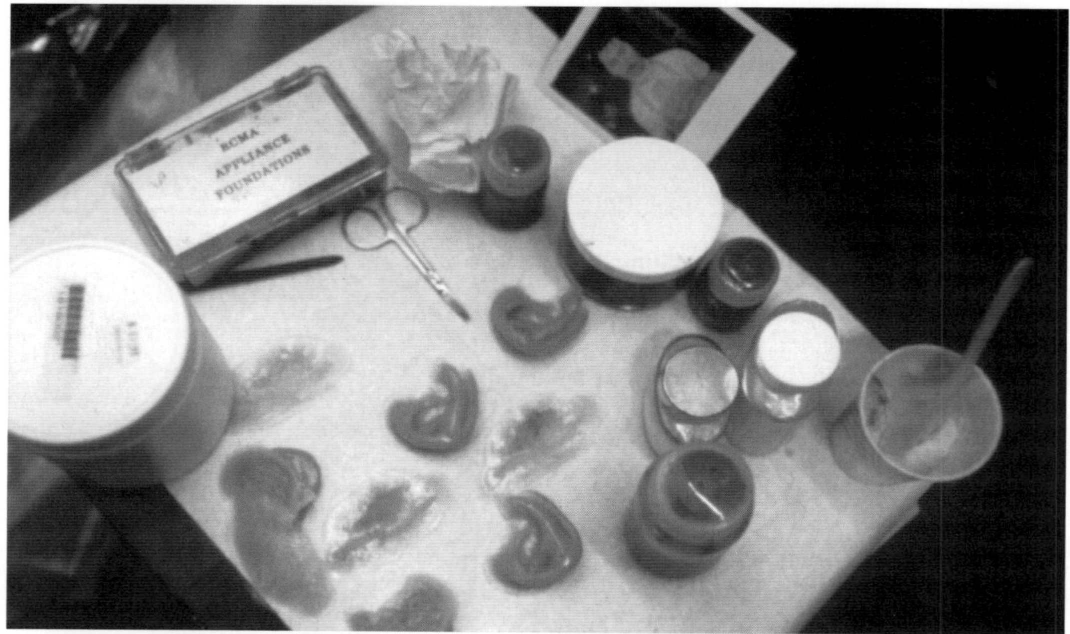

Special makeup: Accessories.

game and that interfaces as many levels of reality. I think, in retrospect, I was still being faithful to that original concept, because really you could see Rushdie's situation as a clash of different realities. The ones who wanted to kill him had a completely different reality and understanding from what he did, so really, in a sense, I believe I was faithful to my original concept, but approached it in an oblique way that I hadn't originally thought I would.

SG: At the same time, *eXistenZ*, as a film, is perhaps your answer to censorship. In *eXistenZ* you, as an artist, create another body orifice and I was just trying to imagine what the censors would have to say about a perversion that doesn't exist and couldn't exist. It's your strong sense of humour once more.
DC: Well, there's a moment when someone puts a tongue into this new orifice and someone puts a finger into this new orifice, and if it were one of the old orifices perhaps it would be censored, but since it's a new one, there are no laws yet dealing with the bioport and the sexuality of that. So you're right. I wasn't thinking of it consciously, but there is certainly an element of that involved, yeah.

SG: More seriously, I think it's an absolutely astounding movie because it's a voyage through your brain, subconscious or otherwise, and at the same time a sort of voyage through your work. There are a lot of elements coming from your other movies. Distorted, transformed, but the happy few will recognise them as such. Was it your intention or not to make something that is absolutely Cronenbergian, totally organic, with no indulgence toward all that has been seen recently about virtual reality and techno and cyber stuff? It has absolutely nothing to do with all these movies.
DC: I was aware. I knew that people would want to categorise it as a virtual reality movie, and I felt that would be a big mistake, for us to accept that

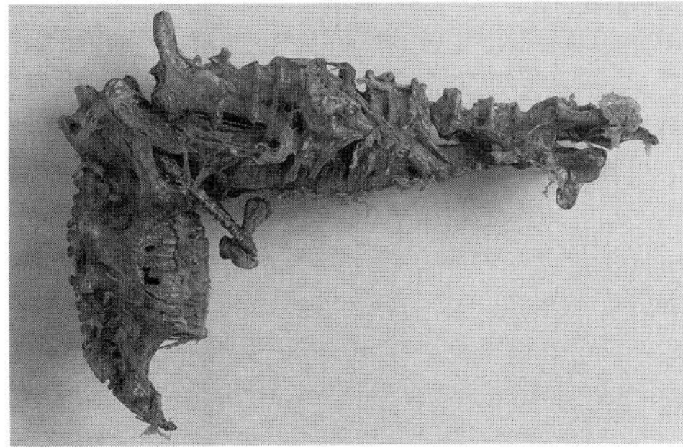

The cartilage pistol: In eXistenZ, this imaginary artefact is redolent of the 'flesh pistol' in Videodrome.

category, because it will lead people to expect something that they're not going to see. As you know from seeing the film, there are no screens in the film. No television screens, no computer screens, no telephones except for one strange one. That immediately means it's nothing like the virtual reality movies. It's a different thing. I wasn't even thinking in terms of doing a sci-fi movie at this point. Every movie now has *Blade Runner* as a touchstone, whether it's *Strange Days* or the Italian film *Nirvana*, they're all *Blade Runer* revisited again and again. It seems to have such a hypnotic influence on young filmmakers. I wanted to deliberately set the film in the countryside, where you could not have the props of the desolate city of the future and so on. So I was not being so innocent and so naïve, because I was defining myself against the films which have been done about the new techno-future. But then there was an innocence there too. I didn't really consciously go back to my other movies, but it's the same. The imagery is still there in me. It hasn't changed, so there's a sense of revisiting some of the concepts and some of the images of the past, but from a different vantage point in my life now.

SG: **At one point in the trout farm section, I connected with *The Fly*, when Brundle is talking of the plasma pool, and then suddenly I felt I was in this plasma pool. So there are so many connections in *eXistenZ* with all your other movies, but perhaps you were not absolutely conscious of that ?**

DC: No, no, I wasn't. Do not forget that this is

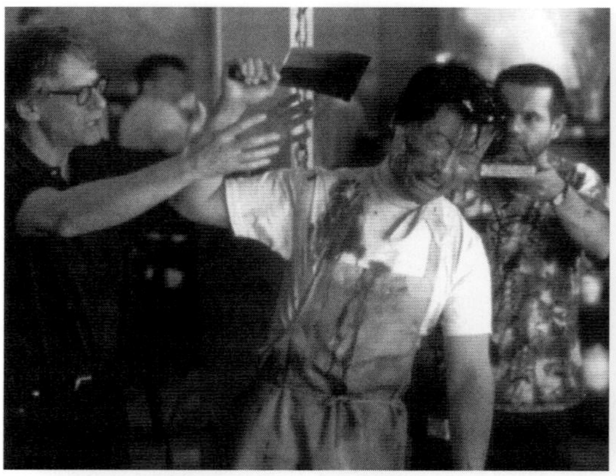

The Chinese restaurant scene: In an allusion to good old gore films, it's decided to kill the waiter to progress the game – and to experience the hate. It's the waiter who pronounces the final phrase: 'Are we still in the game?'

the first completely original script I've written since *Videodrome*. So I had no idea what was going to come out. The script was written before I made *Crash*, at a certain point I had the script for *Crash* and *eXistenZ* together, and I actually thought *eXistenZ* would get made first. It was with MGM at the time, so the sequence would have been quite different. But obviously *Crash* then came together first, and this movie was not made in response to what happened with *Crash*. It's nothing like that. I guess that's my inner landscape, the landscape that you see in my movies, and it connects to all the other ones.

SG: **Talking about that landscape, I wanted you to elaborate a little bit on animals. All the kinds of non-existent animals one can see in your movies. We've seen some in *Naked Lunch*. In *The Fly*, too.**
DC: In *Shivers*, as well. In the first one.

SG: **Of course.**
DC: The parasites.

SG: **I wanted to ask you, because I think it could be important for the understanding of the movie, what's wrong with the phrase 'virtual reality' ? What don't you like? Because I remember another discussion we had long ago . . .**

DC: In fact I do like the term 'virtual reality'. I only dislike it in terms of it categorising this particular movie of mine, because then it becomes connected with many movies we would name that, first of all, were mostly failures, critically and financially, so just as a marketing thing I'd rather not have it called that. But also it is a bit of a naïve term as well, because all reality is virtual. In a sense that's the theme of many of my movies. There is no absolute reality, therefore virtual reality becomes a meaningless term. I understand it, of course, when people are talking about computer simulations and so on. But in the greater philosophical sense, and in the artistic sense, every filmmaker is creating a virtual reality. That is what you do in a film. It's not a reality – people who come in off the streets, they see the difference, but you are drawing your audience into a world that you've created, even if it pretends to be a very naturalistic, realistic world. It isn't. It's complete artifice. Everybody who comes into the cinema knows this. I have a philosophical objection to it as well in that sense, in terms of what an artist does. I do like it as an expression, and in the right circumstances it could be very effective and powerful, but it's starting to lose its meaning because everybody uses it for different things now.

SG: So once again you would agree with what Bill Burroughs was saying: 'There is no real reality.'
DC: I think I discovered that very early on in life as a kid. But you notice what happens with dreams. You notice what happens when you're brushing your teeth and your mind is somewhere else, and you do not remember brushing your teeth. It's such a repetitive task. If someone were to photograph you they would see you brushing your teeth, but that's not your reality. Your reality is in your head. You're thinking about an argument you had with your mother or your wife or somebody, or a discussion. You're not there. Where are you? Which one is more real at that point, the brushing of the teeth or where you are in your head? And which one do you remember? Of course, it has a long philosophical tradition as well, this discussion of multiple realities or what is reality? And that's a constant theme in my movies and for any filmmaker, even if it's unconscious, they're always dealing with that question as we are right now, with this camera and this film. Are these people here or not here? We're pretending they're not here. We're not exactly ignoring, but we're not referring to them. So that is a constant. If, in a film, suddenly an actor looks into the lens, that changes the whole reality of the movie and it becomes a different reality right at that second. You've said, 'Oh, we're noticing the camera.' In what way? I do not see how any artist cannot be dealing with the question of multiple realities as a basic platform from which he launches everything else.

SG: There's something that's really astounding in *eXistenZ*, when characters become 'game characters'. Usually it's another character who discovers it, but some of the characters become conscious they have to change their line. We are almost in Pirandello.
DC: Yes, and I have to say that I read *Six Characters in Search of an Author*, it was one of the things I read while I was writing the script. There were several things. It has nothing to do with a deconstructionist craze, that sort of self-comment. It's something else, it's a different level of discussion of what art is and what a character is as a creation, and what acting is and what actors are. I didn't want to attack it in the current mode, which I think has other reasons for existing.

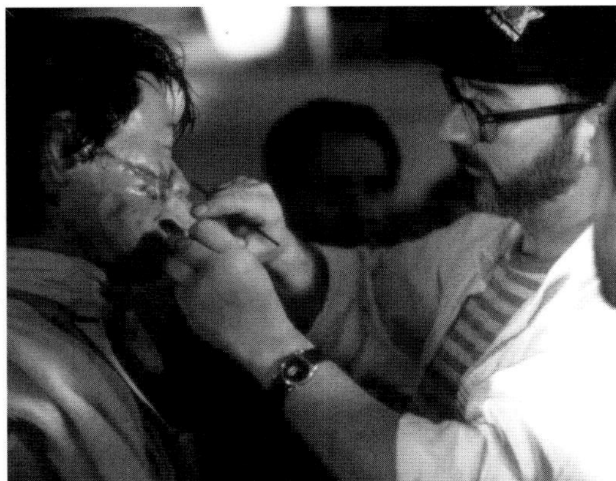

Oscar Hsu (the Chinese restaurant waiter) is subjected to makeup tests (special makeup by Dennis Pawlik).

SG: Once again, one of your major themes appears in *eXistenZ*, and it's a theme of contamination, disease. In a strange way, but very powerful.
DC: Yes, it goes back a long way, right back to my first movie, *Shivers*. The discussion of whether the disease is really a diminished creature, a diseased creature, or is it an enhanced creature, is it a different creature? A disease usually indicates the presence of some other life form. Not always, but often. Some other life form's health is your disease. It's a strange combination. In that earlier film, I was trying to look at disease from the point of view of the disease rather than the diseased creature. It's an interesting exercise. Once again, it's a reality shift. It's a whole different reality. The parasite that lives in your body does not consider itself a disease. The stronger and more healthy it is, the weaker you become. There are two realities that are moving like this. So it's . . . I haven't totally finished with this. I haven't really come to some conclusion, but it constantly recurs, as it certainly does in *eXistenZ*.

From
among the dead
Spider, A History of Violence

There is a profound similarity between *eXistenZ* and *Spider*: in both films, at the end, the main characters have changed significantly. Allegra Geller, 'electronic games goddess', pursued by terrorists, has herself become a terrorist who pursues a great inventor of electronic games. The nice little boy, with a malicious father who killed his wife and replaced her with a horrible prostitute, has become at the end a cold monster, the killer of his own mother. Furthermore, in *A History of Violence*, Tom Stall – whom we first saw at the beginning as the perfect husband, sympathetic, an honest small business owner – has turned into a sadistic killer.

Initially, Cronenberg's theme was transformation, biological and existential. Now it has been 'interiorised', to the extent that we accept his films as psychological studies. Cronenberg has long accustomed his audience to unexpected plot twists, mutations and metamorphoses. But his latest two films are anguished, tortured epics, with characters who – like Bill Lee in *Naked Lunch* – appear to be coming back 'from among the dead'.[1]

Cronenberg's style has purified and evolved into a kind of postmodern classicism, in which the overused special effects have no place at all. Its visible strength is its lyricism, which is extremely hard to find in the cinema of his contemporaries. David Cronenberg's art continues to push him toward new directions. For the moment, we can only be certain that he will not abandon his incisive style of observation, his unsentimental sensitivity, the daring he has exhibited throughout his whole 30-year career, and most of all, his perennially youthful enthusiasm, which is the trademark of the greats.

SG: If there is one movie out of all your works that has been misunderstood, it would be *Spider*. It seems like a Freudian parable, because there's a mother, a father and a son, but the real subject of the movie is someone who's trying to tell a story he will never be able to understand or to analyse. The fantastic element of *Spider* is that he's there when he's ten and when he's 40, as if two parallel worlds had collided. Of course, this situation makes it totally impossible to understand what's happening. It could be the description of an Einsteinian universe where time is as material as space. Although in your movie, sometimes space is not really what it seems to be. I'm thinking of the moment when he lies down and weeps on his mother's grave. Do you think the relative lack of audience response was caused by the complexity of the structure?

DC: It depends on what country, too. A movie like that has a sort of predetermined fate, because it's assumed that it's difficult, it's assumed that it's depressing. This is the key; it's oppressive and sad. Therefore, it will have a limited audience and you release it that way. Then, it comes to pass. I think it only had a 35-print release in the US. So it's sort of one print per city. It's sort of doomed, and it's hard to know what would happen if it got a generous release with a lot of support from critics who understood it. It did get some good critical response, but I don't know how that was used in really promoting the film. Certainly, it got better promotion in Canada

1. To evoke the English translation of the Boileau-Narcejac novel, *From Among the Dead*, which inspired Hitchcock's *Vertigo*.

than in the US. But it's hard to know [of] a pure response directly to the movie itself. There's always the lack of, or surfeit of, surrounding context, which is distorting it, or pushing it, or pulling it, or whatever. It's very hard to go into a movie and not know anything about it. So I have had good responses, complex ones, but I remember casting actors for the role of the father, I remember one English actor who said, 'This is so simple.' And I'm saying this role is actually one of the most complex roles in the movie. That attitude meant he was the wrong actor for that role, even though he was not a stupid man. He just didn't see the trinity of that role in memory, in reality, so yes, it's complex, and yes, it does confound people's narrow expectations and Freudian expectations, because it seems like it's a Freudian parable, and then it's not that at all. What you are left with is perhaps a certain hopelessness, fatalism, and inevitability, which is very sad and I guess very hard for the audiences to take. Maybe it's not something they want to subject themselves to.

SG: **Just imagine you had done this movie in the thirties or in the fifties, you could have had the same kind of actor playing the adult Spider role, but in the script he would have become a ghost. This would have been easier, in a way, for the public.**

DC: Well, maybe. A memory-ghost is something that I experienced, you know. Maybe saying the word 'ghost' is the wrong thing. Do I believe in haunting? Not the traditional way. But am I haunted by the memory of my father, who's been dead for many years? Yes, I am. I hear him, I see him, I smell him. Do I think that's a ghost? No, but it's a memory-ghost. So, I think that in *Spider* we are doing the memory-ghost. I mean he's sort of a ghost – of his own childhood, as an adult, and you can kind of be your own weird inverse ghost – that is to say your childhood is dead, and it is a ghost in a way, but also, when you were a child, you always felt the looming potential of you as an adult. You saw parents, you saw people older, you thought about when I'll get old enough to do this, to do that, so you're also haunted by the ghost of your own adulthood when you're a child. This is a sort of dual memory-ghosting, anticipatory ghosting, going on. I was never tempted to make a real ghost story, because you get into the mechanics of 'ghostness'. What are the rules of being a ghost? Can you see the ghost at all times? And if you want to be conventional, you have to establish the rules of your 'ghostness'. To me, that would be very destructive.

SG: **You have shown in your movies that there are no rules. The convention of memory lane in movies was: when there's a flashback someone must do certain things. In *Spider*, there's no flashback, both are in the same frame and one is repeating the other's sentences.**

DC: And I think that's accurate in terms of how memory works. Without it being a big deal, I think that a movie is a very astute study of memory, and how memory works, and the creative element that's involved in memory, which I think is obviously true. But it's not often shown within a film that way, that creative element, the concept of remembrance of things past, the idea that you would obsessively try to reconstruct it exactly as it happened. First of all, it's impossible, and secondly, I don't think that's ever the memory project, which is to create a new thing.

SG: I **know you share with Burroughs and others the idea that reality doesn't exist, or that it can exist in different circumstances depending on the time and the person. This is one of the subjects of *Spider*, there is no reality. One can try to gather the reality of his past, to collect bits and pieces. But it never really happened. His crime happened, it's almost certain, but all the rest, is it not a story told by, if not an idiot, then a madman?**

DC: Yes, because at the end of the movie, when you could say, 'Ah, he's made a breakthrough into some kind of acceptance of his guilt,' of his culpability, that he did – although it was accidental – murder his mother, then you have to start to think this could be a total construction as well, that suddenly something cracked in him, and now, instead of denying his guilt and instead of having only anger against his father, he has suddenly decided to be the guilty one. But it's a decision. Maybe the emotional situation is that if I am the guilty one, then I can deal with it myself, whereas if I'm always angry with my father, who's probably dead, then I cannot do anything about that anger, except go around and around in circles. But if it's me who's the guilty one, then I can beat myself, I can excoriate myself, and perhaps I can choose to make me the guilty one. But maybe that's just as much a construction, maybe it's completely untrue, maybe there was no crime, maybe the crime was his mother leaving him. We don't know. Maybe she left him after promising that she would never do such a thing.

SG: **There is something in the movie that could lead us to believe that, first of all, when he steals that piece of mirror, the only thing he tries to do is to cut his wrist - which he ultimately doesn't. Then, when he goes to the landlady's room with the hammer, he doesn't murder her either. Perhaps he's absolutely innocent.**
DC: Yes, and the only reason that he is ever in any kind of confinement is because he's so unstable, and perhaps he's not actually ever committed a crime. He's self-destructive.

SG: **That's one of the most beautiful moments in the movie, this story, this tale of the mother spider, which goes and dies away completely from inside. It's absolutely terrible, even if it's not totally true. It's a beautiful metaphor. How come he calls himself 'Spider'? Because he completely identifies with the baby spider left alone?**
DC: And his mother is this 'spider' too. In the movie, the suggestion is that because he loves the spider story so much, she begins to nickname him 'Spider', just without thinking through what it might mean. But the other thing it suggests is that it's the responsibility of the baby spider to carry on, now the mother has died giving birth to him, and now he must grow and be a good adult spider, to continue on. Which is certainly, in human terms, people do feel the weight of their parents, but they also feel the responsibility when their parents die, that they somehow are the ones who keep the memory of their parents alive, because they knew them better than anybody else, they think – although often it's not really true. But they bear the weight of their parents' lives. They're the ones now, if their parents are going to have some kind of immortality, it's through them. So you become the spider now, you're the big boy spider. It's now time for you to soldier on and be an adult spider. But of course he's not having a very good time of it.

SG: **You told me that Ralph [Fiennes] and yourself were really interested in Beckett when you wanted to give substance to Spider's character. What does that mean exactly?**
DC: First of all, it's physical, but also there were times when Beckett almost played the role of a vagrant or a tramp. You know, the photographs of him walking through Paris and stuff, even though often he was very well-dressed, but there was a real identification that he had with the homeless, with the homeless family, or at least a man tormented by his memories.

SG: **He lived many years in a small hotel just on the other side of the Prison de la Sant. It's sort of strange.**
DC: Yes, and he died in a horrible old men's home. He could have chosen not to do that, and I think he had the financial means to not do that, and the fame to not do that, but in a weird way he longed for it. It was like his destiny to become one of his own characters, one of his own vagrants, homeless guys. You know, *Malone Dies*, and it's living in transient boarding houses with a terrifying landlady – this all felt like Beckett territory, partly from life, partly his novels, more than his plays really. It just gave us a focus, a physical one as well, so we kind of did play here in a Beckett kind of way, not overly

imitative, but it just gave us that focus of tone.

SG: By the way, how did you meet Ralph?
DC: Catherine Bailey showed him that script, and I started to connect with her and I was saying I was very interested, and she said you should come to London and you should meet Ralph and me, and see if we like us together and we want to work together. So we went to London with my family. We all stayed at the Cadogan Hotel, which is where Oscar Wilde was arrested, it's famous for that, and it was in the lobby of that hotel that I came downstairs and there were Catherine and Ralph. That's where I met them for the first time. It was funny, because we were all auditioning for each other. We became very good friends, Catherine and I, later we talked and I told her I was hoping that they would like me, and she said she was hoping that I would like them. (*laughs*) So, it was really a mutual audition to see if we felt that we could work together. It was very congenial, very sweet.

SG: Were you also attracted by his inventiveness as a stage actor?
DC: I'd never seen him on stage, I'd only seen him in film. Then, I think, on that same trip, I did see him in *Coriolanus*, and he was very fierce in that play. But I'd seen him in quite a few of his films, I'd never seen him doing anything like *Spider*, but as soon as I met him I could see the vulnerability, and all of the sensitivity and the stuff that you might not see, that he didn't have to play in roles like *French Lieutenant's Woman*, and certainly not in *Schindler's List*. Immediately, once we started to talk about it, I knew that we would have a great time doing it. It was a real challenge for him; there was nothing he had done on stage or in film like that before. But that's the exciting thing, and at that point it is almost like a Beckett performance, like a character from a Beckett play. In film you can afford to be more mute than on stage, but of course Beckett experimented with that as well. So there was even that connection.

SG: It's a little bit different from being mute.
DC: He's not mute. It was written mute, but he started to do the mumbling thing and I really liked that.

SG: On the DVD, a lot of things are more audible. Maybe they corrected the sound, it seemed to me.
DC: It shouldn't be, but in French you translated some of the stuff, and it's possible that in a French dubbed version it might be clearer because somebody decided to make it clearer. He is like those guys in the park who talk to themselves. There is a method in their madness, it's not completely random stuff they're saying, and so there are always connections between what he's saying and what he's thinking and remembering. But I did like it; I just sort of gave him another avenue of expression, that could express both his confusion and his social difficulties and his communication difficulties. I didn't want it to be irritating, you know, it's always a tricky thing. Because he [Fiennes] met some doctors and he showed me some of the stuff that they do, and it's extraordinary, it's very extreme, a little of that goes a very long way on screen, even though it might be accurate in a sociological way, dramatically it would be unbearable. But I think that encouraged him to try to find some verbalisation that could represent that, but not be so overpowering.

SG: What is your method with actors?
DC: Ralph said at a certain point that he got less direction that he's ever had before, and yet felt completely guided and comfortable. And Viggo [Mortensen] and some of the other actors from *A History of Violence*, William Hurt as well, said that they've never been communicated with so little. To me, it's a complete collaboration with the actors. You cast somebody who you think is going to bring a lot to it, and then to try to manipulate them like a puppet, and tell them how to say the lines and stuff, to me is waste of resources. So a lot of what happens, happens when you're discussing the script when you first meet, it happens when you're in preparation, a

lot of it happens when you're doing wardrobe fittings. This is a crucial moment with actors, when they're having their feelings with the wardrobe persons, the discussions about what they might wear, and a costume designer calls me in and says, 'Now, it's this pair of shoes.' And of course, with *Spider*, it's more critical than with the normal clothing situation. Because so much of what you're going to do is revealed to you by your choices in the make-up and you ask yourself: What does the hair look like? How much tobacco will be on his fingers? Is it because he rolls cigarettes he smokes? What colour is the tobacco? In those discussions it's very physical, you are preparing the actor to such a huge extent for being that character. The shoes are often very important to an actor, because then their posture is influenced by the shoes that they wear. So, I think that what happens is that a lot of actors are used to a lot of ego bullshit from the directors. But to me it's minimalist, you say what needs to be said, and then you want your actor to use his own intuition to begin to portray the character. With *Spider*, we did a lot of things about the clothing and the postures and how he would stand and so on, but then we did the first shot, he's walking down the street, and I realise that we never talked about the walk, which is very important. So, after the first take Ralph said, 'What about the walk? Was that the right walk?' and I said, 'Look at it on the monitor, I think it's perfect. It's the perfect spider walk. Kind of defeated, slightly weary, so much there.' I love to do it while we are shooting, I don't do rehearsals, I think that everything changes so completely when you're actually on the set that all of the theories and the stuff that you have is a kind of wasted energy. I don't trust the actors completely, they all want to be directed. They don't want to be uncontrolled, because they can't be, because I know from being an actor in other people's films that you really only have control of your own character, but you don't have control of the movie. You're not there for the other scenes, the other actors don't want to be directed by you. So, you are responsible as an actor for your own character, and you put into it, but ultimately the orchestrator, the maestro, the conductor of the opera has got to be the director, because you don't want to be the one guy who's in the wrong movie. You don't want to be somebody who's in some other film than everybody else, and only the director can make sure that you're in the same movie. He first does that by casting you properly. So that's really all it is. But you invite suggestions and concerns, and then you have to show the actors that you're observing them closely. I often make comments that I could keep in my head, because I think that the actors are doing it wonderfully. But I don't say to myself I don't want to make them too self-conscious, because I think you need to let the actor know, 'I love that thing that you did, I loved that moment when you turned your head,' subtle things. Then they know that they're being watched and observed and appreciated. That's what you give them. And if you think that they're doing something wrong, you don't hesitate, but it's not to humiliate or embarrass. The director is the first audience for that actor'a performance, and from my experience of being an actor, you don't want to be in limbo, you want to hear something, you want to know that something good is going on. And then you get into a rhythm with the actor, and each actor is completely different about how much feedback they need or don't need. Some actors are much more needy than others, and you give them what they need. My job is to give the actors, who hopefully I've cast well, what they need to continue to evolve and find depth and interesting things.

SG: *Spider* is a story about a child who's too young to have sex, but has a lot of fantasies and a lot of very dangerous fantasies, but in a way he's completely asexual. In *A History of Violence*, there's a very heavy sex component, but there are two extremes. The first one is the perfect love between a man and his wife, still in love with each other after maybe twenty years. About the sec-

ond one, a French critic said in *Liberation* that Eddie [Maria Bello] is absolutely disgusted with him, but at the same time his violence and his hidden identity are almost more seductive. And that's why the stairway scene seems so perfect. It shows something that was very present, for example, in *Dead Ringers* – that sex is not simple, it can be mixed with a lot of drives and emotions such as pain, violence, even a form of hatred. Do you think this was absolutely essential?

DC: Yes, not just because they are two pivotal points that are balanced because of course, even beyond what they are, the first scene is also of role play in sex, and so is the second one. We called that married sex and gangster sex. But the married sex is also a fantasy, where they decide to play roles to excite themselves, roles that they never played with each other. So, the whole question of identity in sexuality and violence in sexuality is there in those two scenes. But also, I felt I needed a really visceral, primal moment of connection before and after, to show what happens to them, because just verbal stuff is not enough, a slap is not enough. In Josh [Olson]'s script, she says, 'Fuck you Joey!', slaps him and then goes upstairs and slams the door, and that's it. I felt that's not enough, because your relationship with characters in the movies is often like your relationship with people in your life who are peripheral people. You see them at a party, in a supermarket, on the street, you might see them whacking their kid in a moment of anger, but it's not like someone that you live with. Because it's not much time, this movie has 95 minutes. So how do you pin it? How do you show a real change in the relationship, when you don't have a lot of time to depict the relationship before and after? To me, sex is a critical thing in a relationship, even if it's not there. If it's not there, then it's important that we know it's not there, that we have some idea why it's not there. And is the end result to make a comment on marriage? The only two sex scenes in the movie involve two people who have been married for ten years and have two children. This is not normal for cinema, you know, it's as though once you're married sex is no longer filmable, it's not interesting! (*laughs*) When in fact, here I am, someone who's been married for 30 years, and I could say that's not true, you still have a sex life, and it's not a question of age, it's a question of marriage. So I think that those scenes are very true comments, you could call the movie 'Scenes from a Marriage', in a way it's not so much of a joke to say that. I think there are true things said in the movie about marriage, and parenthood, without it being a 'self-help movie' or something like that. But without those sex scenes, you're faking it, to me you're not figuratively stripping them bare. As you know too, in the movie there's almost no nudity in those sex scenes, but there's a lot of emotional nudity and it's stripping them bare, and the actors were very nervous about those scenes, not because they were prudish, just because they knew they were difficult and that they were going to be very emotional. And, of course, the way movies are shot, the sex on the stair scene takes two or three days. It's physically difficult too; she was generally bruised a lot. But the nervousness of the actors just confirms, for me, that those scenes were essential. Not that they resisted, but they just wanted to get it right and knew that it was going to be emotionally exhausting. Both of the scenes, not just the second one, were difficult that way.

SG: **There are a lot of feminist theories about role-playing; you know, the woman is the eternal victim and the man is a rapist. I know a lot of feminists attack you, for example with *Dead Ringers*, where the female character was supposed to be masochistic. This is the time we're living in, where sex is in no better a situation than it was some centuries ago, when the Catholic Church said there was natural sex and sinful sex. We know that among primates, and even birds, sex is not always natural at all. Do you find it more and more difficult to show that in a film?**

DC: Not really, but it does take a determined effort to ignore the potential. It's a substantial question.

Once a filmmaker – and there are a few American filmmakers, especially living in Hollywood, who politicised themselves to death I think, they became so sensitive – can make a movie without thinking what the reverberations will be among the various activist groups, you have to then plunge deeply into your intuition and your art and leave that superficial world of politicisation behind. You're aware of it, like I'm aware that one or two people called the scene on the stairs a rape scene, and I say, well, then you missed it or I made a mistake. But when I was talking to Howard about the music, I said it has to help make it clear what's going on, but some focus group said even though the music tries to make it romantic, it's still a rape. This is a very young woman writing this, and you say those of us who are more mature, who have had more sexual experiences, have understood the complexity of sexuality and that this is not a rape scene. I mean, it's a much more complex thing going on there. Not at all to deny that you could be married and rape your wife, it's definitely true, the fact that you're married doesn't make it impossible, but the scene is not that. You can see when the eyes of the people get glassy and they click over into political mood. Unfortunately, politics is not the art of the subtle, not when it's public, and anything that is subtle is going to get demolished in politicisation. Which is why I think that politics has no place in art, because you lose the subtlety. And when you lose the subtlety, you are losing the human reality, because it is very subtle and complex, and I can see that in politics you maybe at times cannot afford to be bogged down, because you would be forced into action if you had to address every complexity. But this is art, you know, and this isn't propaganda, this isn't a political statement, this is an artistic statement. So the complexity is there, fortunately, and happily I didn't get very many questions about that scene being a rape, and why, from most of the critics who wrote about the movie after Cannes. I'm a writer and I can anticipate people saying all kind of things, like how can you expect us to have sympathy for the Viggo character if he commits a rape like that? Fortunately, I didn't really get those questions, and I think it's because the subtleties of it were evident. But it is a risk, and it depends on whom you're working with. I've certainly met with studio heads, male and female, who were so politicised it's shocking! People talk about the brutality of the Hollywood studio system, and how they are only interested in making money, but they can really derail themselves by diverging into being a good citizen, which sometimes entails becoming so politicised that it's almost laughable. We can't show that, we can't show that woman that way because that suggests that all women, blah blah, whatever, and you say no, this particular character is not meant to symbolise all women. They have a very primitive idea of how art works and how symbolism works. Fortunately, that is not my experience so far. Of course, the movie hasn't been released anywhere [yet], but based on the reactions of people so far, I don't anticipate that with this movie.

SG: On the other hand, you never know.

DC: Yes. And I think the politicisation stupidity has a particularly nasty taste, unfortunately. Sometimes, there's less of it, sometimes there's more of it. I think the whole feminist thing is not at its highest point, because there was a time when it was laughable. Obviously, the extremist and the militant wing of any political agenda is always laughable; it doesn't mean that the whole agenda is bad, but its shows you how it can go wrong. But I think we might be over that hop with feminism in North America, right now anyway.

SG: *A History of Violence* is a thriller where fate plays an important part . . .

DC: I do not necessarily believe in destiny or preordained fate. I do believe – I'm a Darwinian, you know – that randomness exists as a huge factor. It would have been possible for those two guys to walk into some other place; they just didn't happen to in this case. But at the end of a movie, you sometimes say, 'Of course!' Of course it had to happen like that! You didn't know it before, but at the end you say, 'Of course!' There's a feeling of inevitability to the proper ending to a movie. But as you know, this movie has quite an open ending because things are not resolved, nothing is really resolved. The relationships are not resolved, and even the question of whether Tom can escape the law is not resolved. We don't know there aren't some gangsters who will come after him, we don't know that he's managed to cover his tracks so well, we don't know any of these things.

SG: **And as in many of your movies, we don't really know anything about Tom!**
DC: One of the reasons why I wanted Richie [William Hurt] to be his brother was because we could get some little feel of their past, and when I wrote that stuff about, 'I tried to strangle you in your crib,' it's not so specific because, as Richie points out, maybe not all kids want to do that but a lot of kids do. (*laughs*) So it's not specific enough to count as real background, it just gives you a feel that there was a past there, and that other people lived in Tom's past when he was Joey. It really reflects that idea in the film that you can only know someone so deeply, and that's it.

SG: **You told me that in the graphic novel the characters were much more defined, but there were all the clichés about the mafia, or the mafia as a superfamily where family links are absolutely important, and the only family link that we discover between Joey and his brother is this phrase that he's repeating : 'You cost me a lot.' Which is superb, because you don't really imagine an Italian telling his brother, 'You cost me a lot!' It's true that it gives a dark feel about what family links generally are, what we know, what people feel. But beyond that, don't you feel there's a risk that people will see violence in your movie as an inherently human mode of communication? After all, we're not absolutely sure to be born predators.**
DC: Everything that lives, lives by killing something, and I think every nation has a violent past that involves suppressing or repressing or dominating others. To me, it's more the conundrum of being human and being able to imagine an ideal human existence that doesn't exist, and may not be attainable. No other animal does that, you know. We do that, we say, 'Well, I can imagine a world without violence, without starvation, without cruelty.' I can imagine it because I've seen moments of it, I've seen moments in the city of all of that, so why couldn't that be general? But then to achieve it seems still, after all these thousands of years, to be impossible. And of course even if the Mongols had imagined it, they would have rejected it because they wouldn't want those things, they had a culture in which violence was good. Dominating and killing was good, and starving your enemies was good. So, I do think that combativeness exists at a molecular level, not even just a cellular level. The substance of life on earth is aggression and dominance, and we probably are the only creatures in the universe that are conscious enough to look at that and say, 'Now I want to reject that,' even though it is of the essence of why I exist now as evolved brain. And it's a real conundrum, because I think that the primitive part is still at a cellular level, it's the desire to do that, we have that happening in the brain. I mean, I was reading a book in which the brain was described certainly not as a computer – the idea of a computer as a brain is completely false, and it has lead people into many mistakes. The brain is much more like a rainforest, and there's in fact the same struggle among the cells, and parts of the cells, for dominance as creatures in a rainforest have. The good part is that, if some of those things are destroyed, there are other things that can come to replace them in terms of brain damage and so on. But their sort of mechanistic computer model is completely false, and so even in our brains themselves there's a struggle for dominance. It requires a great intelligence and will to overcome that. I mean, in certain moments I walk down the streets in Toronto and I say, 'This is like an amazing dream!' People are civil, and

there are machines that function, and people that function, and there's a green area and birds, and everything seems to be relatively peaceful and functioning on a human level, even though the birds are having their own struggle.

SG: There are almost no cops in the streets.
DC: Yes, very few, it doesn't seem to be necessary to have police with machine guns in every corner in order to achieve this. And you say, 'Well, that's miraculous, really,' it does induce hope, that could become a worldwide situation. You take that moment and you cling to it, because there is all that bizarre thing of the media reality. While I'm walking down the streets in Toronto, I've got the explosions in Iraq, and the starvation in Darfur, and the torture, and it's all going on simultaneously. It's very confusing, but I think you could definitively make a case for violence as being bedrock human behaviour that will be incredibly difficult to change, because if there is only one human being on the planet who wants to be violent and enjoys it, then it's going to be difficult to eradicate.

SG: Some months ago, I read something really interesting on that subject. Among gorillas, for example, they can control and in a certain way suppress trouble between groups and individuals by all the ceremonies and the rituals and grooming, etc. Maybe if we became more intelligent than we were supposed to become, it's because we replaced grooming, which is a very important social interaction, by language. And language is a perfect political tool to become social. So, how can we explain how this violence – which should have been not quite so important among our ancient ancestors living in Africa – has developed so much since we were peasants perhaps, or maybe before?
DC: I think language has a lot to do with it, because the kind of violence that is experienced or visited on people comes from abstractions – the concept of evil, which the animals don't have, and the ability to dehumanise humans – so that it's almost not even violence against other humans. There are many ways that language, the ability to abstract, has allowed us to build up levels of destruction that no animal ever could manage to generate. There are other problems too, I mean the whole grooming thing does not work in a city of eight million people. It's true that ants have huge cities, and they do have rituals, but that's much more on a level of mechanical instinct, and it's not so when you get to the level of mammal grooming. Then it's much more complex. It has to be a relatively small society. It's like the original version of democracy, where you could have all the citizens of the city actually in one spot talking to each other, because there were just not that many of them.

SG: In the Rousseauist conception of democracy, there's a small group that forms a circle. In the middle of the circle is the one who knows how to talk and convince people. It's true that usually in small groups, tribes, clans, he's not always a self-imposed leader, but he's the one who will more or less express the group's will, as he will in our modern times as a representative.
DC: You should be on the jury at Cannes, to see how that works!

SG: You told me many times you almost never saw your old films again. So this is perhaps an opportunity to take a retrospective look at your cinematic career. You told me that you were sometimes tired of Cronenberg movies, because you can feel trapped. What would you say if you were not directly connected with the making of those movies? What would you say about that career that began with underground student films, then developed in the genre movie, then exploded with commercial success, but was mainly a universal acknowledgment of your cinematic genius?
DC: I can't believe that you're asking this! (*laughs*) And I have no perspective on it. The problem is that I can't see the films, I really can't, in the sense that I can't see them like a normal filmgoer.

So I'm completely at the mercy of the people to describe what they think. I really can't do a critical appraisal.

SG: No, of course! I wasn't asking for a critical appraisal. But what do you mean when you say you're tired of being Cronenberg?

DC: It's interesting to see how, in a movie like *A History of Violence* or even in *Spider*, there is a sublimation of things that are quite overt in my films, which is the whole body obsession, the question of the mutation of the flesh and how that affects identity and so on. All of those things are there in *A History of Violence* and *Spider*, but in a weirdly sublimated form. I think by sublimating them, I'm giving them maybe more power than they have when it's overt. On the other hand, when you ask people what I've done that is uniquely me, that's the stuff they talk about, the body consciousness, those things which people find quite shocking and startling, unusual and original and so on. So it's quite difficult to decide, and it's not just an intellectual decision, it's a visceral one as well, an intuitive one. If I should never make another movie that has those overt characteristics, will my work be diminished? One person who was writing about *A History of Violence* said literally that if he didn't know it was Cronenberg directing, he would never guess, but only one said that. It's not that I necessarily care about that, but it's almost like it's the natural world and superheroes. It's so interesting to see how each superhero has his two or three special things that he can do and the other ones can't do. When you're kid studying insects, you find that insects are just like that: they have one or two tricks that they do, a grasshopper has his legs, he can hop, some wasp has a sting and can fly well, but there are other things that he can't do, and each one has its vulnerabilities and its strengths. So you think of yourself that way in the jungle of cinema; am I giving up my stinger? But I'm not exercising it. Or am I developing some new superpower by sublimating the obvious one and developing some other one? Can I evolve living in my own little jungle, my own little rainforest? I don't know, as I said, part of it is intuitive. So when we talk about *Painkillers*, which I'm willing to talk about – and I have no idea where that's going right now, it's a script that I wrote five years ago – there seems to be a lot of interest in it, and Robert Lantos really wants to produce it, he's been trying to get Pete [Suschitzky] to do it for those five years, and I kept interrupting it with *eXistenZ*, which he produced, with *Spider* and *A History of Violence* – which he didn't – and apparently there is great interest from distributors and he feels he can raise the money. That would be an independent production again, unlike *A History of Violence*, which was all financed through New Line. I'm thinking, well, here's an incredible, intelligent producer who says he can raise the money to do this movie that is my own script, I have final cut, why am I hesitating? There is a reason, but I don't know. There's something that's causing me to have trouble coming to terms with saying, 'Yes, I want to do this, I must do this.' It's very strange, I had a quite similar experience before. Is it the same as that day that I trailed my racecar to the racetrack, the first race of the season in the spring? And enjoyed the beauty of being out in the country, because it's a racetrack in the countryside that I love. The racetrack itself is a road, it goes up and down, in some oaks and pine trees, and it's beautiful. Then, I get out of the car, and I start to unload the racecar, I'm completely alone, and I suddenly don't want to be there. Then I was so shocked. I did not want to be doing that. I wanted to be back in Toronto with my family or whatever, just not there. I was completely shocked and surprised. Racing has been so much a part of my life for about 30 years, not professionally, but still with a great amateur's passion. So maybe that's the response that I'm having to my own script, that I just don't want to be there. It's hard to assimilate.

SG: Actors have loved you for a long time. A lot of actors would love to be in your films.

DC: Yes, I've had great success that way, but I

also maintain a healthy scepticism. I've heard of a lot of actors who love my work, in fact Ed Harris and William Hurt both worked with my sister before they worked with me, and they told her that they would love to work with me. Sure enough, when I contacted them they were very responsive, but sometimes you hear that people want to work with you and they do, but they don't want to play that role. You know, ultimately, an actor is not going to play a role that he really doesn't want to play.

SG: Not only are actors usually very happy to be in your movies, but you're one of the few directors I know who always works with the same crew, more or less.

DC: I've always thought of that as a more European approach than the Hollywood approach, which is always to get whoever was hot, although it's true that there are some Hollywood directors that are pretty consistent in the crew that they work with. First of all, it's more efficient because any clashing of temperaments has happened already, you've worn off the rough spots, you know how each of you works, you know each other's little flaws and foibles, and you've accepted them, and now it's just focusing on the work at hand. And that's where the passion to work with each other goes, instead of extraneous emotional displays or anything. You get excited about the work, and you get excited about the thing that you're creating together, and I'm already getting Ron and the whole editing crew, everybody says, 'We want to do it again, we had such a great time, do a movie, we don't care about which one it is, do it!' (*laughs*) That support is fantastic for a director because it is a collaborative thing, you are the commander of the ship, there's no question about that, but you need the ship! You need the crew, you can't sail it by yourself. You just can't. So it's a wonderful thing to feel everybody coming back together again. It is like a family reunion, a good one, not the Harold Pinter kind, and I take great strength from their support. You don't feel that you're being undermined or backstabbed, or all of those things that you heard about and maybe experienced once or twice. People want it to work, and they're willing to work very hard to make it work and they do it very efficiently. Because of coming in underbudget and with great efficiency, that gives me freedom to do other things, to change things. So, working with that crew can actually affect the art in a very direct way, and your freedom as an artist. So I've never seen any reason not to do that, if I could.

SG: I guess after so many years working with the same basic crew, it saves time.

DC: It completely does, because it's very traumatic to have to choose another director of photography, for example. I've only done it a few times and every once in a while. With *Crash*, for a while, it looked like maybe I couldn't have Peter because he was working on Tim Burton's film *Mars Attacks!*, and then I started to audition others. It's a combination of seducing, because they're artists too, and they don't want to work with you, or they like your work but they don't want to do a movie as extreme as *Crash*. I found it very disturbing, in a very deep way. If I ever took Peter for granted, that would have let me know that I shouldn't, because you realise how complex the relation is between a director and a director of photography. To find the right guy to work with, someone in who you have complete confidence in terms of his art history, and then you also have the technical connection, the humour connection, the temperament, day after day, working at a great pressure, very tired . . . suddenly, you're talking to guys and you don't know how they're going to be under those circumstances. It is like going to war, you want to know that the people around you are reliable.

SG: I've heard so many stories of directors of photography who want to seize power, who want to impose their view.

DC: You can get that from anybody on the set, you know. You can get anybody who either thinks that he should be the director, or wants to be the director, or is just a very domineering kind of personality, you can have a huge struggle on the set. Peter and I have figured out how to do those things, amicably and with good grace and with a feeling of supporting each other. He knows that I understand his problems as a photographer, sometimes I can't accommodate him, but he knows it, sometimes I can. I know the consequences of saying to him, 'I'm sorry I can't give you the ceiling, I can't let you light from the ceiling because I need to see the ceiling.' All of those things, it takes experience, because a young director who's never shot something himself, it takes a while [for him] to understand what it's like to be a cinematographer. So, all of these things are just a source of great strength, to go into a film feeling that you've got all your weaponry with you.

SG: Ron Sanders is one of your longest collaborators, and of course editing is so important in a movie.
DC: It's always interesting when I see a director take editing credit, [as] sometimes they do. I think, in a sense, every director should be able to take the editing credit, because if there's anything that's not working, you, the director, ultimately have to say I'm responsible for all of this, because if I didn't like it I should have said something and changed it. At the same time, you need objectivity, which you can't have, that means the only way you can get that is another sensibility, another person who can surprise you with things. So that's why I ask Ron to edit the film on his own. To begin with, I don't look at it, I don't look at cuts while we're shooting unless there's a scene where maybe there's a problem of reference, maybe we should make this other shot because we don't have it, here's how it looks without it, but normally I don't want to see it until the movie is finished shooting, and then I see the movie that he's cut. Then, we go on and we start working, and we've got incredibly efficient with that. I mean *A History of Violence*, I think it took three weeks to edit, basically. There was always constant finding of stuff, but the basic structure we were very quick in finding. The same with *Spider*. We just got to be very good at it together. Once again, it's not just efficiency, it's creative efficiency, which is a different thing. It's a conservation of energy in the best possible sense. It doesn't mean that we didn't explore a lot of the possibilities, it's just that we can do that incredibly quickly. Of course, the technology helps. But as Ron reminds me, *eXistenZ* was a very difficult edit, it took a lot of complex stuff, whereas *Spider* and *A History of Violence* were very quick and relatively simple, even though they have complex things in them. It's not just a work relationship, obviously we're friends, our children know each other, and it all helps. There's a creative synergy that comes out of all that. It was very interesting, the producers of *Basic Instinct 2*, when I was playing with the idea of doing that, they wanted to strip me of everybody. Their excuse was that they wanted me to have a fresh approach to everything and be stimulated by people and so on. But it was really a power thing, they didn't want me to have my people because they felt that was giving me too much power, if I had people whose loyalty would be with me and not with them, it was a very Hollywood way of looking at it. New Line was not at all like that, they were excited for me to be working with my people. It's a completely different approach. I ultimately had come to think that the *Basic Instinct 2* approach was very perverse. It's like asking a boxer to come into the ring with his hands tied behind his back, because when you're a director, a lot of what you bring is your relationship with other people, and to take those away from me was a very perverse thing.

SG: The last person in the production process – maybe not the least, because there's always something very essential going on – is of course Howard Shore. How do you interact, Howard and you?
DC: First of all, it's a very abstract thing, because

it's hard to find words to discuss music without talking about other music. You can also talk about emotional responses, [but] to be articulate with what music should do in a scene can be a tricky thing. So, once again, if you have a shorthand with somebody, if you have a history with somebody, then you can get right to the basics very quickly. But there is a sort of methodology that we try to stick to, it's pretty straightforward really: I send the script to Howard very early on, and then he comes to visit the set every once in a while, then I show him – not the assembly that Ron does first, because that's still far away from the movie, but maybe my first serious cut. There comes a point where I think OK, this is worth showing to Howard, even though there will be lots of changes. But usually I want to wait until the structure of the film is really there – that is to say the scenes that I've cut out are gone, if I have to transpose scenes, change them around. I really want to be at that point, because that really does affect the structure of the music. We then do what we call a spotting session, that is, Howard will come into the editing room with Ron – and Ron is very musically adept, that's another thing, Ron is not just an editor of visual stuff, he started as a sound editor, and he's also a musician. He's a real rock for me in the sound mix, which is not something people normally think [of] when they think of an editor. He and Howard get along very well and know each other very well. They have this long history, of course, from *The Brood* . . . So, we are all there, the three of us, watching the movie. I screen it for Howard first, he sees the whole thing, and then we do a spotting session, and now we're talking about where would be the music? Why would there be music there? Howard is not the kind of composer who wants to put his mark on the film, no matter what. He wants the music to have a purpose for being there. He's just as likely to say, 'Take that music away!' as he is to put it in. In fact, he composed music for the beginning of *A History of Violence* for the opening scene, first shot. We all agreed it didn't work. That had nothing to do with the quality of music, it just had to do with what it did to the scene. We all agreed that it was better to have no music there, to have it be quiet, and just the music of the car radio. That's the kind of discussions we had: if there was music there, why would it be there? What would it be saying? What kind of instruments would we be using and why? It gets very detailed. You sort of say, 'I think that the music should start just after she says this line,' and then the music starts. And then the discussion will be, 'Well, what would happen if we had it starting halfway through that scene?' Of course, the question of music interweaving with dialogue becomes very critical because it's often not very well done. The music is fighting the dialogue or it's too loud, even just the question of can you hear the dialogue? Do you use timpani and big brass horns in the middle of dialogue? The answer is probably not, because you can't hear the dialogue, or you have to pull the music down so far that it sounds crushed and not full. All of these discussions happen in great detail. Sometimes, even before we have this discussion, Howard will write themes. Howard was in Moscow, conducting a symphony orchestra there to do music for a Korean video game, and at the same time he was composing music for *A History of Violence*. He would write it by hand, and fax it or email it to his crew in New York, where he has his offices, and then they would create a synthesised version of his handwritten score, using simple instruments, and these days they can sound very good, close to the real orchestration. Then they would email it to me in MP3 files, so that I could hear very quickly things that Howard would be thinking of, it wouldn't be composed specifically for the scenes but it would be themes. So, often, when we're spotting now, I've [already] heard some of those and we can say, 'Yes, I can see how this would work with that.' So we're talking about specific music that he's actually composed. We do the temporary mix for a test screen, you definitely want to have music on your movie when you're doing a test preview. But the movie's not finished, and usually the music doesn't even exist, and you're using music from other movies, cut to give some kind of musical support to the film. When we did *A History of Violence*, there were three or four music cues – which is to say discrete sections of music for scenes – that Howard had composed already that were synthesised, they weren't orchestrated, he hadn't gone to London and actually conducted the London Symphony orchestra, or whoever he's working with. So there was actually some of Howard Shore's music in our temporary mix, which is unusual, but because of technology these days you can do that. You can see it's a long, elaborate, delicate process – and then during the sound mix it goes further, because once I've heard synthesised versions of all the cues, and Ron has laid them where he thinks they should go, we can then discuss adjustments to that. And then usually I go to where Howard is recording the music, usually it's London, but not always. This time, because we were trying to get ready for the Cannes festival, we were already starting to do the dialogue pre-mixing. And so every day I'd be connected to Howard by ISTN line. I could see him, and we'd see the movie, he would play me the music over these telephone lines that he'd just recorded. Or he was often in the middle of recording with his London musicians, and then we could discuss things. He could say, 'Now do you want me to record it again using flutes instead of French horns?' Because that would give a softer, gentler version. And I would say yes, or no, or, 'Let's try it,' and then the next day he would play me those things. So, I had still the possibility of making suggestions for changes, as Howard is very collaborative and loves to experiment. By the time that we get into the sound mix I've heard the music a lot, but he leaves me layers to play with because he does pre-mixing as well, but there's always the separate elements. So if I say, 'I love that, but the horns are really bothering me, I think the cue would be better without the horns at all,' it's possible to do that. In *Naked Lunch*, for example, I experimented with Howard by combining some improvisations that Ornette Coleman had done. We actually created in the sound mix some new cues by combining other cues that hadn't existed before. So it can get very creative that way. Howard sends a person who sits in the mix with us, who's responsible for the music and can tell us what Howard was intending in great detail, she's Howard's spy in the mix. If I say, 'Let's try moving this cue five frames later, because somehow something is not working,' then she reports that to Howard. Ultimately, Howard comes to the mix and he hears playback, and then we reserve a few days for him to suggest other things, to make changes, to be upset with what's happened or not, which is not usually the case, and we just play. So it's a very long process and it involves a lot of collaboration.

SG: To take three examples of my favourite Howard scores: the first one would be *The Brood*, the second one *Naked Lunch*, and the third one would be *Crash*. Those three scores are totally different.
DC: And *Dead Ringers* too, I have to say.

SG: Yes, they could have been composed by different people. Each of them gives to the movie a certain atmosphere, and stresses some details, or a whole section of the movie. So have you ever disagreed with Howard? Has he ever proposed music that didn't have the feel of what you wanted to show?
DC: Oh, yeah. I mean, not usually the overall score, but individual cues, yes, sure. Thinking of *The Brood*, which was the first movie I did that had a completely original score: there was a moment I distinctly remember, when Samantha Eggar reseals this growth thing that she has, with external udders and stuff, and I remember not liking the cue that Howard had composed for that. I just didn't think it would work, and so I think we took a cue from somewhere else. That was our first time working together, so there was a lot for both of us to learn about that. I think that was only Howard's second time working on a score. But there are definitely moments where

there are cues [that] I think don't work somehow, and I ask him to change them. Or it can be a happy accident. I mean, the title music for *Crash* was not meant to be the title music, it's six electric guitars meant to be somewhere [else] in the music, and I said, 'I want that for the title music.'

SG: Yes indeed, it's so unusual, so striking.

DC: It is very unusual. You just won't hear that. That's the kind of things that should win Oscars, but never does. But anyway, that affected the visualisation of the opening credits as well. That music, the metallic quality of it, made me think of metallic credits. So, every possible thing has happened. The one thing that hasn't happened is an entire score that I thought was [so] bad, I wanted to go to another composer. This happens a lot in the movie business. Howard himself has replaced some scores that were thrown out by people, some of it is well-known, [so] I won't get into it. An entire score is junked – [it's been] mixed and orchestrated by well-known composers, and then the director, the producer, the studio, whoever, thinks this is not good, this is not helping the movie, in fact it is ruining the movie, and you get rid of that score. If I did that, I would ask Howard to do the new score. But the other mentality is, 'Let's get rid of the composer, and get a new composer, because this old composer maybe doesn't understand the movie.' That's a possible approach; you have found that this composer just has one idea, one take on the movie, and cannot change that, cannot see why there's something wrong with that, or at least cannot see another way of going about it. I've never had that experience, but Howard has had that experience in terms of being the one to come in and replace [the original composer]. But in terms of individual moments where you say, 'I don't think that's working,' Howard is the first to say, 'OK, let's see what else we can do.' He's not there to protect his music only, he's there to make the movie work. People see threads throughout my movies, and I see all those threads connected with Howard's score. I can hear the connections. It doesn't mean that he has not a very strong personality, but he's a Canadian and we have a specific way of expressing our strong personalities. It can still be very strong, but the desire to collaborate, the enthusiasm for collaborating, is really there. The idea of a social structure where people all contribute is very strong in Canada, as opposed to just being the individual, or being the genius. So I think that's part of it, and obviously Howard and I come from the same city, we're very close in age, so the chances that we can [successfully] collaborate are therefore very high.

Epilogue

SG: You said that you wanted to at least try to make a more commercial movie without betraying yourself. One day you told me in Paris, 'I would like to make Cronenberg movies that would be less Cronenberg.' Where does that come from?

DC: It's the 'Brundlefly' problem. Maybe a little less Brundle and more fly, you know, the proportions of the creature. You start to feel trapped by your own mythology, and it's a mythology that comes from several places; part of it comes from inside you, and part of it comes from the way you proceed, and you get put in a box by people, like typecasting. And it seems to be benign, because it's people who say, 'But we want you to keep making scandals, we want you to be that guy who made *Shivers*, we don't want you to be the guy who makes *Naked Lunch* or *Dead Ringers*, because we like that other stuff.' That's putting you in a box, in a prison, in the most gentle and sweet way. It's because they appreciated what you did, and perhaps now that I'm this old they are wanting to relive their own childhood where they grew up watching those movies, and they had an effect on them that they will never recapture, because they are not children anymore. All of those complex things go on. And it could be quite liberating and exhilarating to incorporate into yourself the creative import of other people, which of course in film you do all the time anyway. But it's not as though I've never done *The Dead Zone*, which I didn't write and is based on a best-selling novel, [or] *Dead Ringers*, based on real people, and *M. Butterfly*, based on a play, and of course *Naked Lunch*. So I've done it before. Even *Spider*, which is not an original script, we'd never have written that because it comes out of an English experience that I didn't have. So after *Spider*, it really was two things: it was feeling that *Spider* didn't have enough of an audience, and that it didn't get the distribution, especially in North America, that I would have liked it to have had. It didn't get pushed enough. It's really coming to terms with the nature of the art form as it is right now, which is that, in a narrow world, many films have a 3,000-print release in North America. To have a 35-print movie like *Spider* puts you in a very small box. And you wonder what a movie that had some marketing muscle behind it, a marketing will behind it, would do if it was a film of yours. But it crossed the line that allowed that kind of release. I mean, I've had that really with *The Fly*, almost by accident. That was about an 1100-print release, which for that time was quite big, even though it was a small budget, and it did very well. So I just wanted to have that experience, just to see if there's a way to have it all. Basically, being greedy, you want to be the artist that you want to be with no compromise, and you also want to have a big audience and make some money. Of course, after *Spider*, I was very broke, because that was two years of working without money. I realised I couldn't do that again. I came very close to feeling like a kid and wondering how to pay the rent. So I needed a project that would fulfil all those things. That's very hard to do, and of course you don't know in advance whether it's going to work at the end. At the end, you could even say you have a commercial hit, but secretly you feel depressed about what you've done, because you don't think it's very good.

SG: Nowadays, directors like yourself spend a lot of time reading novels, putting down ideas, and never knowing if they'll find money to do this or that. I know it's been a source of frustration for you. Some of your [unmade] projects have never even been heard of. Could you tell me of some that you still find appealing, that you would like to go back to?

DC: Well, they're not too many. I've been pretty lucky. I've had the experience of being rejected for projects, and it's important to mention that, because sometimes people think that when you reach a certain level of fame or experience, you can do whatever you want. I've tried a few times to get projects that were held by Hollywood studios, and have been rejected. I have no idea of what would have come of that. Of course we know about *Total Recall*, long ago. But there are not too many scripts that I've written myself that didn't get made. Usually, it was because I didn't write them until there was someone who was really a good producer. But *Red Cars* is a script that, whenever I look at it, which is not that often, I really still quite like it. It's about Formula One racing and Phil Hill, the American driver, winning the championship in 1961 for Ferrari. It's a wonderful story. I was very obsessed with racing. Of course, I've done a racing movie, *Fast Company*, about drag racing, which was not my favourite [form of] motor racing, but I enjoyed making that movie. I think if I could get the financing forward, I would make *Red Cars*, even though I stopped the racing myself. I was vintage racing, which is to say I was racing cars from the era of the late fifties, early sixties. So I even would have raced against Phil Hill in 1961. It was a Cooper, a Formula One car, but I've sold all those cars and I've stopped racing, just because it takes so much time. But I did love it. The kind of racing I was doing was club racing, which is a very low-level racing, but I have won races and I have trophies and it was all fun. You can scare yourself, of course, and there's a whole wonderful machine element, the technology, even though it's old technology now – it's vintage technology. You literally get your hands dirty. You tune on the spokes of the wire wheels of your Ferrari, or you tune the carburetors, you change the jets to make the carburetion better. There's a lot of stuff that I could do without being a professional. Engine builder. All car racers fool around with their car. I suppose in Formula One you probably don't, because it's too high-tech, but at the lower levels you do tend to get your hands very dirty. I did love that, and I still have a love for it. So I don't know how I would react if suddenly the money was there for that movie, because I'm more distanced from it in a certain way, but that might be good. I'm not sure. The script was not just for gear heads, it was not just a machine movie, it was about very passionate people, very operatic. Literally operatic, because I created an opera, a Ferrari opera, and I can't imagine why there isn't a Ferrari opera. Maybe I'm going to have to write it. We had men singing on the assembly lines as they created the latest racing Ferrari. That would be a fantastic scene in an opera. It would have been in this movie, even though it's pure fiction. But the movie was based on real people, of course – Enzo Ferrari, Phil Hill, and Wolfgang von Trips, who was a Phil Hill teammate who died at a race in Monza, and that allowed Phil Hill to become world champ. This is full of tragedy and family things, and the mother in their dream sequences is not typical of sports movies (which is maybe why it's hard to finance). But there's a group of people in a company called Volumina in Turin, Italy, who wanted to publish a book that I would do somehow, because they are very inventive publishers. They published a very good book on Peter Greenaway. But as I said to them, I'm not a graphic artist as Peter Greenaway is, and therefore I couldn't do that kind of book. They asked me what I had, and I answered that I had a script, that it couldn't seem to be realised as a movie, but that I would love it to be realised as a book. They got very excited because it's Italian and they're Italian – they're not far from Modena. They're proceeding to create this book, which will be the script of *Red Cars*, done in a very interesting graphic style, an artful way, with many archival photographs of Ferraris, memorabilia, racers, people. They seem to have the cooperation of the official Ferrari archives, which is nice for me, because I'd love to have official Ferrari recognition of the script. It would help me if it is ever going to get made. We intend to present that book at the Venice Film Festival, which is where they presented Peter Greenaway's book. It would be quite fun to go to a film festival when you're only presenting a book, and not a film, even though it's the book of a script! I've never been to Venice before, or to the festival of course. I don't think anybody else is going to make a film like *Red Cars*. For *Total Recall*, it was a different situation and it did get made, although it was not my version, obviously.

SG: I also heard rumours about *The Fly*.

DC: Yes, we seem to be making an opera of *The Fly*, Howard Shore and some people who put operas together. Of course, it's a completely unknown world for me, but having done *M. Butterfly*, the centre of which was an opera, I do have some appreciation for the form of the opera. The idea is that I'll direct it. So it would be a co-production, with probably the Los Angeles opera company and Le Chatelet Theatre in Paris. It's interesting, because they do co-productions in opera too. It's impossible for one company to finance an original work. There are many parallels to the film and many, many differences, of course. So we're hoping it's Placido Domingo who's running the opera company.

SG: But if you ever wrote an operatic story, it was *The Fly*.

DC: Definitely. It's David Henry Hwang who's writing the libretto, who also wrote *M. Butterfly*. Howard and I, we think the music for *The Fly* is very operatic, even as we're going a different way with the music for *A History of Violence*. We were very conscious with *The Fly* that there was a kind of opera going on. But I never really thought necessarily of it as an opera until it was suggested by Howard and Jean-Jacques Cesbron, who's a kind of an opera hustler, he represents various companies, opera performers, and he helps put together opera projects and coordinates them.

SG: I know that opera costs more and more to organise.

DC: Yes, and you work for three years, and then they play for five performances and that's it! You don't know if there's any chance of them ending up in some kind of modern repertory, because that's very rare for a modern opera. One of the interesting things that happen is that you often cannot find singers who want to learn a new opera. They want only to learn the parts of the standard repertory, which they know they will be able to sing for the next twenty years. If they spend the time learning *The Fly*, then there are five performances and they never sing it again. That's not a very good return on their time and effort, so you have to find singers who are looking for a challenge. It's very much an opera version of what you often want with intimate movies. You want to find a star who is interested in not just doing a star turn, but who's interested in something challenging. Sometimes you can find that, and sometimes you can't. It's very fascinating. I have to figure out how to direct an opera, that's part of the fun, because I'm really only just overseeing the writing, and of course, when it comes to the music that's going to be all Howard. Even though I've been involved with the casting, my sensitivity to the singing voice is nothing like my sensitivity to the spoken voice. I have a great sensitivity to spoken voices in cinema. When it comes to singing, I don't have the expertise of someone like Howard. His judgement of the voices of the singers is very sophisticated. Anybody who sings opera is amazing to me, but obviously, even in that rarified world, there are ones who are fantastic, and ones who are just OK. So, the casting of the three premier roles will be very interesting. And then I start to psych into the little, pithy things that have to do with opera, like George Bernard Shaw said, 'An opera is a story in which a tenor and a soprano want to make love but a baritone won't let them.' That's the summary of an opera! These things are strangely clarifying for me. It's not something you think of exactly when you're casting actors, but the bad guy has to be the baritone. What happens if the hero is not a tenor, but is a baritone? We're playing with that. It's very exciting and very challenging, and the possibility for humiliation and failure are huge! But at least, it's on a smaller scale than if you fail with a movie.

SG: It's always interesting for someone who works in cinema to test himself on stage. And opera is really the stage art, because it deals with time much more than a play.

DC: Yes, and yet you also have another problem, that is: how much physical activity can you ask a singer to do and still be able to sing? Can he really hang upside down from the ceiling and sing? I've been seeing some performances which were relatively static, because when the singing was happening, the actors were just standing there basically, and maybe moving around a little bit, then most of the movement was happening between songs. I saw, at Le Chatelet Theatre, a Richard Strauss opera called *Arabella*, which I knew nothing about, and it was fantastic. The music was fantastic, but the production too was fantastic. It was very exciting for me to see that, because it was not static, the set was like a art deco hotel, an L escalator was going up to the ceiling and it was used beautifully in three dimensions, while singing. So it's a great compressed education I'm getting, and everybody who works in films knows that you do learn most of the stuff on the job. You know, the technology moves so fast, and so on. You're always faking it, to a certain extent, because you're always doing something you haven't done before, which is part of the reason you're excited, but it's also scary. You try and experiment with yourself. With opera, of course, it's a big experiment, because I'm coming in knowing just about nothing, and by the time 2007 comes around, I'll be directing one that's based on my own film! (*laughs*) So it's going to be very interesting, and of course it will become a different thing. As important as Howard's music was to the movie, it will be ten times as important to the opera, because it will be right in there with the essence of the voice, and that's exciting too.

SG: **I remember when I was doing research in the Cinematheque library in Toronto, and I found, in your very old scripts, characters and situations and even names that would appear ten or fifteen years later. Who knows what would had happened if suddenly you would have decided to do it at that time? What if you had done something with the material of *Dead Ringers* that was almost fifteen years earlier? Maybe it would have been a masterpiece.**

DC: I doubt it, actually. I've often thought that, because we tried to make that movie ten years before we actually got to make it. And I wonder if I was mature enough in my technique and in my psychology to really make it as good a movie as it turned out to be. I don't know. But how are you relating that to *Painkillers*? Do you think I should wait another twenty years?

SG: **No! But perhaps your creative instinct is right in this case?**
DC: It might be. And yet I find myself saying, when I read it, [that] for all the problems that I see there, it's still more interesting by ten times than the things that I'm getting from my agent. So I have to balance that as well. At the moment that we're speaking, I still don't know whether I will do *Painkillers* or not. Robert [Lantos] would be very upset to hear me saying this, but he knows that I have some inner resistance to it, and he's working very hard as a very kind and smart producer to make me overcome those hesitations, but we'll see.

SG: **When you've worked such a long time on a script, and on casting, when you get a lot of people involved, and then you're shooting the movie, and then you're editing and post-producing the movie – when you feel that the audience was not there – which can happen, maybe because the film was not released properly, or for more mysterious reasons – is it absolutely painful, or have you become a fatalist?**
DC: Yeah, it's funny, I'm a weird combination of optimism and pessimism. I always think that my movies are going to do really well, even when it's obvious, like *Crash* or *Spider*, that they have a limited audience just by their very nature – although *Crash*, as you know, did very well in France.

SG: **But on the other hand, you were surprised by the success of *Scanners* and *The Fly* . . .**
DC: Yes, that's right. So, the possibilities of being disappointed or positively surprised are there. *M. Butterfly* was a disappointment. It had Warner

Brothers, it had the backing, even though it was a low-budget film by their standards, but at that point it was my biggest-budget film. I thought it would do much better than it did, and it didn't get a very good critical response either. But I could see reasons for it that didn't have to do with the film, [that were more to do with] whether I have a very good self-defence mechanism. It might be that you need that, it's sometimes called having a thick skin, but I don't think I have such a thick skin. At the same time, I have inner Machiavellian techniques to protect myself, and so I can think of all the reasons why *M. Butterfly* did not do well that don't have to do with it being a bad film. And then I've always had people who said to me, '*M. Butterfly* is my favourite film of yours,' and I've got the Chinese people who found it incredibly emotional and affecting. So there's always enough support, it doesn't have to be millions of people. I mean it's nice if it's millions of people, because then the film is a big success and it's perceived that way, but creatively, artistically, once all of it is done, I don't want to have a met in me, he said, 'Hey! Are you happy being so marginal? Are you happy with such a small audience?' and I said, 'How big an audience do you need?' I wasn't meaning to be confrontational, I was literally asking the question. When you're a filmmaker, aside from the fact that you want the film to make back its cost and at least make some money for the people who invested in it, how big an audience do you need to be satisfied as a director? If you're only satisfied by having huge number one hits, then you know that's what you're going for. Can you be satisfied being a 'marginal', as I've been called by a couple of other people, including Paul Verhoven? He didn't mean that in a negative way, he meant it literally. So, after *Spider*, I felt that I would like to have a bigger audience for my next one. But it doesn't have to be an overall thing, you can say, 'I'm going to do *Crash*, it's going to be extreme, the fact that it's extreme is what is attractive about it, so there's no point in trying to make it not so extreme.' It means that its budget and its audience will be limited. I accept that, I want to do this movie. So it comes to pass and you do it, and the same with *Spider*. You know *Spider* is not going to be the Number One hit in North America, so you can't be bitterly disappointed, unless you've done a movie for it to be a hit and it's not. Then you might have compromised some of your art in order to be more populist and you get nothing. You don't have the good art and you don't have the money, you don't have a big audience! With *A History of Violence*, I'm very happy with the art part of it, but I'm aware that it is a much more potentially accessible movie than *Crash* – just by the very fact that the characters are more familiar to everybody, especially in the West. And that means that there's a stronger possibility that they can identify with them. They understand these characters, they will be therefore automatically more emotionally involved. I don't do that very often, and obviously there are family concerns in *Dead Ringers* and in *Spider*, but they're so convoluted and tormented that you know that most people won't directly relate to them. So I would be disappointed if *A History of Violence* only did as well as *Spider*. To me, then, that would be a failure, it would mean that something would have gone wrong, because from the beginning it was meant to have a big audience. But we'll see.

SG: Some days ago, I was watching a programme on French TV and they were showing that a lot of so-called 'cult movies' were actually total disasters when they were released. There are big hits totally forgotten five years after, and that will never be re-released except on TV, and 'cult movies', that everybody thinks made billions of dollars, that were flops.

DC: Well, you look at literature. When people talk about great novels, they talk about *Ulysses* and *Moby Dick*. These were all failures in terms of money and now they're considered the cornerstones of literature. It's the same in cinema, there's the technological aspect of movies, and we're in a wonderful place there right now that we were not in 30 or 40 years ago – which is that you can have a movie on your shelf like a book, and you can take it down and look at it, look at your favourite scene, and now see behind the scenes and analyse it all in your house. This has given [us] a whole new mode of perception, which I think is not even still fully assimilated and understood. But for a filmmaker who makes films like *Crash* and *Spider* and *Naked Lunch*, this is a great thing, because it means that the initial box-office response to a film is not so important. It's still important if you want it to be a big hit, but in terms of its life as a creative force, as an influence on other filmmakers, on your life as an artist and the community of artists, it enhances that, and it gives maybe the chance that your movie can be discovered and rediscovered. Young people now, who are famous for having very short memories, they still do discover some of these other films.

SG: And I really don't know if *The Da Vinci Code* will be remembered ten years from now. In France alone, *The Da Vinci Code* sold four million copies, and Proust, I think, sold in the twentieth century like 250,000 copies in France. But of course, Proust is simply the best twentieth century writer.

DC: It's very instructive, you know. I bought a house in the country and the woman didn't take the books away that she had, and they were all sort of Sydney Sheldon bestsellers and that stuff, and you look at it and it's wonderfully pathetic. These books that were bestsellers and everybody was excited about, they're just nothing now, they have no influence, no meaning, they're trash, basically. For someone who is a serious artist, this is very good to see, because you're often tempted to do that because at the time, the excitement, the money, the celebrity and the influence can be very seductive. You just need to step back a little bit and you realise that it's of the moment only, and if you are not that kind of creator, then you don't need that.

SG: Last question, but I think I've already got the answer: could you ever accept not having the final cut on a movie?

DC: Well, I don't have it on *A History of Violence* and I didn't have it on *M. Butterfly*, legally. But I do have it, because the movies will be as I want them to be. I mean, there are very few directors who get final cut officially from a studio. Maybe three, Spielberg and I don't know who else. But one of the attractions that independent producers can offer to a director is final cut, because they say, 'Look, we can't pay you what the studio would pay you, we can't give you the budget and the stars that the studio could afford, but we can give you a lot of things: creative freedom, final cut.' So, for example, if I do another movie with Robert Lantos, I will absolutely have final cut. When I do a movie with New Line, they will not give me final cut and I have to accept that or not do the movie. However, what we can do is have a contractual structure that makes it very difficult for them to re-cut my movie, because we would have to do back-to-back screenings for their version and my version, and do cards, and they would have to show that their version got better scores than my version. So it's not as though they could just take the movie away and re-cut it. They would have to have this proof that their cut was more commercially viable than my cut. They would have to have the will to do that; we've all heard these stories of various Miramax disasters and so on, that couldn't happen legally with New Line. And basically, I'm collaborative up to a point. Their executives would talk to me, wondering if things could be different and better. I would try some things, because there comes a point in editing when you're losing your objectivity anyway . . . so whether it's legally final cut or it's not should become irrelevant. They talk about a director's cut DVD; to me there is only one cut, and it's the director's cut. I've never been in a situation where I felt that I needed to do that, because I've been betrayed or I've had the movie taken away . . . I hope I'll never be in that situation, those are the only reasons – also censorship – for a director's cut DVD. I hope I'll never need to do one. With *A History of Violence*, and the relationship I had with New Line, I don't think it will ever be an actual issue, [since] it has already been a contractual issue. But at the moment every cut in the film is my cut, and I don't see that changing. Obviously, you do have to do a TV version, a free TV version, where the bad swearing is taken away and some of the violence is taken away. All of my movies, final cut or not, have their TV versions that I would not approve, so you see, even the concept of final cut is a very theoretical thing. Do I know that in Finland the Finnish distributor has not just taken one or two little things out [that] the censors were upset about, and he didn't tell me? Any director needs to be able to have the revenue from free TV. Was *Crash* ever shown on free TV? I doubt it. They wouldn't even show it, and I already did a famous Blockbuster version of *Crash*, which is ten minutes shorter than the real version, and on that movie I still have final cut. Kubrick tried very hard to obsessively control every screen, and of course he couldn't. Someone said the projectionist has the final cut, and there's a truth there too. So it's a question of not driving yourself mad, but I don't want the pain of having a movie that someone else has re-cut. I've never had that and it's not an experience I want to have. It hasn't happened, and often it's not a question of legality but a question of personalities. Who is the most obsessive? Who is the most determined? Who is the most Machiavellian? So far, it's always been me. So the movies have basically escaped mutilation, [in] things like free TV. I used to watch movies that way, but since cable channels, who would ever watch that? I don't even look at it. So you now see movies uncut on cable and DVD . . . there's no point in subjecting yourself to free TV, and certainly television is changing because of that. The networks are dying and that's fine. So that particular form of mutilation might well disappear, because people just don't want that, they've now experienced the other things. But as you know, when someone has a DVD of your movie, he pauses it, he skips things that he's not interested in, that's the right of the audience to mutilate your film. They turn the sound down or off, they tune the colours more funny, they like more green . . .

You have to accept this, because all directors do the same thing. They watch a DVD and then suddenly the phone rings and the baby cries, or they're hungry and they stop it, they come back . . . it's not exactly a commercial but it's a stoppage, and you come back . . . I think I'm capable of not losing the movie if I stop it for five minutes and come back. So I mean, it's better than being distracted by a commercial, where you don't want it. I think that the nervous system of the viewer has changed, you're developing some new skills to absorb stuff and channel surfing . . . in a way, the whole question of final cut becomes less hot . . .

Like people 'multi-tasking' on their computer, as they say, and the kids are great at it, because they grow up with it now, and just one source of information is too boring for them. It's not occupying all of their brain. So they need several sources of information, back and forth. But the other interesting thing, too, is that the children watch the movies over and over again. It used to be considered arrogant if a filmmaker said, 'You have to watch my film at least three times.' Now if the kids love your movie, they watch it twenty times. So it's actually a very rich and interesting time for a filmmaker in terms of his audience, and just in terms of personal strategies for survival, there are many ways that you can comfort yourself, especially if you know that your movie is out there somewhere on a DVD, even if it's a bootleg. I remember a long time ago, someone from Cuba saying he had seen my movies in Cuba, where they were banned, but he saw them on a bootleg. When I went to China, people had seen *The Fly*, they didn't even know that I was the director of the movie, people had seen it bootlegged, smuggled; who knows what the quality was like, but it gives it the wonderful, special taste of the forbidden, and that pleased me. Even in piracy and Internet piracy, as a filmmaker you feel, 'I'd rather have my film live than not live.'

It's like evolution and mutation and everything else. Now it's been embodied by sound mixers, the DJs, who sample different songs and mixthem together and create their own songs, and there's a big flurry of concern because it's copyright, because they're using other people's music to make their own music. And there's even film sampling, which I've never seen any of, where there are filmmakers who are taking scenes from all kinds of people's movies. There's a whole subculture of movies that are made, composed, of other people's movies. Do you know that?

SG: I've seen some, but I must say it was usually in art galleries, in Paris. But it's never only sampling. They use sampling to enhance their videos . . .

DC: Yeah . . . but in a way, that sort of process is happening around the world, and there's a sort of international exchange that the technology has made possible, and maybe even inevitable, now. So there is [an] escape [route] for someone whose movie has been changed, or mutilated, or [has had] final cut taken away from him. You still have some of that feeling that it's a new version of 'auteurism', something of you is still there. I haven't had the classic experience of a studio taking my movie away and completely re-cutting it, but even [when] people do that, there's still the shots that you set up, there's something of you.

SG: But you can find on the Net a lot of things that show how you have created a mythology. For example, your *Naked Lunch* gave birth to international Internet mythology – I saw a lot of sites in Japan or Korea . . .

DC: Yes, that's just like the consolation of death and decay, you know. Your molecules, your atoms will eventually be out there, doing whatever they do! (*laughs*) It's not you, but it's part of you. It's similar to that, it's sort of the artistic version of death and decay, which is not necessarily a terrible thing.

SG: There was a Greek philosopher, Hegesias, who said that the most pleasurable state in life is decay.

DC: Well, we'll see . . . (*laughs*)

SG: He was a great philosopher . . .

DC: Who's very decayed right now. So he must know it! (*laughs*)

Filmography

cinema

1966
Transfer
Director/Screenplay/Cinematography/Editing: David Cronenberg; Cast: Mort Ritts, Rafe MacPherson; Filmed outside Toronto; **Duration:** Seven mins. 16mm, colour.

1967
From the Drain
Director/Screenplay/Cinematography/Editing: David Cronenberg; **Cast: Mort Ritts, Stephen Nosko; Filmed outside Toronto; Duration:** Fourteen mins. 16mm, colour.

1969
Stereo
Director/Screenplay/Cinematography/Editing: David Cronenberg; **Naration:** Glenn McCauley, Mort Ritts; **Cast:** Ronald Mlodzik, Jack Messinger, Paul Mulholland, Iain Ewing, Arlene Mlodzik, Clara Meyer, Glenn McCauley; **Produced by:** Emergent Films; **Filmed in Toronto; Duration:** 63 mins. 16mm, b&w.

1970
Crimes of the Future
Director/Screenplay/Cinematography/Editing: David Cronenberg; **Cast:** Ronald Mlodzik, Jon Lidolt, Tania Zolty, Jack Messinger, Paul Mulholland, Iain Ewing; **Production Company:** Emergent Films Ltd., with the participation of the SDICC; **Filmed outside Toronto; Duration:** 63 mins. 35mm, colour.

1975
Shivers/They Came From Within
Director/Screenplay: David Cronenberg; **Producer:** Ivan Reitman, John Dunning; **Cinematography:** Robert Saad; **Editing:** Patrick Dodd; **Music:** Ivan Reitman; **Special effects/Makeup:** Joe Blasco; **Cast:** Paul Hampton (Roger St. Luc), Joe Silver (Rollo Linsky), Lynn Lowry (Forsythe), Allan Migicovsky (Nicholas Tudor), Susan Petrie (Janine Tudor), Barbara Steele (Betts), Ronald Mlodzik (Merrick), Fred Doederlein (Emil Hobbes); **Production Company:** DAL Productions Ltd., with the participation of the SDICC; **Filmed outside Montreal; Duration:** 87 mins. 35mm, colour.

1976
Rabid
Director/Screenplay: David Cronenberg; **Producer:** John Dunning; **Art Director:** Claude Marchand; **Cinematography:** Rene Verzier; **Editing:** Jean Lafleur; **Music:** Ivan Reitman; **Special effects/Makeup:** Joe Blasco; **Cast:** Marilyn Chambers (Rose), Franck Moore (Hart Read), Joe Silver (Murray Cypher), Howard Ryshpan (Dr. Dan Keloid), Patricia Gage (Dr. Roxanne Keloid), Susan Roman (Mindy Kent), Jean-Roger Periard (Lloyd Walsh), Terry Schonblum (Judy Glasberg); **Production Company:** Cinema Entertainment Enterprises (for DAL Productions Ltd.) with the participation of the SDICC; **Filmed outside Montreal; Duration:** 91 mins. 35mm, colour.

1979
Fast Company
Director: David Cronenberg; **Producer:** Michael Lebowitz, Peter O'Brian, Courtney Smith; **Screenplay:** Phil Savath, Courtney Smith, David Cronenberg, based on the history of Alan Treen; **Art Director:** Carol Spier; **Cinematography:** Mark Irwin; **Editing:** Ronald Sanders; **Music:** Fred Mollin; **Cast:** William Smith (Lonnie 'Lucky Man' Johnson), Claudia Jennings (Sammy), John Saxon (Phil Adamson), Nicholas Campbell (Billy 'The Kid' Brooker), Cedric Smith (Gary 'The Blacksmith' Black), Judy Foster (Candy), George Buza (Meatball); **Production Company:** Michael Lebowitz Inc. (for Quadrant Films), with the participation of the SDICC; **Filmed outside Calgary and Edmonton; Duration:** 91 mins. 35mm, colour.

The Brood
Director/Screenplay: David Cronenberg; **Producer:** Claude Heroux; **Executive Producers:** Victor Solnicki, Pierre David; **Cinematography:** Mark Irwin; **Editing:** Alan Collins; **Music:** Howard Shore; **Special Effects and Makeup:** Jack Young; **Cast:** Oliver Reed (Dr. Hal Raglan), Samantha Eggar (Nola Carveth), Art Hindle (Franck Carveth), Cindy Hinds (Candia Carbeth), Henry Beckman (Barton Kelly), Robert Silverman (Jean Hartog), Nicholas Campbell (Chris), Rainer Schwarz (Dr. Birkin); **Production Company:** Les Productions Mutuelles et Elgin International Productions, with the participation of the SDICC; **Filmed outside Toronto; Duration:** 91 mins. 35mm, colour.

1980
Scanners
Director/Screenplay: David Cronenberg; **Producer:** Claude Heroux; **Executive Producers:** Victor Solnicki, Pierre David; **Art Director:** Carol Spier; **Cinematography:** Mark Irwin; **Editing:** Ronald Sanders; **Music: Howard Shore; Special Effects:** Gary Zeller; **Cast:** Jennifer O'Neil (Kim Obrist), Stephen Lack (Cameron Vale), Patrick McGoohan (Dr. Ruth), Lawrence Dane (Braedon Keller), Michael Ironside (Darryl Revok), Robert Silverman (Benjamin Pierce), Asam Ludwig (Arno Crostic); **Production Company:** Filmplan International Inc., with the participation of the SDICC; **Filmed outside Montreal; Duration:** 103 mins. 35mm, colour.

1982
Videodrome
Director/Screenplay: David Cronenberg; **Producer:** Claude Heroux; **Executive Producers:** Victor Solnicki, Pierre David; **Associate Producer:** Lawrence S. Nesis; **Art Director:** Carol Spier; **Cinematography:** Mark Irwin; **Editing:** Ronald Sanders; **Music:** Howard Shore; **Special video effects:** Michael Lennick; **Special makeup effects designer:** Rick Baker; **Cast:** James Woods (Max Renn), Sonja Smits (Bianca O'Blivion), Deborrah Harry (Nicki Brand), Peter Dvorsky (Harlan), Les Carlson (Barry Convex), Jack Creley (Brian O'Blivion), Lynne Gorman (Masha); **Production Company:** Filmplan International II, with the participation of the SDICC; **Filmed outside Montreal; Duration:** 103 mins. 35mm, colour.

1983
The Dead Zone
Director: David Cronenberg; **Screenplay:** Jeffrey Boam, based on the novel by Stephen King; **Producer:** Debra Hill; **Executive Producer:** Dino De Laurentis; **Associate Producer:** Jeffrey Chernov; **Art Director:** Carol Spier; **Cinematography:** Mark Irwin; **Editing:** Ronald Sanders; **Music:** Michael Kamen; **Wardrobe:** Olga Dimitrov; **Special video effects:** Michael Lennick; **Special effects coordinator:** Jon G. Belyeu
Cast: Christopher Walken (Johnny Smith), Brooke Adams (Sarah Bracknell), Tom Skerritt (Bannerman), Herbert Lom (Dr. Sam Weizak), Anthony Zerbe (Roger Stuart), Martin Sheen (Greg Stillson), Colleen Dewhurst (Henrietta Dodd), Nicholas Campbell (Franck Dodd); **Production Company:** Dead Zone Productions; **Filmed near Niagara-on-the-Lake, Uxbridge, Stouffville and Toronto; Duration:** 103 mins. 35mm, colour.

1986
The Fly
Director: David Cronenberg; **Screenplay:** Charles Edward Pogue and David Cronenberg based on the short story by George Langelaan; **Producer:** Stuart Cornfeld; **Co-producers:** Marc Boyman, Kip Ohman
Art Director: Carol Spier; **Cinematography:** Mark Irwin; **Editing:** Ronald Sanders; **Music:** Howard Shore; **Wardrobe:** Denise Cronenberg; **Creation of the Fly:** Chris Walas Inc; **Special effects coordinator:** Lee Wilson; **Cast:** Jeff Goldblum (Seth Brundle), Geena Davis (Veronica Quaife), John Getz (Stathis Borans), Jo Boushel (Tawny), Les Carlson (Dr. Cheevers), George Chuvalo (Marky), David Cronenberg (the gynaecologist); **Production Company:** Brooks Films; **Filmed outside Toronto; Duration:** 96 mins. 35mm, colour.

1988
Dead Ringers
Director: David Cronenberg; **Screenplay:** David Cronenberg and Norman Snider, based on the book *Twins* by Bari Wood and Jack Geasland; **Producer:** David Cronenberg and Marc Boyman; **Executive Producer:** James G Robinson, Joe Roth, Carol Baum, Sylvio Tabet; **Associate Producer:** John Board; **Art Director:** Carol Spier; **Cinematography:** Peter Suschitzky; **Editing:** Ronald Sanders; **Music:** Howard Shore; **Wardrobe:** Denise Cronenberg; **Special effects coordinator:** Lee Wilson; **Cast:** Jeremy Irons (Beverly and Elliot Mantle),

Genevieve Bujold (Claire Niveau), Heidi von Palleske (Dr. Cary Weiler), Barbara Gordon (Danuta), Shirley Douglas (Laura), Stephen Lack (Anders Wolleck), Nick Nichols (Leo), Lynne Cormack (Arlene), Damir Andrei (Birchall); **Production Company:** The Mantle Clinic II Ltd., with the participation of Telefilm Canada; **Filmed outside Toronto; Duration:** 115 mins. 35mm, colour.

1991

Naked Lunch

Director: David Cronenberg; **Screenplay:** David Cronenberg, based on the novel by William S. Burroughs; **Producer:** Jeremy Thomas; **Co-producer:** Gabriella Martinelli; **Director of Photography:** Peter Suschitzky; **Art Director:** Carol Spier; **Editing:** Ronald Sanders; **Wardrobe:** Denise Cronenberg; **Music:** Howard Shore and Ornette Coleman; **Special effects:** Chris Walas, Inc; **Cast:** Peter Weller (Bill Lee), Judy Davis (Joan Lee/Joan Frost), Ian Holm (Tom Frost), Julian Sands (Yves Cloquet), Roy Scheider (Dr. Benway), Monique Mercure (Fadela), Michael Zilnicker (Martin), Nicholas Campbell (Hank), Joseph Scorsiani (Kiki), Robert Silverman (Hans); **Production Company:** Recorded Pictures Company Ltd., with the participation of Telefilm Canada, The Ontario Film Development Corporation, Film Trustees Limited and Nippon Film Development and Finances Inc; **Filmed outside Toronto; Duration:** 115 mins. 35mm, colour.

1993

M. Butterfly

Director: David Cronenberg; **Screenplay:** David Henry Hwang, based on his play, *M. Butterfly*; **Producer:** Gabriella Martinelli; **Executive Producers:** David Henry Hwang and Philip Sandhaus; **Director of Photography:** Peter Suschitzky; **Art Director:** Carol Spier; **Editing:** Ronald Sanders; **Wardrobe:** Denise Cronenberg; **Music:** Howard Shore; **Cast:** Jeremy Irons (Rene Gallimard), John Lone (Song Liling), Barbara Sukowa (Jeanne Gallimard) Ian Richardson (Ambassador Toulon); **Production Company:** Geffen Film Company; **Filmed in Toronto, Beijing, Budapest and Paris; Duration:** 101 mins. Colour.

1996

Crash

Director: David Cronenberg; **Screenplay:** David Cronenberg, based on the novel by J. G. Ballard; **Delegate Producers:** Robert Lantos and Jeremy Thomas; **Director of Photography:** Peter Suschitzky; **Art Director:** Carol Spier; **Editing:** Ronald Sanders; **Wardrobe:** Denise Cronenberg; **Music:** Howard Shore; **Cast:** James Spader (James Ballard), Holly Hunter (Helen Rimington), Elias Koteas (Vaughan), Deborah Unger (Catherine Ballard), Rosanna Arquette (Gabrielle), Peter McNeill (Colin Seagrave); **Production Company:** Alliance Communications; **Filmed in Toronto; Duration:** 100 mins. Colour.

1999

eXistenZ

Director/Screenplay: David Cronenberg; **Producer:** Robert Lantos, Andras Hamori, David Cronenberg; **Executive Producers:** David Henry Hwang and Philip Sandhaus; **Director of Photography:** Peter Suschitzky; **Art Director:** Carol Spier; **Editing:** Ronald Sanders; **Wardrobe:** Denise Cronenberg; **Music:** Howard Shore; **Special Effects Supervisor:** Jim Isaac; **Cast:** Jennifer Jason Leigh (Allegra Geller), Jude Law (Ted Pikul), Ian Holm (Kiri Vinokur), Willem Defoe (Gas), Don McKellar (Yevgeny Nourish), Callum Keith Rennie (Carlaw), Christopher Eccleston (Wittold Levi), Sarah Polley (Merle), Robert A. Silverman (D'Arcy Nader); **Production Company:** Geffen Film Company; **Filmed in Toronto, Beijing, Budapest and Paris; Duration:** 101 mins. Colour.

2000

Camera

Director/Screenplay: David Cronenberg; **Producer:** Jody Shapiro; **Executive Producer:** Niv Fichman; **Director of Photography:** Andre Pienaar; **Art Director:** Carol Spier; **Editing:** Ronald Sanders; **Wardrobe:** Denise Cronenberg; **Music:** Howard Shore; **Cast:** Leslie Carlson (The Actor), Harrison Cane (Lead - as Harrison Kane), Marc Donato (Lead), Kyle Kassardjian (Lead), Natasha La Force; **Production Company:** The Criterion Collection; **Duration:** Six mins. Colour.

2002

Spider

Director: David Cronenberg; **Screenplay:** Patrick McGrath and David Cronenberg; **Producer:** David Cronenberg; **Director of Photography:** Peter Suschitzky; **Art Director:** Arv Grewal; **Editing:** Ronald Sanders; **Wardrobe:** Denise Cronenberg; **Music:** Howard Shore; **Special Effects Coordinator:** Daniel White; **Cast:** Ralph Fiennes (Dennis 'Spider' Cleg), Miranda Richardson (Yvonne/Mrs. Cleg), Gabriel Byrne (Bill Cleg), Lynn Redgrave, (Mrs. Wilkinson), John Neville (Terrence); **Production Company:** Capitol Films with the participation of Telefilm Canada; **Filmed in Berkshire, London and Toronto; Duration:** 98 mins. Colour.

2005

A History of Violence

Director: David Cronenberg; **Screenplay:** Jon Olson, based on the graphic novel by John Wagner and Vince Locke; **Producer:** David Cronenberg; **Director of Photography:** Peter Suschitzky; **Art Director:** Carol Spier; **Editing:** Ronald Sanders; **Wardrobe:** Denise Cronenberg; **Music:** Howard Shore; **Special Effects Coordinator:** Neil Trifunovich **Cast:** Viggo Mortensen (Tom Stall), Maria Bello (Edie Stall), Ed Harris (Carl Fogarty), William Hurt (Richie Cusack), Ashton Holmes (Jack Stall). **Production Company:** New Line Productions Inc and Bender-Spink Inc; **Filmed in Ontario; Duration:** 96 mins. Colour.

television

1970

Secret Weapons (for the series *Programme X*)

Director: David Cronenberg; **Screenplay:** Norman Snider; **Producer:** Paddy Sampson; **Director of Photography:** Andre Pienaar; **Art Director:** Carol Spier; **Editing:** Ronald Sanders; **Wardrobe:** Denise Cronenberg; **Music:** Howard Shore; **Narrator:** Lister Sinclair; **Cast:** Barbara O'Kelly, Norman Snider, Vernon Chapman, Ronald Mlodzik. **Production Company:** Emergent Films Ltd for the Canadian Broadcasting Corp; **Filmed in Toronto; Duration:** 30 mins. Colour.

1971

Based in France, Cronenberg wrote, directed and filmed three TV plays for Canadian television: **Tourettes, Letter from Michelangelo, Jim Ritchie Sculptor.**

1972

On his return to Canada, he then directed six others: **Don Valley, Fort York, Lakeshore, Winter Garden, Scarborough Bluffs, In the Dirt.**

1975

The Victim (for the series *Peep Show*)

Director: David Cronenberg; **Screenplay:** Ty Haller; **Director of Photography:** Eamonn Beglan; **Editing:** Garry Fisher; **Cast:** Janet Wright (Lucy), Jonathan Welsh (Donald), Cedric Smith (the man on the park bench); **Production Company:** Canadian Broadcasting Corporation; **Executive Producer:** Georges Bloomfield; **Producer:** Deborah Peaker; **Filmed in Toronto; Duration:** 30 mins. 2" VTR, colour.

The Lie Chair (for the series *Peep Show*)

Director: David Cronenberg; **Screenplay:** David Cole; **Director of Photography:** Eamonn Beglan; **Cast:** Richard Monette (Neil), Susan Hogan (Carol), Amelia Hall (Mildred), Doris Petrie (Mrs. Rogers); **Production Company:** Canadian Broadcasting Corporation; **Executive Producer:** Georges Bloomfield; **Producer:** Eoin Sprott; **Filmed outside Toronto; Duration:** 30 mins. 2" VTR, colour.

1976

The Italian Machine (for the series *Teleplay*)

Director/Screenplay: David Cronenberg; **Director of Photography:** Nicholas Edvemon; **Editing:** David Denovan; **Cast:** Gary McKeehan (Lionel), Franck Moore (Fred), Harde Linehan (Bug), Chuck Shamata (Rheinhardt); **Production Company:** Canadian Broadcasting Corporation; **Executive Producer:** Stephen Patrick; **Filmed outside Toronto; Duration:** 30 mins. 16mm, colour.